# STOCK
# MARKET
# LOGIC

The author is Editor of:
*Mutual Fund Forecaster*
*Market Logic*
*New Issues*
*The Insiders*
*Income & Safety*
*Investor's Digest*
*Fund Watch*
*Mutual Fund Buyer's Guide*
*Stock Market Weekly*
*Mutual Fund Weekly*
*The Professional Investor*

# STOCK MARKET LOGIC

## A SOPHISTICATED APPROACH TO PROFITS ON WALL STREET

## NORMAN G. FOSBACK

 Dearborn
Financial Publishing, Inc.

STOCK MARKET LOGIC

Library of Congress Catalog Card Number:  76-028826
International Standard Book Numbers:  0-917604-48-2 (hardcover)
0-79310-148-4 (paper)

|  |  |
|---|---|
| First Printing October 1976 | 17,000 copies |
| Second Printing June 1977 | 16,000 copies |
| Third Printing September 1979 | 10,000 copies |
| Fourth Printing November 1980 | 15,000 copies |
| Fifth Printing March 1981 | 16,000 copies |
| Sixth Printing February 1983 | 15,000 copies |
| Seventh Printing June 1983 | 15,000 copies |
| Eighth Printing March 1984 | 16,000 copies |
| Ninth Printing February 1985 | 25,000 copies |
| Tenth Printing April 1985 | 20,000 copies |
| Eleventh Printing September 1985 | 20,000 copies |
| Twelfth Printing April 1986 | 20,000 copies |
| Thirteenth Printing July 1986 | 20,000 copies |
| Fourteenth Printing October 1986 | 25,000 copies |
| Fifteenth Printing January 1987 | 50,000 copies |
| Sixteenth Printing March 1987 | 106,000 copies |
| Seventeenth Printing May 1987 | 101,000 copies |
| Eighteenth Printing January 1990 | 53,000 copies |
| Nineteenth Printing May 1991 | 25,000 copies |
| Twentieth Printing September 1991 | 51,000 copies |
| Twenty-first Printing February 1992 | 105,000 copies |
| Twenty-second Printing January 1993 | 50,000 copies |
| Twenty-third Printing May 1993 | 100,000 copies |
| Twenty-fourth Printing January 1994 | 50,000 copies |

The manuscript was typed by Chris Stotler. The type was set in IBM Press Roman by Shirley Babione and Joan Appel. Manufactured in the United States of America by Arcata Graphics Hawkins, Kingsport, TN.

*Market Logic, New Issues, The Insiders, Insider Indicator, Money Fund Safety Ratings, Income & Safety, Mutual Fund Forecaster, Fund Watch, Investor's Digest, Mutual Fund Buyer's Guide, Stock Market Weekly, Mutual Fund Weekly,* and *The Professional Investor* are trademarks of The Institute for Econometric Research, Incorporated.

iv

"Outstanding action oriented research requires first a thorough knowledge of the problem, and second a thorough knowledge of the applicable scientific theories. Weakness in practical knowledge of the problem leads to academic exercises; weakness in knowledge of methods and theories leads to technically unsound work."

*From The Bank Administration Institute's*
*Evaluation of Pension Fund Investment*
*Performance Measurement*

# TABLE OF CONTENTS

# STOCK MARKET LOGIC

**A SOPHISTICATED APPROACH TO PROFITS ON WALL STREET**

# INTRODUCTION

Few financial endeavors have occupied the time of more men over more years with less success than attempting to "beat the market." So many have tried and failed that it has become popular, especially in academic circles, to believe that no one can consistently outperform the averages.

Nothing could be further from the truth!

Granted, everyone cannot beat the market . . . simply because everyone *is* the market. But that does not preclude the possibility that some investors, utilizing more sophisticated approaches than the public at large, can earn above average returns on their investments. To do so, however, requires the development of a logical investment strategy which takes advantage of the very weaknesses that deny superior returns to most investors.

As a prelude to increased stock market profits, it is necessary to reject the concept that chance alone governs who wins and who loses on Wall Street, while recognizing that most speculators who seek a get-rich-quick solution will end up instead among the big losers. Investors expecting to double their money every year will fail almost without exception, while those with reasonable objectives and a sophisticated and rational approach will usually be well rewarded for their effort. This book is directed toward a definition of what objectives are reasonable and the development of a sophisticated and rational approach to the realization of those objectives.

The first step in building a successful investment strategy is to learn as much as possible about where stock prices in general are headed. **Part One, Stock Market Indicators,** is devoted to an in-depth analysis of the vast array of techniques which have been developed over the years to forecast stock market trends. Computer-aided testing has provided new insights into many traditional indicators and has made possible the development of a number of new market barometers revealed here for the first time.

Although many of the indicators work well enough most of the time, virtually none are always correct and rarely do they all ever point in exactly the same direction. The relatively new science of econometrics provides a number of useful statistical tools for combining information from diverse sources into a single rational forecast. **Part Two, Econometrics and the Stock Market**, describes the integration of the stock market indicators into useful econometric forecasting models, and explains the advantages of an econometric approach to stock market prediction.

At any given moment the odds are about two to one in favor of a bullish forecast being the correct one. A number of possible answers to the then logically ensuing question of what stocks should be bought are explored in **Part Three, Stock Selection Theories**. The seemingly endless number of techniques for picking winners are shown to be but variations on a handful of basic themes, most of which are of dubious value.

There are surely many paths to success, but **Part Four, Stock Selection: From Theory to Practice,** concentrates on an approach that combines a rational theory with a long history of superior results. Evidence is adduced that raises extreme doubts about the validity of the random walk theory.   An old Wall street adage goes, "Don't tell me *what* to buy, tell me *when* to buy it."   In fact, *what* and *when* are two sides of the same coin — both essential to a successful investment strategy.

The next step to making money on Wall Street is learning to apply the tools of portfolio management, covered in **Part Five, A Total Financial Management System.** After defining objectives, several methods, some common and some unorthodox, of improving total returns and adjusting risk levels are explored.

Game theorists call the stock market a "positive sum game" because in the long run the market rises and, in aggregate, all investors make money.   But the money game does not yield uniform profits to all its participants.   Instead it dispenses large gains or losses to a relative handful of participants, leaving most players as small winners.   **Part Six, Measuring the Market:   Keeping Score,** explains how to measure relative performance to learn if your portfolio is doing better than someone throwing a handful of darts at a page of stock listings might do by chance alone; in short, you will be shown how to truly distinguish between winning and losing performances.

**Part Seven, Using Market Logic,** describes a total investment advisory approach utilizing the logical investment framework revealed in this book.

Individuals who own small stock portfolios, or who, for whatever reason, do not wish to devote much of their time to the investment decision-making process, have a ready alternative in mutual funds.   **Part Eight, The Mutual Fund Alternative,** unveils a new method of profit maximization and risk reduction using these popular investment and trading vehicles.

Finally, for those who fear that a random walk still lurks somewhere on Wall Street waiting to trip up investors seeking above average profits, breathe easier.   The concluding **Part Nine, A Run Down Random Walk Street,** allays those fears by tripping up the random walk instead.

**Technical Note: Econometrics** (addressed principally to professional colleagues) provides an overview of the mathematical and computational procedures which are being used today to forecast stock prices at The Institute for Econometric Research.

**Technical Note: Risk** proposes and defines a new risk measure which better meets the tests of common sense and statistical theory than more traditional measures.

A list of **Selected References**, for readers who wish to explore these subjects in greater depth, is supplemented by the author's choice of The Best Investment Books Ever Written.

Finally, the author asks readers to appreciate that any inquiry into the stock market, particularly one that is grounded in statistical analysis, as this one is, can be dated by events. By its very nature a book is not easily revised to reflect all of these changes. To keep readers up to date, the author writes an investment advisory newsletter, *Market Logic*, that regularly publishes new analyses of market timing, stock selection, and portfolio management techniques, including updates of many that are presented here. Please feel free to contact the author for a complimentary issue of the newsletter.

# PART ONE
## STOCK MARKET INDICATORS

## 1 Riches Beyond the Dreams of Avarice

The endless quest by fundamentalists and technicians alike to discover the secret of calling market turns is driven by a knowledge of the incredible returns a completely successful timing strategy would yield.

Consider, for example, that from early 1964 through the end of 1984, the average New York Stock Exchange common stock provided its holders with a total return from dividends and capital appreciation of 11% per annum compounded. By comparison, an investor with the intelligence and foresight to step out of stocks and hold cash during the three bear markets of the period could have earned nearly twice that return — 21% per annum compounded. He could have achieved such a performance without ever picking a single stock or speculating on margin; by merely buying and selling "the market" (which is easier than you might think).

Taking the illustration a step further, an investor who actually sold the market short during the three bear moves (instead of just holding cash) would have reaped an additional profit sufficient to increase the compounded

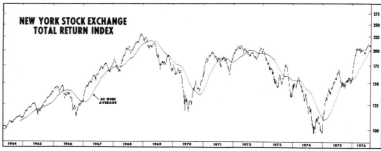

FIGURE 1.        New York Stock Exchange Total Return Index
Weekly range of daily closing prices; May 1964 - July 1976.

return to 27% per annum, a stunning cumulative return of
13,812% (see Table 1).

But let us take our illustration yet a further step. An
investor who perfectly forecast every up and down market
swing of at least 5% during those years, buying just before
each upmove and selling short just before the market was
about to drop 5% or more, would have garnered a return
approaching an astounding 52.4 million percent, equivalent
to nearly doubling his money every year.

Perfectly forecasting even small price swings would
naturally lead to even larger profits, although ultimately
commission costs would equal the size of the swing itself and
eat up all gains.

## TABLE 1

### CYCLICAL MARKET TIMING STRATEGY — MAJOR SWINGS
(April 30, 1964 — December 31, 1984)

| Position | Time Period | NYSE Total Return Index | Theoretical Profit |
|---|---|---|---|
| Long | Apr. 30, 1964 - Apr. 21, 1966 | 101.77 - 147.16 | 44.6% |
| Short | Apr. 21, 1966 - Oct. 7, 1966 | 147.16 - 112.17 | 23.8% |
| Long | Oct. 7, 1966 - Dec. 13, 1968 | 112.17 - 230.51 | 105.5% |
| Short | Dec. 13, 1968 - July 7, 1970 | 230.51 - 117.04 | 49.2% |
| Long | July 7, 1970 - Apr. 12, 1972 | 117.04 - 209.15 | 78.7% |
| Short | Apr. 12, 1972 - Sep. 13, 1974 | 209.15 - 96.55 | 53.8% |
| Long | Sep. 13, 1974 - Dec. 31, 1984 | 96.55 - 890.40 | 822.2% |

Total Compounded Return 13,812%

So the next time you hear someone say that all you need to do is buy good stocks and hold them, think of these comparisons of "buy and hold" with various market timing strategies.

Of course, few investors ever time a single market cycle to perfection, much less repeat the feat year in and year out. And accurately timing all market moves as small as 5% is simply impossible. Indeed, the incredible returns of the short-term trading strategies shown in Table 2 demonstrate how improbable such perfect timing is. Thus, the endless quest for new market timing techniques is based less on a belief that perfection is achievable than on an understanding of how profitable even the slightest success in market timing can be.

### TABLE 2
### ALTERNATIVE MARKET STRATEGIES (1964-1984)

| Strategy | Average Annual Gain | $10,000 Grows To |
|---|---|---|
| Buy and Hold | +11% | $    87,500 |
| Avoiding the Bear Markets | +21% | $   489,700 |
| Long & Short Major Swings Only | +27% | $ 1,391,200 |
| Long & Short Every 5% Swing | +89% | $5.24 billion |

Even readily attainable levels of market timing success can have a dramatic impact on overall returns. For example, an investor who was short for only one-quarter of each of those three bear markets in the past twenty years would have spared himself half the losses incurred by his fully invested counterparts, and his $10,000 would have grown to $237,790 — tripling the profits of buy and hold.

Just what magnitude of returns constitutes a realistic expectation is a function of the degree of forecasting accuracy that can, in practice, be achieved. It might seem likely that accurate market forecasts for the next few days would be relatively easy to achieve, and that any prediction of prices six months or a year in the future would be highly conjectural. Interestingly enough, exactly the opposite is true. As we shall observe later, long-term market cycles are much easier to anticipate than day-to-day wiggles in the averages. Furthermore, besides being exceedingly difficult to predict, small, brief price movements are rendered even less profitable by the burden of repeated transactions costs.

Be it from impatience or curiosity, most investors are unduly concerned about what the market will do in the next few days when their attention would far better be focused on where the market will be in three, six, or twelve months. The answers to questions about tomorrow's ripple may be more interesting, but answers to questions about the major trend are ultimately far more profitable.

Not surprisingly, many of the academic studies that have concluded that successive stock price changes are random (unrelated to one another), have analyzed only very short-term market movements, which do exhibit a large random component. However, when the longer term, which has been all but ignored by random walk theorists, is viewed in the light of market forecasting indicators, it becomes clear that the market does *not* follow a random pattern, and that superior profits await investors willing to follow the guidance of those indicators.

The indicators that have been developed in pursuit of the ultimate market timing index are legion. The following chapters are devoted to descriptions and studies of the most important indicators. The presentations are based not on mere anecdotal evidence but on rigorous and objective analyses of historical reliability.

# 2 The Dow Theory

The venerable Dow Theory is a system of market analysis developed by Charles H. Dow around the turn of the century, and later refined by William Hamilton and Robert Rhea. The theory purports to identify and measure changes in important cyclical trends in stock prices on the basis of movements in the Dow Jones Industrial Average and the Dow Jones Transportation Average (formerly the Dow Jones Rail Average).

To ascertain the present trend of the market with the Dow Theory, an observer must first establish a definite set of criteria to compensate for the theory's lack of specificity. Unfortunately, because stock prices seldom seem to move in uniform, perfectly defined cyclical patterns, it is difficult to develop such criteria. In fact, different Dow theorists have derived radically different criteria for Dow Theory buy and sell signals.

The stated criteria for any set of Dow Theory signals normally include three basic elements. First, the industrial average and the transportation average must confirm one another. A signal by one of the averages but not the other is insufficient to yield a full fledged Dow Theory signal.

Second, following a substantial market decline, a buy signal is established as follows: a rise by each of the averages to points substantially above their major lows; then a decline by each of the averages of some minimum length that does not penetrate their previous lows. (Dow theorists have never quite agreed what the minimum should be.) Finally, each average must rebound from this second intermediate low and establish a new cyclical recovery high.

Third, following an extended market advance, a bear market is signalled in precisely the opposite manner: a decline by each of the averages to points substantially below their major highs; then an advance by each of the averages of some minimum magnitude that does not surpass their previously established highs. (Again, the required minimum varies from Dow theorist to Dow theorist.) Finally, each average must decline from this second top to a new cyclical low.

Table 3 presents a record of major Dow Theory buy and sell signals from 1897 to 1967. Needless to add, this is but one of the versions of Dow Theory signals which have been developed over the years. Other analysts have used different signal parameters (mainly pertaining to the required magnitude of the intermediate moves by the industrial and transportation averages) and have consequently derived different signal dates as well.

## TABLE 3

### DOW THEORY SIGNALS

| Bull Markets | Bear Markets |
|---|---|
| June 28, 1897 - Dec. 16, 1899 | Dec. 16, 1899 - Oct. 20, 1900 |
| Oct. 20, 1900 - June  1, 1903 | June  1, 1903 - July 12, 1904 |
| July 12, 1904 - Apr. 26  1906 | Apr. 26, 1906 - Apr. 24, 1908 |
| Apr. 24, 1908 - May  3, 1910 | May  3, 1910 - Oct. 10, 1910 |
| Oct. 10, 1910 - Jan. 14,  1913 | Jan. 14, 1913 - Apr.  9, 1915 |
| Apr.  9, 1915 - Aug. 28, 1917 | Aug. 28, 1917 - May 13, 1918 |
| May 13, 1918 - Feb.  5, 1920 | Feb.  5, 1920 - Feb.  6, 1922 |
| Feb.  6, 1922 - June 20, 1923 | June 20, 1923 - Dec.  7, 1923 |
| Dec.  7, 1923 - Oct. 23, 1929 | Oct. 23, 1929 - May 24, 1933 |
| May 24, 1933 - Sep.  7, 1937 | Sep.  7, 1937 - June 23, 1938 |
| June 23, 1938 - Mar. 31, 1939 | Mar. 31, 1939 - July 17, 1939 |
| July 17, 1939 - May 13, 1940 | May 13, 1940 - June 15, 1944 |
| June 15, 1944 - Aug. 27, 1946 | Aug. 27, 1946 - May 14, 1948 |
| May 14, 1948 - Nov.  9, 1948 | Nov.  9, 1948 - Oct.  2, 1950 |
| Oct.  2, 1950 - Aug. 31, 1953 | Aug. 31, 1953 - Feb.  4, 1954 |
| Feb.  4, 1954 - Oct.  1, 1956 | Oct.  1, 1956 - May  2, 1958 |
| May  2, 1958 - Mar.  3, 1960 | Mar.  3, 1960 - Oct. 10, 1961 |
| Oct. 10, 1961 - Apr. 26, 1962 | Apr. 26, 1962 - Nov.  9, 1962 |
| Nov.  9, 1962 - May  5, 1966 | May  5, 1966 - Jan. 11, 1967 |

(Source: Harvey A. Krow, Stock Market Behavior, Random House, 1969, p 42.)

Although many analysts have attempted to use the Dow Theory for prediction purposes, its primary function is to identify the present trend of the market, not forecast its future. If the Dow Theory does have a forecasting role to play, it is in predicting the future course of the United States economy. It has a good record in this regard primarily because expectations of future changes in corporate earnings and general business conditions are important factors in current common stock price valuations.

Of course, the companies whose stocks comprise the industrial and transportation averages account for a very significant portion of the total production and movement of goods in the nation's economy. The merger of the two stock price averages into a single integrated system has long been thought to provide an accurate stock market barometer. Primarily because of the difficulties of deriving objective signals, it is overrated. Despite its failings, a pervasive cult has grown up around the Dow Theory over the years and many Wall Street analysts follow the theory on a continuing basis. It should come as no great surprise, then, that when a consensus Dow Theory signal attracts attention in the press, stock prices often temporarily respond to the buying (or selling) pressures induced by the rush of the many Dow Theory adherents into the marketplace. As a consequence, the theory is probably worth noting if for no other reason than to keep abreast of what the Dow theorists are doing. On the basis of rigorous and objective analysis it is not possible to assign any significant forecasting value to the theory.

Although no work has yet been published on the subject, it is quite possible that the Dow Theory's market record could be considerably enhanced by extending the rules to include the Dow Jones Utility Average. (Since the utility average was first calculated in 1929 the original inventor of the theory did not have the average available for inclusion in his system.) Stock prices usually respond to sharp interest rate swings — and utility stocks are particularly interest rate sensitive.   There are two primary reasons for this.   First, utilities borrow large sums of money to finance plant expansion and the interest paid on such loans can have a major impact on their profitability.   Second, utility stocks are relatively conservative investments often purchased mainly for their dividend yield, and constitute an alternative investment medium to corporate bonds.   Thus their price fluctuations are closely attuned to those of interest bearing securities. Because of this dual interest rate sensitivity, utility stocks frequently lead the broad market, and incorporation of the Dow Jones Utility Average into a Revised Dow Theory might well improve the market prediction record.   As it stands today, however, the existing Dow Theory is more a historical curiosity as one of the earliest attempts at technical stock market analysis and less a useful forecaster of future market price trends.

# 3  Yields, P/E's and Other Trivia

The relationship between price and value is clear, but is exceedingly difficult to measure. While price can be observed with certainty, no one can ever be sure what constitutes true value.   Although it may be impossible to objectively determine current value, in the light of hindsight it is clear that price does tend to revolve around it. Consequently, several indicators have been developed which purport to measure value and thereby provide a reference point for the relationship of price to value. The logic is simple:  if the market is undervalued, buy; if the market is overvalued, sell.

*Dividend Yield.*   Long the most popular of valuation measures, the dividend yield is calculated by dividing the indicated dividend rate for the next twelve months by current price.   This figure can be calculated for any market average, or most meaningfully, for all stocks in aggregate.   In this century common stocks have provided an average annual dividend yield of about 4½%, ranging from a low of 2½% to a high of 8%. At times investor enthusiasm has been so great that the market has accepted a much lower dividend yield than normal. When yields are very low, stock prices are, by definition, high, and frequently overvalued as well. The market, then, has nowhere else to go but down, so it is not surprising that, historically, a low market yield has usually been followed by declining prices. Conversely, when the marketplace is rife with pessimism, investors demand a much higher than normal dividend yield to induce them to buy stocks. Since an excessively high yield means that stock prices are abnormally low relative to dividends and are undervalued, the market frequently responds to such situations by climbing higher.

A simple test of the dividend yield as a forecaster of future stock prices is presented in Table 4. Shown are the one year market returns which have ensued from various Dow Jones Industrial Average dividend yield intervals since 1941.

TABLE 4

DIVIDEND YIELDS AND STOCK PRICES (1941 - 1975)

| D. J. I. A.<br>Dividend Yield | S&P 500 Index<br>One Year Later | Probability of<br>Rising Prices |
|---|---|---|
| Under  3% | −10.1% | 0% |
| 3.0% - 4.0% | + 2.0% | 59% |
| 4.0% - 6.0% | + 11.4% | 72% |
| 6.0% - 7.0% | + 15.0% | 87% |
| Over  7.0% | + 37.8% | 100% |
| 35-Year Average | +  7.7% | 68% |

During the 35 year period the dividend yield was under 3% only 19 weeks (in mid-1959 and early 1966) and in every case the average ensuing one year market return was sharply negative. The returns curve relatively smoothly up the dividend yield spectrum with exceptionally high returns following yields around 7%. Identical tests over other time frames reveal that the indicator is a relatively poor predictor of shorter-term price trends, but an excellent forecaster of long-term trends. Indeed, the dividend yield is without peer in forecasting the market two to five years in advance.

Many technicians have been tempted to specify simplistic cutoff points as buy and sell parameters. For example, one analyst writing in *Barron's* suggested that 3½% is the best sell specification. Other technicians have pinpointed critical points such as 3% or 3.3%. As a general rule, the wisest course is to use these levels only as general areas of relative valuation. Precise cutoff points, based on the last few cycles, somehow always seem to miss by an inch in the next cycle. In this case, an inch is as good as a mile, for an investor would be left stranded waiting for that last fraction.

*Price/Dividend Ratio.* The normal way to calculate an effective annual dividend yield is to divide the latest twelve months' dividends, or the anticipated dividend rate for the next twelve months, by the current price, with the result expressed as a percent. A few pseudo-sophisticated technicians invert the indicator and calculate it in precisely the opposite fashion, dividing price by dividend. The result is termed a Price/Dividend Ratio and, in effect, measures the number of dollars the market is willing to pay for one dollar of dividends. In reality, the dividend yield and the Price/Dividend Ratio are, for all intents and purposes, identical; one is merely the reciprocal of the other. For example, a yield of 3% is comparable to a Price/Dividend Ratio of 33.3, a 4% yield is comparable to a P/D Ratio of 25, a 5% yield is the mirror image of a P/D Ratio of 20, and so on.

*Price/Earnings Ratio.* Most analysts view the relationship between dividends and stock prices as of merely passing interest. However, fundamentalists view the market's Price/Earnings Ratio with a sense of urgency normally devoted only to higher subjects of ethics and morality. The Price/Earnings Ratio is calculated by dividing current price by the latest 12 months' earnings per share. Dividend yields and P/E ratios are naturally highly correlated since they both relate a measure of company performance to the same variable . . . the price of the stock. Dividends are, after all, paid out of earnings and, all other things equal, they will move in similar trends. Dividends do have one notable advantage, however: stability. Earnings fluctuate seasonally and to a great extent, even randomly. Company managements seek to moderate these fluctuations by maintaining a dividend payout proportioned to the long run prospects of the company. "Managing" earnings is easy — any good accountant can do it. But distributing cold cash to stockholders requires a hard economic decision — once paid out it is irretrievable.

It can also be argued, persuasively, that in the long run earnings mean nothing to stockholders unless they are ultimately paid out in dividends. A company can go on exclusively reinvesting earnings in future growth only so long. At some point shareholders must receive tangible fruits of the earnings reinvestment if it is to be of any value to them.

Price/Earnings Ratios become distorted during severe economic contractions. Under normal conditions, a persistent decline in prices relative to earnings results in a falling Price/Earnings Ratio. A low P/E, in turn, is generally bullish. The 1930 s were an exception. The economic depression was so deep that when the market bottomed out in 1933, earnings had declined even more drastically than stock prices and the Dow Jones Industrial Average's P/E was over 30. A ratio of that magnitude would normally reveal extensive overvaluation of stocks and would be considered extremely bearish. In 1933 the high P/E Ratio merely reflected abnormally low earnings, not excessively high prices. In fact, stock prices were extremely low and undervalued. (In contrast the D.J.I.A. dividend yield accurately reflected the market's undervaluation by rising to over 10%.)

Thus, while the Price/Earnings Ratio may be a fairly good yardstick of the relative prices of common stocks, it is generally inferior to the dividend yield as a market forecasting tool.

*Book Value.* Still another interesting measure of relative value is the relationship between common stock prices and company net worth. Net worth, or book value, per share is calculated by adding up all of a company's assets (things owned), subtracting all of its liabilities (things owed), and dividing by the number of common shares outstanding. The statistic is a theoretical measure of what a company is worth. If the price of a stock is far below its book value per share, the stock is considered undervalued and should be purchased. Conversely, when the Price/Book Value Ratio is high, a stock may be significantly overvalued and should be sold (all other things being equal, of course).

The problem with this approach is that "net worth" may not represent what a company is in fact worth. After all, an asset is only worth what one can get out of it. If a company has a high asset value but never earns any money nor pays any dividends to its stockholders, it is worth very little to the stockholders. Furthermore, book values are often extremely artificial, reflecting only what company managements and accountants wish to put into them. Companies which are absolutely identical in all other respects can have drastically different balance sheets and hence, book values, simply as a result of accounting gimmickry. What is true for individual companies is, by extension, also true for the market. The relationship between market indexes and aggregate book values has therefore always been an extremely erratic one, and predictions of future changes in the former from current levels of the latter is a risky undertaking.

*Q-Ratio.* In an inflationary environment, book values are understated because the real values of assets rise. Economists call this actual value "replacement value." Stock price divided by replacement value yields the Q-Ratio. While superior to indicators that merely use book value, it is almost impossible to calculate, and is of greater interest to theoreticians than to practicing investors.

*Conclusion.* Of the four fundamental indicators — yield, P/E, book value, and Q-Ratio — the first is by far the best.

# 4 Leading Economic Indicators

Stock prices usually fluctuate in response to changing *anticipations* of economic events which affect the welfare of companies, not in response to the events themselves. Historically, the stock market has demonstrated an ability to presage the economy by six to twelve months. Traditionally declining well in advance of economic contractions and turning up prior to the start of economic expansions, the market is an acknowledged leading indicator of the general economic cycle.

A few analysts argue that the stock market might even be too good a predictor of the economy. (As economist Paul Samuelson once observed, "The market has predicted nine of the last four recessions.") And occasionally it does indeed go off on its own seemingly mad and irrational tangents. When this occurs, such as in 1961 and '62, it reacts to correct its own excesses. But most of the time it maps economic swings remarkably well and has a respectable forecasting record.

Numerous other economic series also exhibit leading characteristics. The National Bureau of Economic Research (NBER) has developed several dozen series which tend to lead the economy at cyclical turning points. From the overall list of these leading indicators, they have focused on a select eleven (one of which is the stock market), which seem to provide better economic forecasts than all the others. These eleven indicators, listed in Table 5 (page 18), compose what is often termed the NBER "short list."

## TABLE 5

## THE NBER "SHORT LIST"

| Subject | Leading Indicator |
|---|---|
| Capital Expenditures . . . | Contracts and orders for plant and equipment (constant dollars) |
| Consumer Sentiment . . . | Index of consumer expectations |
| Durable Goods . . . . . . . | Changes in manufacturers unfilled orders for durable goods (constant dollars) |
| Employment . . . . . . . . | Weekly initial unemployment claims |
| Housing . . . . . . . . . . | Index of new private house building permits |
| Labor Utilization . . . . . | Average work week of production workers |
| Money Supply . . . . . . . | M2 (constant dollars) |
| New Orders . . . . . . . . | New orders of consumer goods and materials (constant dollars) |
| Prices . . . . . . . . . . . . | Percent change in sensitive materials prices |
| Production Capacity . . . | Percentage of companies reporting slower deliveries |
| Stock Prices . . . . . . . . | Standard & Poor's 500 Stock Price Index |

In the constant quest for the Holy Grail of market timing, analysts have attempted to ascertain whether one or more of these leading indicators presages not only general economic activity, but stock prices as well. If such a relationship does exist, its value to investors is obvious.

One of the best efforts was reported by Jesse Levin in the *Financial Analysts Journal* (July-August, 1970). Based on a study of seven economic peaks from 1923 to 1960, Levin discovered that a majority of the eleven leading indicators, other than stock prices, peaked ahead of stock prices. The best leader was new house building permits, with money supply and new orders close behind.

The NBER defined seven economic contractions between 1923 and 1968. The market generally led the economic turns, and a majority of the other leading indicators led stock prices at every economic cycle peak. (At the four subsequent economic peaks, from 1969 to 1983, common stocks continued to lead the economy, with a majority of the other leaders beating stocks at the top two times.)

## TABLE 6

### CHARACTERISTICS OF ECONOMIC CYCLE PEAKS

| Peak of S&P 500 | Peak of Economic Cycle | Stock Price Peak vs. Economic Peak | % of Leading Indicators Peaking Ahead of Stocks |
|---|---|---|---|
| Mar. 1923 | May 1923 | 2 Month Lead | 60% |
| Sep. 1929 | Aug. 1929 | 1 Month Lag | 83% |
| Feb. 1937 | May 1937 | 3 Month Lead | 67% |
| June 1948 | Nov. 1948 | 5 Month Lead | 86% |
| Jan. 1953 | July 1953 | 6 Month Lead | 67% |
| July 1956 | July 1957 | 12 Month Lead | 91% |
| July 1959 | May 1960 | 10 Month Lead | 60% |
| Averages . . . . . . . . . . | | 5 Month Lead | 73% |

On average, 73% of the other eleven leading indicators turned down before stock prices, and in every one of the seven cycles at least a majority started declining before the market. A similar analysis of economic troughs discloses that stock price upturns were also generally preceded by increases in a majority of leading indicators.

While it therefore appears that some leading economic indicators lead not only economic turns but stock market turns as well, in point of fact there are a number of severe constraints to their practical application as market forecasting tools. It is not really so surprising that they showed good leading characteristics during the forty year period because the NBER selected them from among scores of other indicators after extensive testing and manipulation for that very reason. And seven cycles is a very small sample on which to draw large conclusions. The real question is, Can the indicators be relied upon for forecasting accuracy outside of the basic study period?

Indeed, everything went wrong during the early 1970s. The widely followed NBER short list composite index peaked in mid-1974. Not only did it fail to predict the recession, but it lagged far behind the turn in stock prices as well. The Standard & Poor's 500 Index, itself a component of the composite index, turned down a full year and a half earlier while the broad market, as measured by the New York Stock Exchange Total Return Index, actually peaked in early 1972, more than two full years in advance of the composite. In early 1975 the staff of the NBER sat down to figure out what went wrong.    Their best explanation was that the rampant price inflation of the last few years biased many of the indicators.    After making "ex-post" adjustments for inflation, the NBER noted that the leading indicator composite peaked in early 1973, concurrent with the top in stock prices and prior to the actual economic turn. This belated discovery was, of course, small consolation to investors who had already lost upwards of half their investment capital by following the "lead" of the leading indicators.  There is no assurance that some other problem may not crop up in future cycles.

Another problem manifest in the use of leading indicators is data reporting lags. While stock prices are known instantaneously, most economic indicators are computed but once a month and some only quarterly.    Virtually all of them, regardless of their frequency or infrequency of calculation, are reported to the public with substantial lags, in some cases months later.  Yet others are initially reported in preliminary form and then regularly revised weeks, months, or even years later.    It does little good to know that an indicator has peaked in advance of the market if that fact is not known until some time after the market peak.

Yet another problem is the determination of what constitutes a turn in an indicator.  Is it sufficient, for example, for a leading indicator to render a sell signal when, after rising continuously for a lengthy period of time, it turns down for a single month?    The answer to the question is important because, just as with stock prices, leading economic indicators exhibit random fluctuations.    Not every downtick or uptick signifies a lasting turn in the prevailing trend.  So, it may be the better part of wisdom to observe two or three or even more months of data before stating that an actual reversal has  occurred.  But the longer the wait, the more lag is imputed into the leading indicators themselves. These lags, when added to the original data reporting lags, tend to further decrease their usefulness as market timing devices.

In conclusion, it is fair to say that as good as stock prices may be as a leading indicator of general economic expansion and contraction, other non-stock price measures may perform the task just as well and possibly even better. But it is quite another thing to assume that these indicators will in themselves be of value in predicting stock prices. Since the relationship between the market and any indicator is less than precise, it is preferable to at least start with indicators that are unambiguous and immediately available. The leading economic indicators are wanting on both counts.

# 5   Will the Real Money Supply Please Stand Up?

Many economists believe money supply is the single most important factor in national economic planning, but until about ten years ago the average investor had never heard of this term. Public interest in the subject has now carried to such an extreme that some market participants eagerly await the release of the weekly money supply statistics prior to making market decisions.

Money supply is the total of all money held by the public. The simplest form of money is cash; that is, currency and coin in circulation. Since cash in circulation is very stable and the average household or business holds most of its money in the form of constantly fluctuating checking account balances, the basic definition of money supply usually includes the total of all cash plus checking account balances, (demand deposits at commercial banks) held by everyone in the country except other banks and the government.

This basic form of money supply is called M1, or "narrow money supply." A slightly wider definition called, appropriately enough, "broad money supply," or M2, is the sum of several types of savings plus M1.

Most analysts concentrate their attention on M1 or M2, but a number of further refinements are also popular. For example, when large time deposits, term repurchase agreements, and institutional money market fund balances are added to M2, the result is called M3. Alternatively, a variety of other instruments can be added to M3 with the result called L (for Liquid assets). If all this sounds baroque, take heart — even economists are bewildered.

DEFINITIONS OF MONEY SUPPLY*

M1 = Currency, travelers checks, demand deposits (i.e., checking account balances) and other checkable deposits.

M2 = M1 + overnight repurchase agreements and overnight Eurodollars, non-institutional money market mutual fund balances, money market deposit accounts, savings deposits, and small time deposits.

M3 = M2 + large time deposits, term Eurodollars and repurchase agreements, and institutional money market mutual fund balances.

L  = M3 + U.S. savings bonds, short-term Treasury securities, bankers acceptances, and commercial paper.

*January 1990

Money supply does play a key role in the overall scheme of economic policy, but its relationship to the stock market is primarily that of a coincident, not a leading, indicator. Current knowledge of many indicators imparts information about future changes in stock prices, but current knowledge of money supply behavior mainly imparts information regarding the current trend of the market.

The correlation between past money supply movements and future stock price changes is so weak that it is more fruitful to base price level forecasts on alternative monetary variables such as interest rates, Federal Reserve policy actions, and bank reserve positions.

Put another way, rising money supply usually accompanies rising stock prices (and vice versa), but the rate of increase in money supply has little bearing on how much stock prices will rise in the future.  Indeed, in the 1972-1974 cycle it appears that investors so well anticipated the forthcoming upturn in both money supply and the economy that the market turn preceded the other two.

The size and growth of money supply is indirectly influenced by the Federal Reserve System through its direct control over the reserves of member banks, the discount rate, and through open market operations.  The exact mechanics of that influence are so complex that there is widespread disagreement as to which is cause and which is effect.

One simple view is that high money supply growth leads to lower interest rates due to an excess of money available for lending.  But, on the other hand, rapid monetary expansion has usually been followed by inflation, which in turn leads to higher interest rates.

Monetary growth at first stimulates business activity, but eventually prices rise by almost the same amount as the monetary growth and the level of economic activity benefits hardly at all.  Usually an initial period of rapid monetary growth is followed about six months later by real economic growth, followed a year or more after that by an increasing rate of inflation, followed still later by a period of monetary restraint designed to alleviate that inflation, with the final consequence being recession.

The United States and much of the world recently completed just such a cycle.  The seeds of inflation in the mid-1960s grew into the boom of the late 1960s and early 1970s and finally bore the bitter fruit of a severe and protracted recession.

Since an expansionary monetary policy has opposite effects over the short and long terms, a constant rate of moderate growth would seem ideal.  Dr. Milton Friedman of the University of Chicago and his many followers advocate just such a policy.  These "monetarists" believe money supply is causal and most other economic conditions are mere effects.

A somewhat different view is taken by "fiscalists" who

believe government spending policies cause the changes in levels of national prosperity. They view money supply changes as merely one of the many effects of federal fiscal policies.

The two schools of thought are not really so far apart as it might appear because large government deficits, such as we now face, usually are financed by a rapid expansion of the money supply, enabling banks and others to purchase the government securities which are issued to finance deficits.

One of the great burning issues of the day (and decade) in economics is what rate of money supply growth is necessary to achieve general prosperity without inflation.

Many economists believe inflationary pressure is created when the long run growth of M1 exceeds 3% per annum and growth rate policies as low as 1% are supported. Recent experience suggests, however, that even a 3% growth rate would result in such a sluggish pace of business activity that unemployment would remain at politically unacceptable levels. A money supply growth of 6% annually is thought by some experts to be sufficient to alleviate unemployment without creating "too much" inflation.

It might seem, therefore, that a reasonable middle course would be to keep M1 growing near the middle of the 3% to 6% per annum range. For a number of reasons, it is not that simple. First of all, not everyone agrees on the salutary effects of constraining money supply growth within the 3% to 6% range. Secondly, there is almost no agreement among experts as to the length of time over which money supply growth rates should be calculated in order to be meaningful. Some practitioners place weight on monthly changes while others argue that trends shorter than six months, or even a year, are meaningless.

The result is "something for everyone." For example, a few years ago, six then-prevailing and popular versions of money supply viewed over four different intervals led to two dozen possible rates of monetary growth (see Table 7).

## TABLE 7

### MONEY SUPPLY:  ANNUAL GROWTH RATES

|  | Latest Month | Latest Quarter | Latest 6 Months | Latest 12 Months |
|---|---|---|---|---|
| Demand Deposits | 5.1% | 6.7% | 2.1% | 2.2% |
| M1 | 4.3 | 6.9 | 3.9 | 3.8 |
| M2 | 7.9 | 9.7 | 7.5 | 7.0 |
| M3 | 12.3 | 12.2 | 9.5 | 7.5 |
| M4 | 4.4 | 5.9 | 7.2 | 8.4 |
| M5 | 9.6 | 9.5 | 9.2 | 8.4 |

Thus it could be said with equal accuracy that money supply was creeping upward at 2% per annum or exploding at a rate exceeding 12% per annum.

Another element of confusion is introduced by the adjustment of money supply data to remove the effects of inflation, producing data that is called "real" money supply. The adjustment is usually accomplished by dividing the published (or "nominal") money supply data by an inflation deflator based on a price index to obtain the effective, or real money supply. The resultant series expresses money supply in terms of its dollar purchasing power. As the inflation adjustment can be made using a variety of possible price indexes and time intervals, the potential array of monetary growth statistics becomes almost infinite.

Obviously this is not a situation conducive to rational policy formulation. Fortunately we are only concerned with identifying and measuring indicators that are related to the stock market. We are therefore able to ignore those aspects of money supply which are of interest only for their very gradual and long term effects on the national economy and can concentrate on those money supply movements most highly correlated with stock price trends. Extensive testing shows the best indicator to be real M2; i.e., broad money supply adjusted for inflation.

In Figures 2-3 the upper line is nominal M2, and the lower line is real M2. Although the former rose rapidly throughout the 1974-1975 economic recession, and during both downward and upward stock market legs, the latter paralleled the 1974 bear market decline and turned up shortly after the stock market trough at year-end.

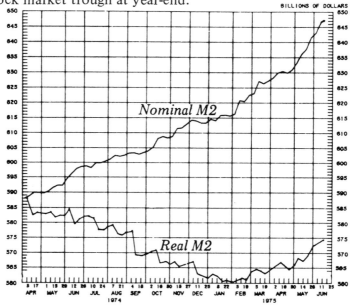

FIGURES 2-3. Broad Money Supply (M2) — Nominal and Real (weekly); April 1974 - June 1975.

This roughly coincidental relationship with stock price trends has been repeated on numerous occasions during the last three decades, making real M2 a highly useful stock market indicator. It is important to bear in mind, however, that money supply is only a moderately good indicator of future stock price changes. Its basic value is in confirming the current trend.

The nation's money supply statistics are compiled in all their dimensions as of each Wednesday and reported by the Federal Reserve System after a lag of about nine days. Two sources within the Federal Reserve System itself provide excellent weekly summaries to the public at nominal charge:

(1) "U.S. Financial Data," Federal Reserve Bank of St. Louis, P. O. Box 442, St. Louis, Missouri 63166; and (2) "Statistical Release H.6," Board of Governors, Federal Reserve System, Washington, D. C. 20551. Many other government publications contain the data as well, but these are the two best.

# 6 Free Reserves

Free reserves are a measure of the liquidity of the nation's banking system. When banks are highly liquid, they have a large quantity of funds on hand for lending and are able to finance individual business growth and, ultimately, broad economic growth as well. On the other hand, when banks are fully loaned out, they are said to be illiquid and are less able to provide the financing necessary for further economic expansion.

The connection to the stock market readily follows. Economic growth translates into sales growth for individual companies, which in turn provides earnings and dividend increases, expectations of which lead to rising stock prices. Similarly, economic contractions induced by poor bank liquidity mean declining sales, earnings, and dividends, and hence a falling stock market.

All banks belonging to the Federal Reserve System (which includes most large commercial banks) are required to leave fixed portions of their deposits as reserves with the Federal Reserve Bank in their region, primarily as a safety measure. Member bank free reserves are calculated by subtracting (a) their legally required reserves, and (b) their borrowings through the Federal Reserve System, from their total cash reserves. The result can be either a negative or a positive amount, but when net free reserves are negative, they are commonly called "net borrowed reserves."

The Federal Reserve System surveys the reserve position of its member banks once a week. The banking week ends on Wednesday and the aggregate reserve position is reported to the public the following evening.

By virtue of their power to establish the minimum legal reserve requirement for their member banks, the regional Federal Reserve Banks can control the system's actual reserve position. Commercial banks tend to hold total cash reserves in an amount approximately equal to that legally required of them by the Federal Reserve System. To hold more cash than required would mean foregoing the making of income producing loans and investments. This induces banks to keep their levels of excess cash reserves very low; so low that they sometimes actually become negative. When individual banks do fall short of their required reserve levels, they must promptly raise the difference. One way is to borrow from the Federal Reserve itself. As a result, changes in the free reserve series tend to be well correlated with the banking system's volume of borrowing from the Fed.

In turn, the extent of borrowing from the Fed is highly dependent upon the relationship between the discount rate (the interest which the Fed charges banks on the money it loans to them) and other market rates of interest such as those on U. S. Treasury Bills and "federal funds." As the banks wish to maximize their profits, they usually borrow from the Fed only when it is to their financial advantage to do so; that is, when the discount rate which they must pay the Fed for borrowing is less than the rate they would have to pay for overnight borrowing from other banks in the federal funds market or the interest income they would lose if they had to sell treasury bills from their portfolio. Hence, the spread between the federal funds rate and the discount rate and the spread between the treasury bill rate and the discount rate are both closely tied to the volume of bank borrowings from the Fed and to the net free reserve position of the nation's banking system. Since net free reserves are a good predictive indicator of stock price trends, these interest rate spreads should also be excellent stock market harbingers and, in fact, they are. (See Chapter 12, "Bills, Funds and Discounts.")

To calculate a Free Reserve indicator for market forecasting purposes, care should be exercised in its construction and testing on several counts. For example, during World War II the banking system held extremely large quantities of net free reserves as the public economized and saved their money in furtherance of the war effort. The magnitude of the free reserve position, several billion dollars, was so great as to in retrospect cast it as a "special case" and suggests the advisability of omitting that period from any statistical analysis of the series.

It should also be noted that while the net free (or borrowed) reserve position tends to revolve around zero, the overall level of the series has expanded as the nation's banking system has increased in size. This trend can be largely eliminated by dividing the dollar amount of net free (or borrowed) reserves by total bank reserves. Expressed as a percent, the Free/Total Reserve Ratio provides an excellent measure of the extent to which banks are capable or incapable of providing the funds necessary for business growth and economic expansion. Table 8 shows the average three, six, and twelve month stock market performances since World War II following a net free or net borrowed reserve position. (The actual indicator used is a ten week exponential moving average of the Free/Total Reserve Ratio.)

TABLE 8

FREE RESERVES AND MARKET PERFORMANCE (1946 - 1974)

| | S&P 500 Index % Change | | Probability of Rising Prices | |
|---|---|---|---|---|
| Time Period | Net Free Reserves | Net Borrowed Reserves | Net Free Reserves | Net Borrowed Reserves |
| 3 months | + 3.0% | 0.0% | 72% | 48% |
| 6 months | + 6.1% | −0.3% | 80% | 44% |
| 12 months | +11.4% | +0.1% | 80% | 46% |

The post war record reveals that a net free reserve position has been followed by rising prices approximately four out of five times, while a net borrowed reserve position has more often led to a market decline than a rise.

Similar analyses demonstrate that positive changes in the Free/Total Reserve Ratio usually lead to rising stock prices, while negative changes in the ratio are more generally followed by market declines. In other words, trends toward better or worse liquidity are nearly as important as actual states of good or bad liquidity.

The best of all possible worlds, then, is a net free reserve position that is expanding. During the last 30 years, such a situation has been followed by major bull market trends 94% of the time. Conversely, a combination of net borrowed reserves and a worsening trend has been followed by major bear markets 55% of the time, a good record, but one which suggests that the indicator is more reliable when it is bullish than when it is bearish.

# 7   Reserve Requirements

When the Federal Reserve System really means business and desires to force a significant change in the trend of interest rates and/or the monetary aggregates, it changes the bank reserve requirement. The reserve requirement instrument is so powerful and so rarely used that a change invariably has a significant and continuing impact on stock prices.

The minimum cash reserve levels which all member banks of the Federal Reserve System must carry by law are established by the Open Market Committee of the Federal Reserve System and vary for different classes of banks. Commercial banks located in the larger metropolitan centers (known as "city banks") must maintain a greater percentage of cash reserves than banks located in less urban areas (known as "country banks").

Commercial banks possessing different quantities of demand deposits (checking account balances) are also subject to different reserve requirements.  As a general rule, the larger the bank, the higher is the required reserve ratio.  Most of the nation's deposits are concentrated in a few hundred large city banks and the reserve requirement established for those banks is the most significant one.  The reserve requirement on deposits in these large commercial banks has been as high as 26%, a rate established in 1948.  Since then the general trend has been down and the 16.5% level set on January 20, 1975, was the lowest in forty years.

Although a comprehensive analysis requires consideration of many factors, as a general rule a given proportionate change in the reserve requirement ratio is capable of causing an equivalent change in the nation's money supply.  For example, if the reserve requirement ratio is decreased from 20% to 19% — that is, by 5% in terms of the amount of the change relative to the beginning requirement — the money supply will ultimately rise by about 5%, assuming no offsetting factors.

Note the inverse relationship between the direction of the reserve requirement change and the direction in which money supply moves.  The less cash banks are required to keep on hand, the more money they can lend out to foster future economic and monetary growth.  Hence, decreases in the reserve requirement constitute an easing of monetary policy and are bullish for stock prices, while increases in the reserve requirement represent a tightening of monetary conditions and are viewed bearishly by the market.

*Reserve Requirement Increases.*  Since 1936 the Federal Reserve System has announced increases in the reserve requirement for large city banks on eleven occasions.  Table 9 (page 32) reveals the response of the stock market to these increases.  On balance, the market has tended to commence declining within two weeks of an announced reserve requirement increase.  The rate of price decline has thereafter accelerated sharply with the largest loss in evidence fifteen months after the announcement.

TABLE 9

RESERVE REQUIREMENT INCREASES
AND MARKET PERFORMANCE

| Time Period | S&P 500 Index Percent Change | Time Period | S&P 500 Index Percent Change |
|---|---|---|---|
| 5 Days: | + 0.3% | 3 Months: | − 1.7% |
| 10 Days: | − 2.3% | 6 Months: | − 5.3% |
| 15 Days: | − 0.7% | 9 Months: | − 8.1% |
| 20 Days: | − 0.3% | 12 Months: | − 8.5% |
| | | 15 Months: | −13.3% |
| | | 18 Months: | − 9.1% |

*Reserve Requirement Decreases.* The Federal Reserve System has announced reductions in the required reserve ratio for large city banks 15 times since 1938. Almost invariably the market has responded by staging a dramatic advance. As evidenced by the summary data contained in Table 10, prices have moved upward from the very first week of the change.

TABLE 10

RESERVE REQUIREMENT DECREASES
AND MARKET PERFORMANCE

| Time Period | S&P 500 Index Percent Change | Time Period | S&P 500 Index Percent Change |
|---|---|---|---|
| 5 Days: | + 0.6% | 3 Months: | + 8.2% |
| 10 Days: | + 1.4% | 6 Months: | + 19.9% |
| 15 Days: | + 1.4% | 9 Months: | + 25.2% |
| 20 Days: | + 1.7% | 12 Months: | + 29.0% |
| | | 15 Months: | + 33.2% |
| | | 18 Months: | + 37.2% |

Since 1960 the Fed has deemed it wise to lower the reserve requirement for large city banks on only two occasions, each of which occurred at an exceptionally good market buying point. The Fed announced a cut on November 13, 1974, from 18% to 17½% and a still larger cut two months later on January 20, 1975, from 17½% to 16½%. The fact that stock prices responded by staging one of the most vigorous advances in history came as no surprise to experienced Fed watchers. Previous reductions in the reserve requirement have also been announced at the generally excellent market buying points of April 1938, late summer 1942, April and August 1949, mid-1953 and 1954, early 1958, and late 1960. On every one of these occasions the market responded with a strong advance. Of the 15 reserve requirement reduction announcements, there has never been a single instance following which the market was not higher six, nine, twelve, fifteen and eighteen months later. Indeed, the market has never risen less than 20% in the eighteen months following an announced reserve requirement cut.

In conclusion, it may be stated categorically that a reduction in the reserve requirement on demand deposits for large city banks is the single most bullish event in the world of stock price behavior.

# 8  Discount Rate

The discount rate is the interest rate which Federal Reserve Banks charge their member banks for direct loans.

When deposit shifts cause a temporary deficiency in a commercial bank's cash reserve position, it is required to raise funds to make up for that deficiency. Three primary sources of cash are available. The bank may sell treasury bills from its portfolio, thus reducing the quantity of interest-earning assets on hand. Alternatively, it may borrow overnight deposits from other banks (in what is called the "federal funds" market), for which it must pay interest. Finally, it may borrow from the Federal Reserve System itself, using what is known as the "discount window." With this last alternative, the discount rate governs the interest the bank must pay the Federal Reserve.

As a general rule, banks will use the lowest cost alternative, be it from the interest foregone when selling treasury bills or the interest that must be paid to borrow in the federal funds market or at the discount window. The Fed prefers to loan money to member banks for only brief periods of time or as a last resort. It seriously frowns on banks which borrow continuously or do so out of a pure profit motive. The popular view held by market analysts is that the Fed uses the discount rate to control market rates of interest, and that a change in the discount rate is therefore a key leading indicator of monetary trends. In fact, the relationship is quite the reverse. As the Federal Reserve System seeks to discourage banks from using the discount window, it normally sets the discount rate at a level which is in line with, and preferably a bit higher than, the alternative treasury bill and federal funds rates.

In other words, the discount rate is a follower of market interest rates, not a leader.

If the discount rate serves as anything but a passive instrument of Federal Reserve policy, it is probably only through its minor announcement effects. Occasionally the discount rate may be changed as a signal to banks that the Federal Reserve System is easing or tightening monetary policy in other areas.

Nonetheless, the stock market has traditionally viewed discount rate changes as harbingers of future monetary policy, not as the passive elements they generally are. In fact, stock prices do tend to rise following reductions in the discount rate and do tend to fall after discount rate increases. This phenomenon simply reflects concomitantly changing market interest rates.

For the record, the empirically observed relationship between discount rate changes and the stock market show that during the three month period immediately following a decrease in the discount rate, stock prices have tended to rise at the well above average rate of about 7% (1% to 2% per quarter is the long term norm). In the following three quarters the rate of gain has been a bit lower, about 3% to 4% per quarter, but still above average.

In the twelve months following increases in the discount rate, the stock market has also risen, but at a below average rate of less than 1% per quarter. Hence, a discount rate increase tends to act as a depressant on stock prices but not as an actual negative force. Or, more precisely, discount rate increases tend to mirror increases in market rates of interest which are the actual depressants on stock prices. Since it is always preferable to select the most direct indicator available, discount rate changes must defer to other interest rates as superior monetary forecasters of future stock market behavior.

# 9 Margin Requirements

The margin requirement is the minimum down payment required on purchases (or short sales) of stock.

By virtue of its authority to regulate the margin requirement, the Federal Reserve System is capable of enticing or discouraging the flow of speculative capital into the stock market. According to theory, the monetary authorities are thereby able to stabilize stock prices, preventing speculative extremes in both directions.

The Fed was first empowered to control the rate in 1934. Since then the margin rate has been as low as 40% and as high as 100%. It was fixed at 50% from January 3, 1974, into the 1980s. Despite the long time lapse since that last adjustment, the market's responses to margin changes is so significant that all investors should be aware of the historical record.

*Margin Requirement Increases.* Since the 1930s the Federal Reserve System has exercised its power to increase the minimum margin requirement twelve times. Requirement increases force speculators to put up more of their own capital to buy stock, thereby reducing both leverage and potential rewards. In theory, this should discourage new stock purchase commitments. In addition, the greater initial capital requirements reduce the total number of shares of stock which can be purchased. The resulting reduction of total market demand should cause downward pressure on stock prices. Table 11 indicates that the market's *initial* response to the bearish Federal Reserve action has traditionally been appropriately negative. But then, in a trend opposite to the theoretical expectation, the market has usually

TABLE 11

MARGIN REQUIREMENT INCREASES
AND MARKET PERFORMANCE

| Time Period | S&P 500 Index Percent Change | Time Period | S&P 500 Index Percent Change |
|---|---|---|---|
| 1 Day: | − 0.5% | 1 Month: | + 1.1% |
| 2 Days: | − 0.4% | 3 Months: | + 4.9% |
| 3 Days: | − 0.2% | 6 Months: | + 8.3% |
| 4 Days: | − 0.3% | 9 Months: | + 10.8% |
| 5 Days: | − 0.4% | 12 Months: | + 14.4% |
| 10 Days: | − 0.3% | 15 Months: | + 10.2% |
| 15 Days: | + 0.3% | 18 Months: | + 10.6% |

recovered its lost ground. By the end of one month it has moved up 1%, an above normal rate of gain. The market has generally continued to rise at an above average rate for one full year following a margin increase. Not until more than a year after the initial action has the market generally started to decline.

Of course, individual market cycles have deviated from the average. For example, the margin rate was increased on November 24, 1972, just prior to the great market collapse of 1973-1974. A margin increase on February 21, 1946, also immediately preceded a sharply downward market. (The 1946 event can probably be dismissed as a one-time aberration since the Fed jacked the requirement up to the then unprecedented extreme of 100%, effectively prohibiting all margin activity.) All of the remaining ten margin requirement increases have occurred well before the market topped out — indeed, too early to have been of any help at all in timing market peaks.

It is also worth noting that the market has virtually always advanced vigorously in the months just prior to a margin increase; in fact, significantly so. In the immediately preceding six months, prices have advanced 15% on the average, while the full one year gain before the Fed has taken action has averaged 27%. That rate of excessive price growth is normally just what the Fed desires to temper when it injects a margin increase into the market atmosphere.

*Margin Requirement Decreases.* The margin rate has been lowered ten times since 1937. The Federal Reserve System has invariably made these reductions following protracted declines in the market. The lowering of margins has sometimes been instituted prior to a significant trough in prices, while on other occasions reductions have occurred somewhat after the market has formed a trough. On balance, though, margin requirement reductions have been a slightly leading indicator of market bottoms. Table 12 details the historical experience of market prices following the ten margin decreases.

TABLE 12

MARGIN REQUIREMENT DECREASES
AND MARKET PERFORMANCE

| Time Period | S&P 500 Index Percent Change | Time Period | S&P 500 Index Percent Change |
|---|---|---|---|
| 1 Day: | − 0.3% | 1 Month: | + 0.3% |
| 2 Days: | − 0.5% | 3 Months: | − 2.3% |
| 3 Days: | − 1.0% | 6 Months: | + 3.4% |
| 4 Days: | − 1.8% | 9 Months: | + 7.7% |
| 5 Days: | − 1.9% | 12 Months: | + 12.5% |
| 10 Days: | − 0.4% | 15 Months: | + 16.3% |
| 15 Days: | − 0.6% | 18 Months: | + 18.5% |

Contrary to theory, the market has declined slightly on average in the days and weeks immediately following the margin cuts, a reflection of the slightly leading tendency of the indicator. After a couple of months, prices have usually initiated a strong uptrend and have continued to rise at an above average rate for more than a year.

Indeed, only the most recent margin reduction on January 3, 1974, can be judged an absolute failure in predicting a market upturn. By that date the broad market had been in a downward trend for 21 months. The Federal Reserve System presumably acted in the hope of stemming what had already been a sharp bear market collapse. Stock prices defied tradition and continued to trend lower for most of the balance of 1974. In retrospect, the speculative excesses which built up prior to the 1972-1974 bear market can be seen to have been so great that a very lengthy and substantial price decline was necessary to correct them.

If it is acknowledged that the last crash was a unique event, it is likely that in the future the purchase of stocks following a margin reduction should once again prove to constitute a profitable investment strategy.

# 10  Three Steps And A Stumble

The "Three Steps And A Stumble" rule states that when the Federal Reserve System tightens monetary policy by increasing one of its basic policy variables (Discount Rate, Margin Requirement, or Reserve Requirement) three times in succession, the market should "stumble" and fall down. The rule implies that a minimum of three restrictive changes in a single variable are required to knock the market down.

The "Three Steps And A Stumble" rule has been triggered just twelve times since the first signal in 1919. The signal dates, along with an analysis of their leads and lags of market peaks, are noted in Table 13. The third signal was triggered by three reserve requirement increases and the fourth by three margin boosts.   All the rest are products of three successive discount rate increases.   Signals have led market turns more frequently than lagged them.

### TABLE 13

### "THREE STEPS AND A STUMBLE" SIGNALS (1914-1983)

| Signal | Date of Signal | S&P 500 Peak | Lead or Lag |
|---|---|---|---|
| 1 | Nov.  3, 1919 | Nov.  3, 1919 | Coincident |
| 2 | July 13, 1928 | Sep.  7, 1929 | 14 Month Lead |
| 3 | May  1, 1937 | Mar.  6, 1937 | 2 Month Lag |
| 4 | Jan. 21, 1946 | May 29, 1946 | 4 Month Lead |
| 5 | Aug. 13, 1948 | June 15, 1948 | 2 Month Lag |
| 6 | Sep.  9, 1955 | Aug.  2, 1956 | 11 Month Lead |
| 7 | Mar.  6, 1959 | Aug.  3, 1959 | 5 Month Lead |
| 8 | Dec.  6, 1965 | Feb.  9, 1966 | 2 Month Lead |
| 9 | Apr. 19, 1968 | Nov. 29, 1968 | 7 Month Lead |
| 10 | May   4, 1973 | Jan. 11, 1973 | 4 Month Lag |
| 11 | Oct. 26, 1977 | Sep. 21, 1976 | 13 Month Lag |
| 12 | Nov. 14, 1980 | Nov. 28, 1980 | Coincident |
| | | Median: | 3 Month Lead |

Table 14 shows a more explicit record of market action following the signal dates.   The rule appears to have merit, although the direction of stock prices after the signals has not been uniformly downward, nor has the average extent of the

### TABLE 14

### "THREE STEPS AND A STUMBLE" & MARKET PERFORMANCE

| Time Period | S&P 500 Index Percent Change | Number of Times Market Advanced |
|---|---|---|
| 5 Days: | + 0.4% | 3 out of 12 |
| 10 Days: | − 0.1% | 3 out of 12 |
| 15 Days: | − 0.4% | 6 out of 12 |
| 20 Days: | −1.4% | 5 out of 12 |
| 3 Months: | − 0.3% | 6 out of 12 |
| 6 Months: | − 1.1% | 6 out of 12 |
| 9 Months: | − 5.2% | 7 out of 12 |
| 12 Months: | − 5.0% | 8 out of 12 |
| 15 Months: | −4.0% | 7 out of 12 |
| 18 Months: | − 6.5% | 6 out of 12 |

declines been especially severe.    A "Three Steps And A Stumble" signal tends to act as a depressant to stock prices. Eventually all sell signals have led to substantial price declines − about 30% on average, although in some cases a long delay has ensued before the decline has materialized. (In 1928, a 14 month, 70% rise in prices followed the sell signal before the market declined.   By then the Fed was already assuming a contrary stance of monetary ease.)

The long run significance of "Three Steps And A Stumble" sell signals may be alternatively illustrated by assuming a hypothetical investment policy of shorting stocks during the twelve months following each of the ten initiations of the bearish rule.   Based on the performance of the Standard & Poor's Composite Index, the simulation produces a total portfolio growth from $10,000 to $13,486 over the cumulative twelve year holding period.   That equates to an annual rate of return of 2.5%.   While the net return would be trivial after adjustment for trading costs, the fact that a short selling strategy would result in any paper profits at all, suggests anew that periods following "Three Steps And A Stumble" signals would be good ones to temporarily step out of stocks and into riskless money market investments.

The weakness of the "Three Steps And A Stumble" rule lies in its highly variable prediction lead time. The Fed begins taking restrictive action well before the economic and stock market booms near completion.   Indeed, the rule's requirement of three steps rather than just a single step up in any one of the key rates is a concession to this fact − but only a compromise.   It is apparent that occasionally a rule of four or five (or only two) steps up in one of the rates would improve the lead or lag time and furnish superior sell signals, although the specific occasions on which the adjustments should be applied are not determinable in advance.   In sum, "Three Steps" signals constitute a warning that the market is basically overpriced, even though the serious investor must look elsewhere for more precise timing indicators of market tops.

# 11 Two Tumbles
## And A Jump

The "Two Tumbles And A Jump" rule states that when the Federal Reserve eases the monetary climate by decreasing one of the three basic policy variables (Discount Rate, Margin Requirement, or Reserve Requirement) *two* times in succession, conditions are favorable for an ensuing "jump" in stock prices. It was first proclaimed by the author in 1973.

The rule was then next triggered on January 9, 1975, following the Fed's second consecutive cut in the discount rate. The market shot upward from that point, with the S&P 500 Index increasing 32% after one year and reaching a peak interim gain of 34%. Though impressive, as noted in Table 15, it was only an average "Two Tumbles And A Jump" performance.

TABLE 15

"TWO TUMBLES AND A JUMP" SIGNALS (1914-1983)

| Signal No. | Date of Signal | S&P 500 Index Maximum % Gain Within One Year | S&P 500 Index Maximum % Loss Within One Year |
|---|---|---|---|
| 1 | Dec. 23, 1914 | + 82% | 0% |
| 2 | June 16, 1921 | + 41% | − 6% |
| 3 | June 12, 1924 | + 42% | 0% |
| 4 | Nov. 15, 1929 | + 28% | − 23% |
| 5 | June 24, 1932 | +137% | − 4% |
| 6 | May 26, 1933 | + 31% | − 8% |
| 7 | Sep. 14, 1942 | + 48% | 0% |
| 8 | Mar. 30, 1949 | + 16% | − 11% |
| 9 | Apr. 16, 1954 | + 36% | − 1% |
| 10 | Jan. 24, 1958 | + 34% | − 3% |
| 11 | Aug. 12, 1960 | + 20% | − 7% |
| 12 | July 10, 1962 | + 24% | − 6% |
| 13 | Dec. 4, 1970 | + 17% | 0% |
| 14 | Dec. 6, 1971 | + 22% | 0% |
| 15 | Jan. 9, 1975 | + 34% | − 1% |
| 16 | June 12, 1980 | + 22% | − 1% |
| 17 | Dec. 3, 1981 | + 11% | − 18% |
| | Median . . . | + 31% | − 3% |

Had an investor bought at each "Two Tumbles And A Jump" signal date and sold the position one year later, he would have realized a handsome return. Although he would have been invested for only 17 of the last 69 years, an initial $10,000 investment would have grown to $542,304 by year-end 1983. Alternatively, an investor who disdained the market during those 17 years and held stocks only through the remaining 52 years would have seen an original $10,000 investment shrink to just $6,450. The "Two Tumbles" rule more than captured the entire market rise since World War I.

The great bull markets of every decade have been accompanied by "Two Tumbles And A Jump" signals. Even the November 15, 1929, signal was propitious, for it precisely caught a 28% six month rally between the quick, panicky crash in the fall of 1929 and the real crash of mid-1930 to mid-1932. The December 3, 1981, signal was early, but it preceded the largest market breakout in half a century.

Furthermore, as noted in Table 16, on average the 17 "Two Tumbles" signals have yielded impressive gains across

TABLE 16

"TWO TUMBLES AND A JUMP" AND MARKET PERFORMANCE

| Time Period | S&P 500 Index Percent Change | Number of Times Market Advanced |
|---|---|---|
| 5 Days | + 0.8% | 10 out of 17 |
| 10 Days: | + 1.7% | 12 out of 17 |
| 15 Days: | + 3.5% | 14 out of 17 |
| 20 Days: | + 3.6% | 13 out of 17 |
| 3 Months: | +11.3% | 14 out of 17 |
| 6 Months: | +16.1% | 16 out of 17 |
| 9 Months: | +21.5% | 16 out of 17 |
| 12 Months: | +30.5% | 16 out of 17 |
| 15 Months: | +34.4% | 16 out of 17 |
| 18 Months: | +34.4% | 16 out of 17 |

all holding periods. In fact, it is one of the very, very few indicators in existence with a near perfect half-century record.

Economic theory holds that the Federal Reserve System can snap an economic or stock market expansion quite easily by taking restrictive monetary action, but that it has a much more difficult time reversing a contraction. The theory is often described in terms of "pulling or pushing on a string." (It is obviously easier to pull a string than to push one.) According to the theory, when the economy is operating at or near full capacity or when the market is straining toward new heights, the strings are tight and the Fed can pull them around at will. When the economy is depressed, the strings are slack, and the Fed has great difficulty pushing them in the direction and with the force it desires.

Although this theory seems plausible, it is not supported by the "Stumbles" and "Tumbles" rules. While the expansionary "Two Tumbles And A Jump" rule has a truly superlative record of forecasting market and economic upturns, the restrictive "Three Steps And A Stumble" rule has only a moderately good record of forecasting downturns.

Strangely enough, it is the latter which has gained a relatively wide following in the investment community, while the former has escaped "discovery" until relatively recently. Even technical analyst Edson Gould, one of the most vocal supporters of the "Three Steps" rule, has pointedly remarked that restrictive Fed actions are more significant than actions of moderation. The evidence casts considerable doubt on that hypothesis.

# 12 Bills, Funds, and Discounts

The interrelationships between three key interest rates — federal funds, treasury bill, and discount — provide important clues to future stock market performance.

Each of these rates is related to the process by which Federal Reserve System member commercial banks adjust their cash reserves to the levels mandated by the Fed. Three basic reserve adjustment alternatives are available to the banks: (1) They may buy or sell U. S. Treasury Bills. (2) They may borrow or lend money to other banks in the overnight federal funds market. (Although these "loans" involve only bookkeeping entries with no cash changing hands, interest is still paid.) (3) Banks needing more reserves may, as a last resort, borrow money from the Federal Reserve System at the discount rate.

The respective levels of the three interest rates dictate which alternatives a bank chooses. When the treasury bill and federal funds rates are below the discount rate, banks in need of additional cash reserves liquidate T-Bills from their portfolios or borrow from one another — and Federal Reserve loans to member banks are nil.

Alternatively, when the federal funds rate is bid above the discount rate, it means that some banks are willing to pay a premium to obtain reserves. They may have one of two motives for paying such a premium. The first is to avoid the Fed's scrutiny of their lending policies that is a normal part of the discount process. The second is that the banking system as a whole is so illiquid (strapped for cash) that the few banks with extra reserves demand a generous return to induce them to loan funds to the banks which are squeezed by a reserve deficiency. Either situation symbolizes tight monetary conditions and is bearish for the stock market. Historically, the federal funds and treasury bill rates have usually held below the discount rate. When the reverse has occurred, the stock market has been exceptionally vulnerable.

Figure 4 presents a graphic illustration of the relationship between the federal funds and discount rates during the critical five-year period 1928-1932. Although historians now realize that the nation's monetary and economic situation was inherently unsound in the late 1920s, the stock market, oblivious to all adverse signs, spurted upward to seemingly ever higher highs before the bubble finally burst. Note that in early 1928 the federal funds rate moved above the discount rate, a condition that persisted into the fall of 1929. This was dramatic warning that the banking and financial systems

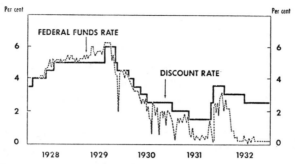

FIGURE 4.    Federal Funds Rate (weekly) and Discount Rate (effective dates); 1928 - 1932.

were in severe trouble.  In retrospect no other single indicator so dramatically predicted the ensuing crash.

More recently investors have disciplined themselves to watch monetary and economic conditions with greater care. To some degree the result has been a reduction in the lead time of many key indicators.  As a close examination of the 45 year interest rate chart contained in Figure 5 reveals, a

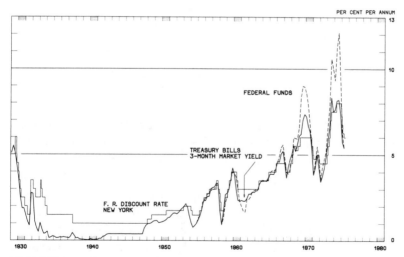

FIGURE 5.    Federal Funds Rate (quarterly), Treasury Bill Rate (quarterly), and Discount Rate (effective dates); 1930 - 1974.

positive spread between the federal funds and treasury bill rates and the discount rate has developed into a coincident rather than a leading indicator of market declines. The treasury bill rate moved above the discount rate at year-end 1952, signalling the market decline which commenced in January 1953. One or both of the treasury bill and federal funds rates (the latter available in chart form only since 1955) also surged above the discount rate in 1957, early 1960, 1966, 1969-1970, and 1972-1974. All of these penetrations coincided with periods of sharply declining stock prices.

Figure 6 magnifies the federal funds — discount rate relationship between 1968 and 1975, eight years of generally,

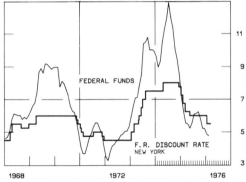

FIGURE 6.    Federal Funds Rate (monthly) and Discount Rate (effective dates); January 1968 - February 1975.

though not continually, declining stock prices. Not coincidentally, the federal funds rate spent most of this period well above the discount rate. Only during the rising markets of mid-1970 to mid-1971, late 1971 to mid-1972, and from late 1974 onward did the federal funds rate generally hold below the discount rate. Even the moderate mid-1975 correction was accompanied by a minor penetration by the federal funds rate through the discount rate. At all other times a bearishly positive federal funds — discount rate spread prevailed and stock prices usually fell.    In this entire critical eight year period, this interest rate spread has a nearly flawless record.

(A related indicator, the Prime Rate - Federal Funds Index, also has a near-perfect record during the last fifty years.)

# 13 Yields, Yields, Yields

*Yield Curve.*   A yield curve is a relationship between market yields of interest bearing securities of different maturity lengths.   (The maturity is the date on which the issuer of the security must pay back its face amount to the security holders.)  The most representative yield curve construction is based upon securities issued by the U. S. government:   treasury bills which mature in less than one year, treasury notes with one to five year maturities, and long term treasury bonds which mature in over five years.

Normally, the longer the time to the maturity of a security, the higher its yield.   Thus, treasury bills usually yield less than treasury notes, which in turn generally provide lower yields than treasury bonds. This is called an "upward sloping" yield curve.

There are two reasons for such an upward sloping yield relationship.   First, the longer the time to maturity, the greater is the risk that the "real" rate of return (the simple annual rate of return minus the annual rate of inflation) might be negative;   that is, a "real" loss.   The longer a security is to be held the more opportunity there is for the actual inflation rate to diverge from the expected rate.

Second, there is the possibility that investors might not be able to hold a security to maturity.  At maturity, of course, the security holder will receive par value (usually $1,000 or a multiple thereof).   But a sale before maturity for any reason introduces the chance of a capital loss.   The longer the time to maturity, the greater is the possibility that a sale might be required and that a capital loss on the security might necessarily be incurred.

In summary, the possibility of incurring losses in nominal or real dollars entitles holders of longer maturing securities to higher yields than those received by holders of short maturity securities. Thus an upward sloping yield curve is normal and is bullish for the stock market.

Any deviation from an upward sloping yield curve is bearish. If treasury bills yield more than notes or bonds, or if notes yield more than bonds, something is amiss. The phenomenon may indicate an abnormal need for short term funds by the government or private enterprise to cope with near-term liquidity problems. Or it may reflect an exacerbation of short term inflationary pressures. Or, in yet a third case, it may reflect a policy of monetary tightness by the Federal Reserve System.

All of these situations have bearish implications for stock prices, because liquidity problems, inflationary pressures, and monetary stringency upset the normal day to day course of business, harming companies, workers and consumers in the process, and ultimately penalizing profits and dividends, the cornerstones of a fundamentally strong stock market. Consequently, while a normal upward sloping yield curve usually precedes and accompanies rising stock prices, deviations from the normal curve more frequently precede and accompany falling prices.

Strictly speaking, a yield curve of government securities should be calculated using all available government bills, notes, and bonds (there are dozens of each on the market). While such an indicator can fairly easily be developed with econometric techniques, an excellent weekly approximation of the full yield curve can be derived by relating yield indexes of just three types of government securities: three month (90 day) treasury bills, three to five year treasury notes, and ten year or greater treasury bonds (see end of discussion for data sources).

During the last 35 years, a normal upward sloping yield curve based on these three yield indexes has been accompanied by primary bull markets nearly 80% of the time. An abnormal yield curve has been accompanied by sustained uptrends only 45% of the time and by major downtrends 55% of the time.

As noted in Table 17, the implications for actual future market changes have been just as profound. Market performances over subsequent three, six, and twelve month periods

TABLE 17

YIELD CURVE AND FUTURE STOCK PRICES (1941-1975)

| Yield Curve | S&P 500 Index 3 Months Later | S&P 500 Index 6 Months Later | S&P 500 Index One Year Later |
|---|---|---|---|
| Normal | + 3.0% | +6.0% | + 11.5% |
| Abnormal | − 0.5% | −0.8% | − 0.7% |
| 35-Year Average | + 1.9% | +3.8% | + 7.7% |

are clearly superior when the yield curve is normal and upward sloping than when it is abnormal and downward sloping. The yield curve is one of the very few indicators equally adept at predicting the market for each of these periods, a valuable supplement to its excellent mapping of major bull and bear market trends.

The best source of weekly yield statistics is the *free* Federal Reserve Bank of St. Louis publication, "U. S. Financial Data." Their treasury bond yield series is particularly useful because it eliminates so-called "flower bonds" which may be used at par in payment of estate taxes. A flower bond purchased prior to death for, say, $850 may be used just as though it were $1,000 cash when estate taxes are paid. Due to this added reward potential, flower bonds carry a lower than average yield, a feature which biases the yield curve relationship if they are included in an index of long term treasury bond yields.

*Dealer Loan Rate.* One little known but extremely useful guide to money market conditions is the Dealer Loan Rate — the interest rate charged by money center banks for overnight loans to major bond dealers on the riskless collateral of U. S. government bonds. No one indicator can ever tell the whole monetary story but the Dealer Loan Rate is one of the most sensitive interest rates in existence. More often than not, it leads most other market rates, especially at critical turning points. Unfortunately, in early 1975 The Federal Reserve terminated publication of the rate in their regular statistical releases. Today it is used by the Fed for internal purposes only and is quite difficult to obtain.

*Interest Rate Spreads.* A valuable supplement to the yield curve indicator is the "interest rate spread," which is calculated by subtracting the yield of a short term fixed income security from the yield of a long term, fixed income security. An interest rate spread for government securities can be computed by subtracting a short term treasury bill yield from the average yield of long term treasury bonds. A corporate sector spread can be derived by subtracting the average yield of high grade, short term corporate debt, such as commercial paper, from the average yield of high grade corporate bonds.

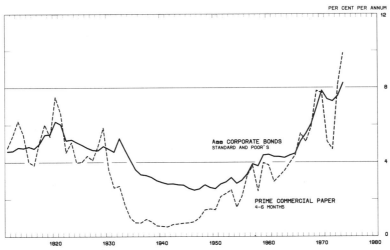

FIGURE 7.    Corporate Interest Rate Spread — High grade bond yield (annually) and commercial paper rate (annually); 1911 - 1974.

(An alternative to the commercial paper rate is the "prime rate," the rate of interest banks charge their most credit worthy customers. Until the last few years, the prime set the standard for market rates of interest on high grade corporate issues. Today that situation is reversed, and the prime is little more than an anachronistic *follower* of market yields. The commercial paper rate is a superior bellwether rate.)

The average of the government and corporate sector yield spreads is an excellent measure of the structure of interest rates in the U. S. economy.

Just as an upward sloping yield curve is bullish for the market, so is a positive interest rate spread. The more positive the spread, the more favorable is the market environment. It follows that a trend toward a larger positive spread is also favorable for the market, as is an accelerating rate of positive improvement. A comprehensive spread indicator should thus include the average interest rate spread, its change, and its rate of change.

Based upon this model, the interest rate spread indicator has accurately signalled many periods of both rising and falling stock prices. Within the last quarter century, periods of extremely favorable spread readings (all bullish elements in gear – large spreads, and positive changes and rates of change) commenced in July 1950, September 1953, March 1958, August 1960, October 1964, August 1967, December 1970, and January 1975. In every case common stock commitments ultimately proved to be exceptionally rewarding.

The most bearish readings (caused by negative spreads and negative changes and rates of change) were flashed in April 1957, May 1966, throughout 1969, and early in 1974. While the indicator obviously did not signal every period of sharply declining prices in the last 25 years, there were no false signals. Whenever the indicator reached a bearish extreme, the market invariably responded by moving sharply lower.

*The Not Quite So Confident Confidence Index.* Lacking critical inside information from a member of the President's Council of Economic Advisors, or perhaps a peephole into the Federal Reserve Board's meeting room, or some other source of inside information from the nation's economic elite, the best alternative is to emulate the behavior of those who seem to be the most financially sophisticated. Their actions should be a positive harbinger of the direction of future market prices. One of the oldest and most widely followed measures of sophisticated sentiment is the Confidence Index, developed by *Barron's* in 1932.

Since it was developed over forty years ago the index has garnered a large following and been the subject of frequent analysis. The most common belief is that turns in the Confidence Index tend to lead turns in the stock market by 60 to 120 days.

The Confidence Index purports to measure the relative yields, or prices, of different grade corporate bonds. The index is calculated by relating the yields of high grade bonds to the yields of intermediate grade bonds:

$$\frac{\text{Average Yield of High Grade Conservative Bonds}}{\text{Average Yield of Intermediate Grade Speculative Bonds}}$$

An understanding of how the index works is facilitated by expressing it in terms of price rather than yield, the one being a function of the other. The Confidence Index may then be defined by the following ratio:

$$\frac{\text{Average Price of Intermediate Grade Speculative Bonds}}{\text{Average Price of High Grade Conservative Bonds}}$$

According to the index's underlying theory, when bond investors are confident of economic trends, they are more willing to place their funds in high yielding speculative bonds, thus bidding up their prices and increasing the ratio of speculative bond prices to conservative bond prices. On the other hand, when bond investors are fearful of future economic trends, they transfer funds from speculative bonds, which fall in price under the added supply pressure, and buy safer high grade bonds which increase in price from the added demand. This has the effect of reducing the Confidence Index Ratio.

It would not be untoward to inquire what possible relevance bond buyers have to the stock market. The question has been asked quite frequently of late as the index has yielded one wrong market call after another. The theoretical answer is, bond buyers (often representing multi-billion dollar institutions), are substantial investors in all types of financial assets, including common stocks. The confidence or lack of confidence these "sophisticated" investors have in the economy and the financial markets is believed to have positive relevance to the equity market.

In the last few years, the index has fallen on hard times. Indeed it has seemingly been worthless as a market predictor. Upward and downward trends in the Confidence Index, supposedly denoting greater or lesser speculative enthusiasm on the part of sophisticated investors, have occurred in a virtually random fashion vis-a-vis subsequent stock market trends.

Aside from its rather circuitous underlying theory, the problems with the index seem to lie mainly in the bonds which are used in its construction. While *Barron's* average of ten high grade corporate bonds is a fairly representative, although far from perfect sample, the speculative bond average has always been something of a mishmash. Until June 1976 the "intermediate" grade bond average was a "low" grade average consisting of a fantastic conglomeration of forty mixed issues: specifically, ten high grade railroad issues, ten second grade rails, ten utilities, and ten industrials. Note that thirty of the bonds were railroad and utility obligations, two sectors which have been beset by their own peculiar and well publicized problems during the last several years. The price and yield fluctuations of these thirty bonds were probably tied as directly to the unique problems of the two industries as to the speculative bond market in general. The other ten bonds in the forty issue average were supposedly ten speculative industrial company issues. A number were of even higher quality than the high grade conservative bond average to which they were ultimately related in the index ratio.

To rectify this problem, in the summer of 1976 *Barron's*

replaced the forty low grade bond average with the current ten bond intermediate grade average. Sadly, little attention was seemingly put into new bond selection. Companies with representation in the speculative average are Alabama Power, Beneficial, and Caterpillar, all issues of a quality superior to most of the bonds in the supposedly high grade group. The complete list of the high and intermediate grade bonds is presented in Table 18.

TABLE 18

CONFIDENCE AND INDEX BOND COMPONENTS
AND S&P RATING (JANUARY 1990)

| High Grade Conservative | | Intermediate Grade Speculative | |
|---|---|---|---|
| Bond | S&P Rating | Bond | S&P Rating |
| ATT 8-3/4s '00 | AA | Alabama Power 9-3/4s '04 | A |
| Anheuser Busch 8-5/8s '16 | AA | Beneficial 9s '05 | A |
| Baltimore G&E 8-3/8s '06 | AA | Caterpillar 8s '01 | A |
| DuPont 8-1/2s '06 | AA | Commonwealth El. 9-1/8s '08 | BBB |
| Exxon 8-1/4s '01 | AAA | Firestone 9-1/4s '04 | A |
| GE 8-1/2s '04 | AAA | GTE 9-3/8s '99 | A |
| GMAC 8-1/4s '06 | AA | Honeywell 9-3/8s '09 | A |
| IBM 9-3/8s '04 | AAA | Union Carbide 8-1/2s '05 | BBB |
| Illinois Bell 7-5/8s '06 | AAA | USX 7-3/4s '01 | BBB |
| Procter & Gamble 8-1/4s '05 | AA | Woolworth 9s '99 | A |

The "improvement" has not really improved anything. The net result of the change is still a next to meaningless market indicator; a not quite so confident Confidence Index.

*Stock Versus Bond Yields and "Will-Go."* If long term corporate bonds yield 8% and common stocks provide an average dividend yield of only 4%, the bonds are twice as profitable and also less risky; ergo, stocks should be sold. Right? Although that is the implication of the bond yield — stock yield spread, the record suggests greater risk in following the indicator than in ignoring it. The spread disregards the all important factor of dividend and earnings growth, an essential component of the total long run return of common stocks. A strategy of buying stocks when the average dividend yield became greater than the average bond yield and selling stocks when their average dividend yield declined to less than the average bond yield seemed to have some validity in the 1920s, '30s, and '40s. More recently the spread has been continuously negative since 1958. Stepping out of stocks at that time would have proven most unwise as the Dow has since more than doubled.

A simple five-week moving average of the stock yield — bond yield spread constitutes the increasingly popular "Will-Go" Index. Although trends in the Will-Go Index *reputedly* predict trends in stock prices, this indicator is actually without significant forecasting ability. All it really measures is changes in interest rates and changes in stock prices, the latter being the most important factor in stock yield changes. Serious market students should look elsewhere for useful market forecasting tools.

*Barron's Bond/Stock Ratio.* The Bond/Stock Ratio represents an alternative calculation of the basic bond yield—stock yield spread. It is computed by dividing the interest yield on *Barron's* ten high grade bonds by the earnings yield on *Barron's* fifty stock average. (An earnings yield — calculated by dividing latest twelve month earnings per share by current stock price — is the reciprocal of a Price/Earnings Ratio.) Although the indicator measures the valuation of company earnings, not dividends, like the yield spread indicator, it ignores the all important element of future earnings growth. In this case half a loaf is worse than none, and the Bond/Stock Ratio, too, can be ignored by market timing students.

# 14 Total Shorts/Total Volume Ratio

The Total Shorts/Total Volume Ratio (TS/TV) measures the market sentiment of the greatest risk takers on Wall Street — the short sellers.

Most beginning market students are puzzled by the concept of short selling. The confusion need not exist because it is really a very simple operation. As everyone knows, the normal investment procedure is to buy stock and then, at a later date, sell it. If the sale price is above the purchase price, the investor makes a profit. If the sale price is below the purchase price, the investor incurs a loss.

Short selling's basic point of departure from the normal long operation is that in shorting, the sale of the stock comes first and the purchase last. The game is scored the same way. A profit is realized only if the stock is purchased at a price less than that at which it was sold. The confusion which often resides in the short selling operation is, how does the investor obtain the stock to sell it if he has not previously purchased it? The answer is simple. He merely borrows someone else's stock certificate and sells it. (Your brokerage house usually has drawers full of stock certificates they don't mind lending to you.) After he closes out the operation the short seller returns the certificate to the lender.

To draw an analogy, if you borrowed your neighbor's car and sold it to another party, and then later purchased another car and returned it to your neighbor, you would have essentially engaged in a short selling operation. Of course, your neighbor might be rather upset if you returned to him an automobile inferior to the one he originally lent you. Such a problem does not exist when selling short stock because all shares of a given issue are interchangeable.

Selling short ordinarily requires an above average quantity of intestinal fortitude. Because the speculator is dependent upon a *decline* in prices to make a profit, it goes against the American grain and has frequently been subject to criticism. More importantly, short selling flies in the face of that which is inherently in favor of ordinary stock speculation; namely, the concept of limiting one's loss to 100%, while exposing his position to a theoretically infinite gain. A short seller reverses this highly favorable risk/reward ratio, exposing himself instead to unlimited loss. After the initial sale has been executed, there is no limit to how far up prices can move and how much the offsetting purchase will ultimately cost. The most he can gain is 100%, and that would be realized only in the rare event that the stock price declined to zero.

Short selling is a highly speculative endeavor, and most participants engage in it only when they are extremely confident that prices will decline. Not surprisingly, emotion enters into their decision making process. Indeed, most short selling usually occurs after prices have already declined substantially, providing the speculator with what amounts to an emotional crutch. Only after a significant price drop is he normally able to muster enough courage to start selling short. Unfortunately, it is a simple function of logic that the more prices have already declined, the closer they are to their ultimate lows and a subsequent reversal. This theory is borne out by reality. Most short selling activity occurs not prior to price declines, but after price declines and prior to large market rallies. It is precisely because a short sale reflects an extreme in speculative sentiment that derivatives of aggregate short selling data are often highly useful in forecasting future stock price trends.

The ratio of total short sales to total volume is therefore a contrary indicator of speculative sentiment. Whenever the Total Shorts/Total Volume Ratio has been high, prices have risen, not fallen. And when selling short stocks has been a more appropriate strategy, the ratio has been low instead.

During the last forty years, the TS/TV Ratio has fluctuated between 1% and 10%. Most of the readings near the lower end of that range occurred several decades ago, and the ratio has since exhibited a strong secular (i.e., long term) uptrend. Failure to adjust for this trend renders the indicator virtually worthless for market timing purposes. For example, in 1941 a reading of about 2.3% was considered normal, neither bearish nor bullish. By 1976 a normal ratio would have been approximately 7.8%. The secular uptrend has raised the average level of the ratio at a rate of about 0.15% per year.

There is also a seasonal bias to the ratio around year-end.

During the last few weeks of December and the first several weeks of January, total market volume usually increases significantly, thereby diminishing the TS/TV Ratio to below normal levels.  The greatest diminution of the ratio occurs during the very last week of the year.

After adjustments for trend and seasonality, the Total Shorts/Total Volume Ratio has yielded several excellent signals, particularly on the buy side. Just within the last few years, clearly defined peaks in the ratio were registered at the important intermediate and primary market troughs of March 1968, June 1970, August 1971, November 1972, June 1973, October 1974, and October 1975.

One criticism lodged against the indicator is that it reflects not only speculative bearish sentiment, but also the non–speculative, even conservative, action of professional arbitrageurs.  Arbitraging often occurs following the announcement of company mergers and acquisitions. It is the responsibility of the free market to adjust the price of the newly acquired company to the price which is being offered by the acquiring company.  Arbitrageurs profit from small discrepancies in price by purchasing the under-valued security (of the acquired company) and selling short the over-valued security (of the acquiring company).  When the under and over-valuation is eliminated by this demand and supply pressure (i.e., when the prices converge), the arbitrageur closes out his position.  Arbitrage induced short selling activity also results from minor undervaluations of convertible bonds and preferreds, and common stock warrants.  The divergences from normal valuation are eliminated by purchasing the convertible security and selling short the common.

The argument is not without merit and some adjustment is required.  Arbitrage induced short selling activity usually increases near market tops when merger activity and the issuance of new securities is at a fever pitch, influencing the Total Shorts/Total Volume Ratio toward a less bearish reading than would otherwise be the case. It is to the credit of the indicator that it overcomes these biases and still provides many excellent market calls.  On the other hand, merger and arbitrage activity fades as bear markets progress, leaving this indicator relatively free of bias to signal the bottom reversal.

The TS/TV Ratio has also been criticized because it lumps the short sales activities of sophisticated floor specialists with that of unsophisticated public speculators.    Although measures of the relative levels of short selling by such groups are indeed useful indicators themselves, it appears that in the aggregate all market participants tend to overdo short selling at bottoms and tend to ignore the opportunities at tops. Thus the TS/TV Ratio is a good market forecasting indicator.

# 15  Short Interest Ratio

The Short Interest Ratio (SIR) is one of the oldest and most popular measures of public market sentiment.  In its traditional form, its generally perceived forecasting value is probably somewhat exaggerated, but it lives on and has provided many excellent market signals.

The ratio is calculated by dividing the mid-month New York Stock Exchange short interest (that is, the number of shares that have been sold short and not yet repurchased) by the average daily trading volume on the Exchange during the preceding four weeks.  A reading of 1.00 indicates that outstanding short positions are equivalent to about one day's trading activity.  Similarly, an SIR of 2.00 indicates that the outstanding short interest is the equivalent of two days' trading volume.  (A 2.00 SIR would apply to a 20 million share short interest accompanied by an average daily trading volume of only ten million shares.)

High ratios have usually been followed by rising markets, and low ratios have traditionally been succeeded by falling stock prices.  In the last quarter century Short Interest Ratio readings greater than 1.75 have had especially bullish implications, while SIR readings below 1.00 were seldom followed by spectacular upside performances.

The short interest is computed by the New York Stock Exchange on approximately the 15th of each month and reported to the public four trading days thereafter. As there is a five trading day lag between transaction executions on the Exchange and the "settlement" date for all trades, in effect the Exchange tabulates a short interest of five trading days prior to the 15th, creating a total lag before the data finally becomes available to the public of almost two full weeks. Despite this lag, the Short Interest Ratio has proven to be an excellent market forecaster.

Its predictive value is two-fold. First, short sellers, who hope for declining prices, are usually wrong at key market turning points. A high short interest relative to market volume reveals pessimism by the short sellers, but the market usually goes against them by moving higher. When short selling is relatively unpopular, and the short interest and SIR are low, as frequently occurs after a period of steadily rising stock prices, a price decline usually follows.

The second reason for the SIR's forecasting success is that short sales, once made, can be covered only by an offsetting purchase of stock and thus a short position is ultimately a source of market demand. The larger the short interest (and the higher the Short Interest Ratio) the more shares must eventually be bought in the future and the greater is the prospective demand for stocks. Not surprisingly then, extremely high SIR's are often followed by rising markets, induced in part by short sellers covering their open positions. When the short interest is low, this source of future demand for stocks is proportionately reduced and prices are more likely to fall, or to at least rise at a below average rate.

Despite its popularity and generally good historical record, the traditional Short Interest Ratio contains a few flaws. For one thing, although it primarily purports to measure the month to month significance of the short interest position, in fact trading volume fluctuates much more broadly than the short interest itself. Ostensibly a sophisticated measure of the short interest, the SIR (short interest divided by volume) is instead largely dominated by what should be its less important volume component — the "tail wagging the dog" syndrome. The easiest way to correct this deficiency is to divide the monthly short interest by more than merely the average of the past few weeks' NYSE volume. The more months of volume used, the less relative importance a sharp change in trading activity in any one period will have on the volume average. At least several months, and possibly even a year or more, of recent volume data should therefore be used. After all, the short positions comprising the reported short interest are not all the result of trading during the latest month.

Yet another problem with the traditional SIR is monthly seasonality bias. An indicator distorted by seasonal irregularities will certainly provide less than optimal market predictions. The bias in the traditional SIR stems from seasonality in both its components:   the short interest and the New York Stock Exchange volume.   Standard statistical procedures have been used to construct seasonal adjustment divisors. These divisors can be used to eliminate seasonal bias from each of the series.   They are provided in Table 19.

### TABLE 19
#### SIR SEASONAL ADJUSTMENT DIVISORS

| Month | Short Interest | NYSE Volume | Short Interest Ratio |
|-------|---------------|-------------|---------------------|
| Jan. | .95 | 1.12 | .85 |
| Feb. | 1.00 | 1.09 | .91 |
| March | 1.00 | 1.03 | .98 |
| April | 1.00 | 1.00 | 1.01 |
| May | 1.02 | 1.06 | .96 |
| June | 1.02 | 1.02 | .99 |
| July | .99 | .95 | 1.04 |
| Aug. | .98 | .87 | 1.13 |
| Sep. | .99 | .86 | 1.15 |
| Oct. | 1.00 | .96 | 1.03 |
| Nov. | 1.04 | 1.02 | 1.02 |
| Dec. | 1.03 | 1.09 | .94 |

For example, the January SIR seasonal adjustment divisor of 0.85 indicates that, on average, the reported SIR for that month is 85% of normal and needs to be adjusted upward by dividing the reported SIR by 0.85. August and September readings are much too high and require extensive downward adjustments.

The short interest itself shows significant seasonality in three months: November, December, and January. This can be attributed to heavier than normal short selling for tax purposes during the last two months of the year and off-setting covering transactions early in the new year. The seasonality of NYSE volume, on the other hand, is not only much stronger, but is also pervasive throughout the year. Abnormally high volume occurs in December, January, and February (traditionally months of extensive portfolio re-structuring) and unusually low volume is in evidence during the summer months of July through September (when some investors are vacationing).

Extensive computer analysis of several alternative versions of the SIR shows that the most theoretically sound, as well as the best, market predictor, is one based upon the exact relationship between the seasonally adjusted monthly short interest and average daily NYSE volume over the past one year. (Since an entire year's volume is used, its intra-year seasonality bias has been effectively eliminated.) This improved indicator, called appropriately, the Improved Short Interest Ratio (or Improved SIR), provides market prediction accuracy about double that of the traditional SIR. It is here based upon sophisticated econometric calculations but it can be approximated by simply dividing the seasonally adjusted short interest by average daily NYSE volume over the past year.

A detailed comparison between the Traditional and Improved Short Interest Ratios is presented in Table 20. Observe first that both are excellent indicators. Well above average three, six, and twelve month market gains ensue from bullishly high indicator readings. Far below average, even

TABLE 20

## TRADITIONAL AND IMPROVED SHORT INTEREST RATIOS
## AND MARKET PERFORMANCE (1947 - 1975)

| Current Level of Indicator | Traditional SIR Indicator | | Improved SIR Indicator | |
|---|---|---|---|---|
| | S&P 500 3 Mo. Later | Probability of Gain | S&P 500 3 Mo. Later | Probability of Gain |
| Under 1.00 | + 0.4% | 54% | − 1.6% | 39% |
| 1.00 to 1.25 | − 0.1% | 50% | + 0.9% | 55% |
| 1.25 to 1.50 | + 2.4% | 63% | + 1.3% | 61% |
| 1.50 to 1.75 | + 3.5% | 77% | + 4.1% | 74% |
| Over 1.75 | + 4.9% | 77% | + 6.8% | 94% |
| 28-Year Average | + 1.9% | 62% | + 1.9% | 62% |

| Current Level of Indicator | S&P 500 6 Mo. Later | Probability of Gain | S&P 500 6 Mo. Later | Probability of Gain |
|---|---|---|---|---|
| Under 1.00 | + 0.8% | 53% | − 2.9% | 37% |
| 1.00 to 1.25 | + 1.8% | 60% | + 2.1% | 59% |
| 1.25 to 1.50 | + 4.1% | 66% | + 3.0% | 69% |
| 1.50 to 1.75 | + 4.7% | 74% | + 6.6% | 74% |
| Over 1.75 | +10.3% | 86% | +13.5% | 98% |
| 28-Year Average | + 3.8% | 66% | + 3.8% | 66% |

| Current Level of Indicator | S&P 500 12 Mo. Later | Probability of Gain | S&P 500 12 Mo. Later | Probability of Gain |
|---|---|---|---|---|
| Under 1.00 | + 2.4% | 53% | − 4.4% | 34% |
| 1.00 to 1.25 | + 5.2% | 66% | + 3.4% | 58% |
| 1.25 to 1.50 | + 7.9% | 67% | + 7.3% | 72% |
| 1.50 to 1.75 | + 8.3% | 70% | +11.1% | 78% |
| Over 1.75 | +17.0% | 91% | +24.9% | 97% |
| 28-Year Average | + 7.4% | 68% | + 7.4% | 68% |

negative, market performances follow bearishly low readings. Similarly, very high probabilities of price gain follow from high SIR readings and very low chances of gain succeed low readings.

Just as noteworthy in Table 20 is the superior forecasting

record of the Improved SIR relative to the Traditional SIR. While the latter is an excellent indicator in its own right, its record seems mediocre in comparison to the record of the Improved SIR. In a very bullish market environment, the Traditional Short Interest Ratio indicator might, for example, provide only a moderately bullish reading because of its seasonal bias and its dependence on a single month's volume. The Improved Short Interest Ratio, on the other hand, would normally correctly classify the market as very bullish. In general the improved ratio better forecasts extreme market changes and eliminates false signals.

Improved SIR readings over 1.75 are followed by rising prices between 94% and 98% of the time, about as close to perfect as one can expect in the stock market. And readings under 1.00, while not *always* followed by falling prices, exhibit enough significant bearish propensities to suggest the appropriateness of a defensive investment posture.

In sum, both the Traditional and Improved Short Interest Ratios are valuable forecasting tools in their own rights. The Improved SIR is nonetheless a major improvement on its Traditional counterpart and is an indicator well worth inclusion into any market forecasting system.

A few analysts have suggested that a Short Interest Ratio based upon the Dow Jones Industrial Average has a forecasting ability superior to the Traditional Short Interest Ratio. The DJI Short Interest Ratio can be computed (rather laboriously) each month by adding up the short interest of each of the 30 Dow stocks and dividing that total by the total of the average daily trading volumes of each of those stocks. It is doubtful that the DJI SIR can furnish extra forecasting power sufficient to offset the nightmarish calculations involved in its computation . . . and of course the next step would be a separate SIR for the *500* stock S&P Composite. The Amex SIR, for which data is available, is just too erratic for forecasting purposes. Improvements to the NYSE Short Interest Ratio already suggested in this chapter are superior and in the long run will make the indicator more reliable.

# 16 Specialist
## Short Sales Ratio

Because various classes of investors react with different degrees of sophistication to past and present market behavior, analysis of their actions often yields valuable clues to future market performance.

A particularly sophisticated group are the NYSE specialists who are charged with the role of balancing incoming buy and sell orders to create fair markets in the stocks in which they specialize. It is often necessary for them to trade in these stocks to maintain orderly markets. Weekly data on the total trading activity of all specialists is made available to the public by the Securities and Exchange Commission with a two week lag. The data permits outsiders to gain valuable insights into the market views of these astute traders.

The ratio of Specialists' Shorts to Total Shorts (SS/TS) is an especially useful derivative of this data. Specialists are normally quite savvy in their short selling activity, and the greater the volume of their shorting relative to all other shortsellers, the more likely it is that prices will subsequently decline. Conversely, when specialists cut back on their short selling, the implication is that they are bullish relative to all other short sellers, and the market should rise.

The record as presented in Table 21 on page 66 shows that the theory is indeed valid. The presentation is based upon simple one week SS/TS ratios, although the indicator can be improved by averaging the weekly readings over a five or ten week period to smooth out random fluctuations.

The SS/TS intervals have been constructed so as to include a roughly equivalent number of weekly readings (about 350). Readings in the upper quintile are usually followed by below average market performances. In contrast, readings below 45% are extremely bullish, with the odds on rising prices over

## TABLE 21

### SS/TS AND MARKET PERFORMANCE (1941-1975)

| Specialist Short Sales Ratio (SS/TS) | S&P 500 Index Three Months Later | Probability of Rising Prices |
|---|---|---|
| Under 45% | + 4.2% | 76% |
| 45% to 50% | + 2.6% | 63% |
| 50% to 55% | + 2.2% | 62% |
| 55% to 60% | + 1.1% | 58% |
| Over 60% | − 0.5% | 52% |
| 35-Year Average | + 1.9% | 62% |

| Specialist Short Sales Ratio (SS/TS) | S&P 500 Index Six Months Later | Probability of Rising Prices |
|---|---|---|
| Under 45% | + 8.4% | 85% |
| 45% to 50% | + 5.6% | 69% |
| 50% to 55% | + 3.6% | 64% |
| 55% to 60% | + 1.8% | 59% |
| Over 60% | − 0.2% | 53% |
| 35-Year Average | + 3.8% | 66% |

| Specialist Short Sales Ratio (SS/TS) | S&P 500 Index One Year Later | Probability of Rising Prices |
|---|---|---|
| Under 45% | + 17.1% | 84% |
| 45% to 50% | + 10.6% | 72% |
| 50% to 55% | + 6.7% | 70% |
| 55% to 60% | + 3.7% | 59% |
| Over 60% | + 0.4% | 54% |
| 35-Year Average | + 7.7% | 68% |

the ensuing three months better than three to one. The six and twelve month returns are even more impressive, with comparable bullish readings almost six to one in favor of a market gain.

The "under 45%" interval naturally includes some readings which are unusually extreme. As a rule, the farther below 45% the ratio falls, the more bullish are its forecasts. Based on historical experience, if the weekly ratio were to drop anywhere below 35%, the probability of a rising market over the following three, six, and twelve months would be near 100% and would suggest annualized rates of return during each holding period well in excess of 25%, three times the long run norm.   Generalized results for just the one year holding period are presented in Table 22.  The average one year market gain for all ratio readings below 45% is +17.1%. Note how much higher the returns are following especially extreme readings.

TABLE 22

EXTREMELY BULLISH SS/TS READINGS AND
MARKET PERFORMANCE (1941-1975)

| Specialist Short Sales Ratio (SS/TS) | S&P 500 Index One Year Later | Probability of Rising Prices |
|---|---|---|
| Under 35% | + 25.9% | 100% |
| 35% to 36% | + 23.9% | 94% |
| 36% to 37% | + 17.3% | 81% |
| 37% to 38% | + 16.0% | 76% |
| 38% to 39% | + 22.9% | 89% |
| 39% to 40% | + 13.4% | 81% |
| 40% to 41% | + 14.6% | 72% |
| 41% to 42% | + 15.4% | 85% |
| 42% to 43% | + 16.8% | 88% |
| 43% to 44% | + 12.8% | 78% |
| 44% to 45% | + 13.4% | 79% |

Future market losses associated with 1% intervals of the Specialist Short Sales Ratio for readings above 60% show a similarly smooth trend.

There is a slight seasonal bias to the data around the end of the year, at which time the Specialist Short Sales Ratio tends to be higher than normal.   The bias is not large enough to warrant seasonally adjusting the data.

# 17 Non-Member Short Sales Ratio

Just as following sophisticated "winners" like the specialists can lead to profits, it pays to bet against habitual losers. One such group of chronic losers is the non-member short sellers, also called "public" short sellers. When these speculators, defined as persons who are not members of the New York Stock Exchange, get bearish enough to substantially increase their short sales activity, the market almost invariably responds by going against their wishes and rising.

The group isn't any more successful at the other extreme. When they turn relatively optimistic and drastically decrease their short selling, as is their wont after most market rallies, they are usually proved wrong again by a substantial market correction.

The Non-Member Short Sales Ratio (NMSR) is calculated by dividing non-member short sales by total market short sales. Sectors other than specialists contributing to the total are floor traders and other NYSE members. Occasionally erratic weekly fluctuations suggest the advisability of smoothing (averaging) the ratio over several weeks . . . about ten weeks appears sufficient.

The ten week average ratio is generally bullish when it is over 25% and bearish when it is under that level. The more extreme the reading, the more likely it is that the non-member short sellers are wrong, and the more substantial should be the ensuing market move.

The record of the indicator over the past 35 years is most impressive. Table 23 correlates three month market returns with various percentage intervals of the ten week average ratio.

Although the odds on a three month market gain are nearly nine in ten when the indicator is over 35%, they are less than one in two when the ratio is under 20%. In fact, the record indicates that prices are likely to decline somewhat following a ten week average ratio below 20%. The relationship between the level of the ratio and the expected return on stock prices is fairly smooth. Although not indicated in the table, this relationship generally holds for ratio readings outside the 20% and 35% points as well. Readings of less than 15%, for example, are even more bearish than the "under 20%" interval on the table would indicate.

TABLE 23

### NMSR AND THREE MONTH
### MARKET PERFORMANCE (1941-1975)

| Non-Member Short Sales Ratio (NMSR) | S&P 500 Index Three Months Later | Probability of Rising Prices |
|---|---|---|
| Under 20% | − 1.1% | 48% |
| 20% - 25% | + 0.5% | 54% |
| 25% - 30% | + 3.3% | 68% |
| 30% - 35% | + 4.5% | 75% |
| Over 35% | + 5.9% | 88% |
| 35-Year Average | + 1.9% | 62% |

The six month prediction record (Table 24) is also consistent across all levels of the ratio and affirms the three month

TABLE 24

### NMSR AND SIX MONTH
### MARKET PERFORMANCE (1941-1975)

| Non-Member Short Sales Ratio (NMSR) | S&P 500 Index Six Months Later | Probability of Rising Prices |
|---|---|---|
| Under 20% | − 0.9% | 51% |
| 20% - 25% | + 0.8% | 52% |
| 25% - 30% | + 5.8% | 73% |
| 30% - 35% | + 8.2% | 85% |
| Over 35% | + 12.1% | 96% |
| 35-Year Average | + 3.8% | 66% |

results. Extremely bullish readings have resulted in rising

prices over the ensuing six months 96% of the time and average returns more than three times as great as the 35-year norm. Readings below 20% suggest declining prices and a far below average probability of gain.

This indicator's value is reaffirmed by the one year returns (Table 25) which, among other significant results, show a perfect up market prediction record for bullish ratio readings above 35%.

TABLE 25

NMSR AND ONE YEAR
MARKET PERFORMANCE (1941-1975)

| Non-Member Short Sales Ratio (NMSR) | S&P 500 Index One Year Later | Probability of Rising Prices |
|---|---|---|
| Under 20% | − 0.6% | 53% |
| 20% - 25% | + 2.5% | 54% |
| 25% - 30% | + 9.3% | 74% |
| 30% - 35% | + 16.5% | 83% |
| Over 35% | + 24.3% | 100% |
| 35-Year Average | + 7.7% | 68% |

Adding support to the long term historical record are the indicator's more recent timing achievements. The ten week Non-Member Short Sales Ratio has accurately called every significant market move of the past several years. After impeccably predicting the market declines of 1972 to 1974, the ten week average jumped to a highly bullish 38% in early October 1974, coinciding nicely with the major market trough. The indicator then gradually declined until the very week of the July 1975 intermediate market top when the ten week average ratio hit an extremely bearish 14.5%. Stock prices immediately dropped. The Non-Member Short Sales Ratio then reversed course and proceeded upward, rising to a bullish peak of 28% on October 3 of that year, pinpointing the actual autumn intermediate low of the market. By spring 1976 the indicator had once again fallen to 14.5%, the identical level it reached at the beginning of the 1975 summer correction.

The indicator's recent and long term record reflects a high degree of forecasting precision. While not infallible, the Non-Member Short Sales Ratio has a far better than average prediction record.

*Refined Indicator.*    Both the Specialist Short Sales Ratio and the Non-Member Short Sales Ratio are time tested market forecasting tools. A superior treatment of the data, and the one preferred by the author, is the ratio of weekly non-member short sales to the combined weekly shorting activity of all NYSE members on the trading floor (i.e., specialists and floor traders). This treatment eliminates from consideration the short selling activity of members trading off the floor for their own accounts, which can be influenced by non-speculative arbitrage transactions and option hedge strategies. The new ratio is superior to both the Non-Member and Specialist Short Sales Ratio individually. It is also greatly influenced by recent market behavior and an even more refined guide to future market performance can be derived by adjusting the Non-Member/On-Floor Short Sales Ratio for recent market trends.

*Member Short Sales Ratio.*    Some analysts treat the basic Non-Member Short Ratio in the opposite form, calculating a Member Short Sales Ratio.    Since anyone who is not an exchange member is, by definition, a non-member, the Member Ratio behaves in the identical fashion as the Non-Member Ratio but simply moves in the opposite direction. If the Member Ratio is 75%, the Non-Member Ratio is 25%. If the Member Ratio is 80%, the Non-Member Ratio is 20%. The two always add up to 100%, and which one is used is irrelevant.

*Non-Member Volume Ratio.*    Other analysts relate non-member short sales to total exchange volume rather than to total exchange short sales. The series lacks stability, having trended sharply upward during the last three decades. Comparisons between current and historical values are difficult and this particular indicator form would best be avoided.

# 18  Member Off-Floor Balance Index: Once in a Generation Buy Signals

The best possible bull market indicator would be one that unerringly signals every market upswing. Lacking that (which we do, because it probably doesn't exist), one might wish for an indicator that signals only the greatest buying points of each generation, but does so flawlessly.

The Member Off-Floor Balance Index, which measures trading activity by all members of the New York Stock Exchange other than specialists and floor traders, is such an indicator.

Major buy signals from the index are so rare, they literally come just *once in a generation*. If there exists the elusive "they" whom market commentators often credit with a mysterious ability to control stock prices, "they" are probably these savvy NYSE members. The balance between purchases and sales reveals the expectations of these highly sophisticated market participants. Historically, massive buying has always been massively bullish. Such buying is so infrequent that the member trading data is ignored by virtually every Wall Street analyst.

Usually these exchange members are net sellers of common stocks. There are a number of reasons for this peculiarity. The most important factor is arbitrage activity, as members take advantage of lower commission rates to profit from minor price differences between markets. For example, they may purchase convertible securities in an over-the-counter transaction, convert them into listed common stocks, and then sell the common in the open market. Only the sales on the exchange are reported in NYSE member trading statistics.

Another contributing factor to the net selling is the private unrecorded purchase of large blocks of common stock off the exchange and the subsequent distribution of the stock in smaller lots on the exchange. Other types of transactions can be isolated that also result in sales of shares on the exchange with no recorded offsetting purchases. Accordingly, the Member Off-Floor Balance Index has a historical bias toward net selling.

When these members do buy on balance, especially in large quantities, history has demonstrated that it pays to heed their actions. On only two occasions in the past four decades prior to 1974 have these sophisticated investors partaken in massive common stock buying. The first was in 1942, just as a four year, five fold upmove commenced in the unweighted market averages. The second, in 1949, entailed what was up to that time the greatest buying splurge in exchange history by off-floor members. Out of it emerged a 19 year super bull market.

With such a record of long term market timing, investors should have taken particular notice in 1974 when, following six years of general market decline and amid a condition of severely depressed security prices, the Member Off-Floor Balance Index indicated net buying comparable to the levels in 1942 and 1949.

From February through July 1974, the group purchased over 23 million shares of stock. In August and September "they" added another 14 million shares to their portfolios.

On September 13, 1974, the very week that the unweighted Total Return Indexes reached their ultimate bear market lows, the S.E.C. reported that net buying by off-floor members had reached the greatest intensity since October 1949 (when the DJIA was at 185). By the end of 1974 the group had bought still another eight million shares on balance. In all, a total of 45 million shares of net buying was registered on the Exchange between February and December of 1974. During that 47 week period, the Index showed net buying in 44 weeks — a record unsurpassed in market history. Finally, in 1975 these members resumed their normal net selling after a buying peak in February. (By that time cumulative net purchases since early 1974 totalled 46.1 million shares.)

With a market timing record that superb, investors can only eagerly await this sophisticated group's next buying spree. But don't hold your breath waiting. It may not come for another generation.

# 19 Odd Lotters

If only we could identify investors who are always doing something wrong, we could simply do the opposite and forever be right. Enter the odd lotters.

An "odd lot" is a block of stock consisting of fewer than 100 shares. Most odd lot transactions are initiated by small investors who lack sufficient funds to purchase a "round lot" of 100 shares of stock. Market "sophisticates" have traditionally viewed the small investor with scorn, maintaining that his market judgments are invariably wrong. More recently the justification for their derision has been questioned.

*Odd Lot Volume Ratio.* Once upon a time, the ratio of total odd lot volume to total NYSE volume was an extremely popular market indicator. When the ratio was high, unsophisticated odd lotters were active market participants and prices were supposed to fall. Similarly, a low ratio revealed disinterest by the error-prone odd lotters and heightened the prospects for a sustained market rally. During the last two decades, odd lot trading has diminished considerably in relative terms, introducing an uncontrollable downward trend to the ratio and rendering it useless for market forecasting purposes. Whereas odd lot activity accounted for as much as 15% of total NYSE volume during the mid-1940s, it constitutes only about half of 1% of trading today. The remaining 99.5% of volume in listed securities is done in round lots.

*Odd Lot Balance Index.* Today, the market sentiment of the odd lotters is most commonly measured by the Odd Lot

Balance Index. The Balance Index is calculated by dividing the volume of shares sold in odd lots on a given day or week by total odd lot purchases. (Sales and purchases don't match because they are executed independently.) When the ratio of odd lot sales to purchases is above 1.0, odd lotters are selling stock on balance. According to market lore, prices should thereupon move upward against their wishes. When the sales/purchases ratio is less than 1.0, odd lotters are buying on balance and, according to the theory, stock prices should decline rather than go up as these mini-investors would hope.

During the 1950s and early 1960s, the Balance Index showed that odd lotters were indeed more often wrong than right. They usually sold heavily near market bottoms when they should have been buying and bought on balance near market peaks when they should more appropriately have been liquidating positions. In the mid-sixties, something went askew with the theory. Since then, odd lotters have been among the savviest traders on Wall Street, invariably buying at bottoms and selling heavily at tops.

Extensive computer testing on several decades of odd lot trading, using a number of variations of data transformation suggested by odd lot followers, reveals that the Odd Lot Balance Index is largely devoid of consistent market forecasting ability.

*Odd Lot Short Ratio.* Until the late 1970s, the Odd Lot Short Ratio (OLSR) was the most reliable technical indicator in existence. The indicator reflected the sentiment of a group that was always wrong. Like lemmings rushing to the sea, cycle after cycle the odd lot short sellers were hell-bent on self-destruction.

As short selling offers an extremely poor reward-risk relationship, anyone who engages in short selling must either be remarkably intelligent (to profit therefrom) or incredibly naive (to even try). The odd lot short sellers fall into the latter class. They probably consist of two types of unsophisticated speculators. One is the small trader who, because of his limited funds, must deal in small quantities of shares. The second is a more substantial investor who sells short in odd lots merely to assure that his short sale will be executed at the next increase in price. (A round lot short sale, being of a lower priority on the exchange floor than regular sales, may get executed at a less favorable price.) Both of these speculators, the small trader and the pseudo-sophisticated master of market gimmickry, are wrong in their market judgments.

The indicator was optimally calculated by dividing odd lot short sales by the average of odd lot purchases and total sales. This series has averaged about 1.2% over the last few decades, but has ranged from as low as 0.1% to upward of 6.0%. Since the odd lot short sellers were always wrong, a high ratio signified heavy short selling and a subsequently rising market. On the other hand, a low OLSR reading indicated a relative dearth of odd lot short selling, a bearish condition.

Between 1941 and 1975, the OLSR was nearly infallible. For example, the market never failed to rise in the 12 months following a ten-week average OLSR reading of 4% or greater, averaging a 23% advance. On the other hand, the market rose in the following year less than one-third of the time that the OLSR was below 0.5%. The average 12-month market loss following such a low reading was over 6%.

The OLSR's omniscience came to a sad conclusion with the advent of listed put options. No longer did small, pseudo-sophisticated bears need to sell short an odd lot of stock; they could simply buy a low-priced put option. It was thus necessary to bid a fond, though regretable, adieu to this once great market timing tool.

# 20 High Low Logic Index

The High Low Logic Index was invented by the author in 1979. It represents a significant addition to the repertoire of breadth and divergence indicators.

The High Low Logic Index is easy to calculate, and its logic is as easy to grasp. It may be computed daily or weekly, and with either NYSE or Amex data, or with both. (All of the analyses in this chapter are based on the NYSE.) The Index is simply the *lesser* of the two following percentages:

(1) New highs as a percent of issues traded.
(2) New lows as a percent of issues traded.

In one recent week, 227, or 10.7%, of the 2,128 issues traded on the NYSE established new 52-week highs. Meanwhile, 122 stocks, or 5.7%, set new annual lows. The weekly High Low Logic Index simply equals the *lesser* of the two percentages, or 5.7%.

The rationale behind the Logic Index is simple. Under normal conditions, either a substantial number of stocks establish new annual highs or a large number set new lows — *but not both*. As the Logic Index is the lesser of the two percentages, high readings are therefore difficult to achieve.

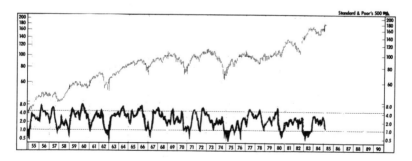

FIGURE 7A. Ten-week exponential moving average of NYSE High Low Logic Index (versus Standard & Poor's 500 Index) with two horizontal dashed lines highlighting particularly bullish readings below 1% and extremely bearish readings above 5%; 1955-1985.

(In fact, the 5.7% reading cited above is more than twice the 2.7% average weekly value of the last 40 years.)

When the Index attains a high level, it indicates that the market is undergoing a period of extreme divergence — many stocks establishing new highs *and* many setting new lows as well. Such divergence is not usually conducive to future rising stock prices. A healthy market requires some semblance of internal uniformity, and it doesn't matter what direction that uniformity takes. Many new highs and very few lows is obviously bullish, but so is a great many new lows accompanied by few or no new highs.

Superior prediction from the Logic Index can be generated by smoothing the weekly values over several weeks. (A 10-week exponential moving average is useful.) As shown in Table 26, readings above 5% on the smoothed Index reveal extreme market divergence and are bearish. Readings below 1% reveal great uniformity and are especially bullish.

## TABLE 26

### HIGH LOW LOGIC INDEX
### 10-WEEK MOVING AVERAGE (1944-1980)

| High Low Logic Index | NYSE Total Return Index | |
|---|---|---|
| | 3 Months Later | 6 Months Later |
| Under 1% | + 7.6% | + 14.4% |
| 1% to 2% | + 5.4% | + 11.0% |
| 2% to 3% | + 3.3% | + 6.2% |
| 3% to 5% | + 1.9% | + 4.9% |
| Over 5% | - 1.4% | - 0.1% |
| 40-Year Average | + 3.6% | + 7.6% |

Measured on a one-week basis, Logic Index readings below 1% and above 7% are extreme. A double-digit reading is rare and has nearly always been followed by sharply declining stock prices. Such a reading has presaged *every* major bear move in the last quarter century. Table 27 presents all weekly readings above 10% between 1941 and 1980.

All-time bullish weekly lows of the minimum possible 0% occurred in September 1966 and December 1970, both of

TABLE 27

HIGH LOW LOGIC INDEX
ALL DOUBLE DIGIT WEEKLY READINGS (1941-1980)

| July 28, 1950 | 11.2% | June 3, 1960 | 11.4% |
|---|---|---|---|
| April 6, 1956 | 10.8% | Mar. 23, 1962 | 10.8% |
| April 13, 1956 | 12.0% | Mar. 30, 1962 | 10.2% |
| April 20, 1956 | 11.0% | Feb. 18, 1966 | 10.3% |
| April 27, 1956 | 11.7% | April 15, 1966 | 11.5% |
| May 11, 1956 | 10.6% | May 2, 1969 | 11.2% |
| June 14, 1957 | 10.1% | April 21, 1972 | 10.2% |
| Oct. 9, 1959 | 10.0% | April 28, 1972 | 12.8% |
| April 1, 1960 | 10.2% | Feb. 15, 1980 | 12.2% |
| April 22, 1960 | 10.2% | | |

which accurately identified excellent buying points.

The Logic Index is also useful for predicting short-term market trends. Table 27A presents the record of the daily NYSE High Low Logic Index from 1965 to 1980 (approximately 3,700 daily readings). The Index has been smoothed with a ten-day exponential moving average.

*Caveat:* Since early 1978, new highs and new lows have been reported on a consistent 52-week basis. Prior to that time, a new high or low was measured in the context of a stock's price history from the beginning of the year, except from New Year's until mid-March, when the reference point was January 1 of the *prior* year. Hence, the earlier method produced base periods ranging in length from 2-1/2 to 14-1/2

TABLE 27A

HIGH LOW LOGIC INDEX
10-DAY MOVING AVERAGE (1965-1980)

| High Low Logic Index | NYSE Total Return Index: | | | |
|---|---|---|---|---|
| | 1 Day Later | 5 Days Later | 10 Days Later | 20 Days Later |
| Under 0.25% | +0.19% | +1.00% | +1.88% | +3.46% |
| 0.25% to 1.00% | +0.02% | +0.14% | +0.30% | +0.65% |
| 1.00% to 2.00% | 0.00% | -0.02% | +0.05% | +0.21% |
| 2.00% to 3.00% | -0.01% | -0.08% | -0.26% | -0.56% |
| Over 3.00% | -0.18% | -0.87% | -2.17% | -3.25% |
| 16-Year Average: | +0.03% | + 0.18% | + 0.37% | +0.76% |

months. As the base period expanded during each year, the relevant price ranges of individual stocks grew wider, increasing the difficulty of setting either new highs or new lows. It is surprising, and gratifying, that the indicator's historical record is as accurate as it is in the face of this obstacle. As all future data will be consistent, the forecasting value of the High Low Logic Index should grow.

# 21  The Fosback Index:
## A Fund Timing Indicator

*Mutual Fund Cash/Assets Ratio.* Every month the Investment Company Institute compiles detailed statistics on the portfolios of over 400 mutual funds. The Mutual Fund Cash/Assets Ratio is produced by lumping together the cash and cash equivalents (treasury bills, commercial paper and other money market instruments) for all the funds and dividing that sum by the total assets of all the funds. ("Money market" funds should be excluded from the calculations.)

Since mutual funds supposedly represent "smart money" under professional administration, one might presume that they would be able to call market turns quite closely and adjust their portfolios accordingly. Just the opposite is the case. As a barometer of investor psychology, the mutual fund cash ratio acts as a contrary indicator. Professional money managers tend to be wrong at market extremes.

When the fund managers expect the market to rise, they become fully invested in common stocks and the ratio of cash and equivalents to total assets is low. The market usually falls. When the funds are bearish, they hold a high proportion of cash to total assets. The market invariably rises. Indeed, the fund managers seem less sophisticated at times than the small investors whose monies they are managing. The public has traditionally been most willing to acquire mutual fund shares when the market is low and likely to rise, and has shown a propensity to redeem shares when the market is high and most liable to fall. (This phenomenon can be measured by a statistic known as the Sales/Redemption Ratio. While this ratio has achieved some popularity with market analysts, it is contaminated by long and variable trends which makes interpretation of it exceedingly difficult, if not impossible. As a result, the Sales/Redemption Ratio has no proven predictive capacity and is vastly overrated as a market forecasting tool.)

The Cash/Assets Ratio is also a measure of money potentially available for stock market investment. When the funds are so bullish that they hold only small amounts of cash in reserve, they lack "buying power" to move the market higher, possibly one reason why the market does not, in fact, move higher. When fund managers are most bearish and loaded with cash, they have completed their selling and their actions have already exerted their negative effects on prices. Sooner or later, a desire to become fully invested will once again result in those reserves being committed to the market — providing fuel for the next bull cycle.

Today the assets of all open-end mutual funds amount to less than one-third of the assets of private non-insured pension funds, and represent a decreasing portion of the total. Fortunately, the cash reserve positions of pension funds closely track the mutual funds. The mutual fund data, available monthly, can be used as an effective proxy for the pension fund data, which is only available quarterly and with a substantial delay.

During the last 22 years (the data first became available in 1954), the Mutual Fund Cash/Assets Ratio has varied between 4% and 14%. Observations in the upper range have been concentrated in recent years as a consequence of a secular uptrend in the ratio. This uptrend has rendered the raw data relatively ineffective for forecasting purposes and led many followers of the ratio to very prematurely forecast market bottoms during the 1969-1970 and 1973-1974 bear cycles.    Although the Mutual Fund Cash/Assets Ratio has reached an extreme at every key market turning point, its rising trend prevents identification of those extremes except by hindsight.    The primary cause of the trend is the rising level of interest rates.    The higher interest rates are, the stronger is the pressure for funds to withdraw money from stocks and invest it in safe, short term, high yielding cash equivalents such as treasury bills, commercial paper, and CD's.    It is no accident that the long term uptrend in the cash ratio has so closely paralleled the long rise in interest rates.

*The Fosback Index.*    The mutual fund cash/assets data can be improved by factoring the level of interest rates out of the raw Cash/Assets Ratio and calculating the percentage of cash holdings relative to total assets in a manner which reflects only the fund managers' stock market judgments. The effect of the attraction of alternative interest bearing securities is excluded.    The adjustment mechanism forms the basis of the Fosback Index (also called the Fund Timing Index), a major breakthrough in stock market prediction.

The Fosback Index has a zero neutral point, with positive percentages indicating extra cash held by funds and negative readings signifying an actual deficit of money available for the stock market.    (Of course, the funds will always have some cash and equivalents on hand.    A negative reading merely indicates they don't have enough.)

The    Fosback    Index    is    an    exceptionally    powerful forecasting tool, but is relatively simple to calculate.    It first involves estimating how much cash the mutual funds *should* be holding, based on market interest rates. (The commercial paper rate is a good guide because commercial paper is the funds' favorite haven for cash reserves.)    An analysis of the last 22 years shows that if no interest return were available on idle cash, the funds would still hold about 3.2% of their assets in the form of cash to meet daily cash flow requirements, including redemptions and expenses.    Historically they have held further cash reserves equal to about seven-tenths of the quoted commercial paper rate.

For example, if the commercial paper rate were 5%, the funds would be expected to hold cash reserves equal to seven-tenths of that rate, or 3.5%, plus the minimum cash holding of 3.2%. . . a total normal cash holding of 6.7%. The Fosback Index is then calculated by *subtracting* this estimated *normal* cash/assets ratio from the current *actual* cash/assets ratio. If the actual ratio is, say, 9.2% and the normal ratio is 6.7%, the funds would be holding 2.5% extra cash. The final Fosback Index can alternatively be expressed in dollar form by multiplying total fund assets by 2.5%. If total assets are $40 billion, extra cash would be equal to $1 billion (2.5% x $40 billion).

The science of econometrics will be described in detail in Part Two. However, you might be interested to know that the calculations described above represent an elementary but quite elegant *econometric model.*

## TABLE 28

### EXTREME FOSBACK INDEX READINGS
### AND MARKET PERFORMANCE (1954-1975)

| Date | Fosback Index | NYSE Total Return Index Three Months Later | NYSE Total Return Index Six Months Later |
|------|------|------|------|
| July, 1958 | 2.8% | + 12.8% | + 26.1% |
| Nov., 1966 | 2.5% | + 17.4% | + 28.3% |
| July, 1970 | 2.9% | + 19.9% | + 35.4% |
| Aug., 1970 | 3.3% | + 11.1% | + 46.4% |
| Sep., 1970 | 3.1% | + 7.2% | + 34.2% |
| Oct., 1970 | 2.5% | + 18.7% | + 34.7% |
| Nov., 1970 | 2.5% | + 31.8% | + 35.2% |
| Oct., 1974 | 3.7% | + 5.3% | + 30.2% |
| Nov., 1974 | 3.2% | + 25.6% | + 42.4% |
| Dec., 1974 | 3.2% | + 44.4% | + 59.3% |
| Feb., 1975 | 2.8% | + 13.5% | + 11.2% |
| Mar., 1975 | 2.7% | + 10.3% | + 2.3% |
| Average Return | | + 18.2% | + 32.1% |

In its 22 year history, the Fosback Index has risen to at least 2.5% only a dozen times. On every one of those twelve occasions, a substantial market advance ensued. The record at market tops is not quite as good since funds usually work down to a low cash position far in advance of the market peak — too far, in fact, to provide accurate timing of the actual market high. Nevertheless, the overall record shows The Fosback Index to be a superior predictive indicator.

Data for the basic Mutual Fund Cash/Assets Ratio is compiled as of the last day of each month and released by the Investment Company Institute with a lag of about three weeks.  A portion of the statistical summary is usually reported in the financial press the following day.  The complete report may be obtained from the Investment Company Institute, 1600 M Street, N.W., Washington, D.C. 20036, for $36 per year.

# 22 Advisory Sentiment Index: Betting Against the Experts

It may seem disconcerting that those who would render investment advice to others are likely to be wrong themselves, but in the aggregate, stock market advisory services are indeed wrong in their market forecasts at major turning points.   Fortunately, all is not lost.  Advisory services are usually right during sustained market trends.   These conclusions are derived from an analysis of the published market forecasts of investment advisors as formalized into an indicator which is popularly termed the Advisory Sentiment Index.

The Advisory Sentiment Index measures the proportions of stock market advisory services which are bullish and bearish on the market's future trend. The indicator was first developed

TABLE 29

## ASI AND MARKET PERFORMANCE (1963-1976)

| Advisory Sentiment Index (ASI) Bearish Extremes — Buy Signals | | | Advisory Sentiment Index (ASI) Bullish Extremes — Sell Signals | | |
|---|---|---|---|---|---|
| Date | ASI | Market % Change to Sell Signal | Date | ASI | Market % Change to Buy Signal |
| | | | Apr. 23, 1965 | 90% | − 7.4% |
| July 30, 1965 | 41% | + 25.1% | Jan. 26, 1966 | 91% | −18.3% |
| Oct. 19, 1966 | 28% | + 49.3% | Sep. 20, 1967 | 71% | − 1.8% |
| Apr.  3, 1968 | 14% | + 18.1% | June 12, 1968 | 70% | − 1.0% |
| Sep.  4, 1968 | 32% | + 11.8% | Dec. 25, 1968 | 69% | − 8.7% |
| Mar. 21, 1969 | 26% | +  3.5% | May 16, 1969 | 61% | −17.3% |
| Aug.  1, 1969 | 20% | +  6.5% | Nov. 14, 1969 | 63% | −28.6% |
| May 15, 1970 | 31% | + 41.2% | Mar. 26, 1971 | 85% | − 8.4% |
| Aug.  6, 1971 | 50% | +  8.3% | Sep. 10, 1971 | 82% | −12.8% |
| Nov. 26, 1971 | 50% | + 22.7% | Dec. 15, 1972 | 85% | −24.8% |
| June  8, 1973 | 39% | + 17.1% | Oct. 12, 1973 | 69% | −20.9% |
| Nov. 30, 1973 | 36% | + 10.3% | Mar. 22, 1974 | 64% | −29.6% |
| Aug. 23, 1974 | 29% | − 2.9% | Nov. 22, 1974 | 64% | − 8.4% |
| Dec. 23, 1974 | 43% | + 37.9% | Feb. 21, 1975 | 79% | + 13.1% |
| Aug. 15, 1975 | 46% | + 25.7% | Feb.  6, 1976 | 92% | N/A |
| Compounded Gain: + 1006.9% $10,000 Grows to: $110,687 | | | Compounded Loss: − 86.3% $10,000 Shrinks to: $1,374 | | |

(ASI Source: Investors Intelligence, Inc., Larchmont, New York)

by Chartcraft, Inc. and has been reported in *Investors Intelligence* advisory service since 1963.    The Institute for Econometric Research also regularly calculates and publishes an index based upon its own sample of 70 to 80 advisory letters.

Not unlike many private investors, stock market advisors often find themselves caught up in current market trends and unable to yield objective opinions on the likely course of future stock prices.    When the marketplace is filled with doom and gloom, advisors, too, are likely to be extremely pessimistic and bearish on the market.    (They may even help cause the depressing atmosphere.) Mass pessimism is likely to accompany a primary market low. This is the classic contrary opinion theory — there is no one left to become bearish so selling becomes less aggressive. It follows that advisors are most bearish — and wrong — just as the market is about to bottom out. When the investing public is most optimistic, so, too, are the vast majority of advisory services. (Again, the advisors' bullishness may well be a contributing factor to the public's.) According to the theory of contrary opinion, such a condition is likely to accompany a major market peak — proving both advisors and the public wrong again.

Table 29 (page 85) marks extremes of advisory sentiment from 1963 to 1976. The Advisory Sentiment Index is defined as the number of bullish advisors as a percent of those expressing a definite opinion on the market's major trend. Market performance is measured by the unweighted New York Stock Exchange Total Return Index.

On the surface, the Advisory Sentiment Index appears to be an excellent contrary indicator. Extremes of sentiment virtually always coincide with the commencement of market trends in the opposite direction. However, noting this fact and acting on it are two different matters, for the question arises, how high is high on the sentiment index and how low is low? It is a relatively simple matter to observe indicator and market extremes with the benefit of hindsight. It is not so simple to observe such an extreme and correctly identify it as such at the moment it is occurring. For example, an index reading of 69% marked the close of the 1968 bull market, but it would have been unprofitable to universally use that level to judge ensuing bull markets, for the index sometimes held above 69% for many months before finally topping out at a much higher level. Alternatively, it is easy to note the bullish extremes of 90% and 91% established in 1965 and early 1966, respectively. But anyone who waited for that peak to be repeated would have missed calling every top in the next decade. Until 1976 every subsequent bull market peaked without the ASI reaching that extreme.

It is also important to note that advisors are likely to be right during extended market trends because they are generally quick to change position when prices go against them. Analysis reveals that advisors are right on trends just about as often as they are wrong on turning points.  It all nets out to an indicator which is about half right and half wrong and difficult to use for forecasting purposes even when it is right.

Not the least of the problems in utilizing the Advisory Sentiment Index lies in deciding which advisors to rank bullish and which to rank bearish, as their forecasts are frequently hedged.  Furthermore, it is not unusual for a given advisor to be bearish short term and bullish long term or vice versa. (There are intermediate terms as well to help complicate the analysis.)

In conclusion, when the Advisory Sentiment Index approaches a very extreme level, a contrary approach could well pay off for the investor.  However, as such a generous dose of subjective judgment is required to make that determination, the indicator probably cannot be used objectively with any great success.

# 23 Put/Call Ratio

The Put/Call Ratio measures the sentiment of speculative option traders.  A high Put/Call Ratio indicates that option buyers favor puts, and are bearish.  Historically, their pessimism has been ill rewarded, as the market has instead forged higher.  A low Put/Call Ratio signifies a relative dearth of put buying and a preponderance of bullish call buying.  The record shows that option buyers' optimism is usually short-lived, as the market declines instead.

A call is an option to buy common stock;  a put is an option to sell common stock.  A call buyer hopes prices will rise;  a buyer of a put option wishes prices to fall.  Both calls and puts receive their value from the price of the stock itself and option speculators' judgments of the future course of the stock's price movement.

Consider, for example, the valuation of a call option. If a stock sells at $25 and a speculator owns an option to purchase that stock for only $20, the value of the option is $5. Any price less than $5 would prompt a massive purchase of call options, an immediate payment of $20 and a resale of the acquired stock at $25, for a profit. Hence the theoretical value of the option is $5. Actually, because of a variety of other factors, the option price will usually be somewhat above $5.

One of these factors is the possibility of large percentage gains. If, in our example, the stock rises in price to $30, the option to buy it at $20 is worth $10. (Paying $10 for the option plus $20 for the stock by exercise of the option is akin to paying $30 for the stock in the first place.) Note that while the common stock has advanced 20%, from $25 to $30, the option value has doubled, from $5 to $10, a 100% gain and five times the percentage stock gain. This is obviously a highly leveraged and profitable situation.

Of course, there is a corresponding risk. If the stock declines from $25 to $20, the call option would be theoretically worthless. While a common stock investor would lose only 20% of his original investment, a call buyer would lose his entire investment. (Put options are diametrically opposite to call options. The space will not be devoted here to explaining their reward and risk opportunities. Suffice to say that the buyer of a put option only makes money when the stock declines in price, whereas the call option buyer makes money when the stock moves up.)

Option buyers are plainly a special breed. They shoot for large, highly leveraged profits. In return they risk catastrophic loss of capital. It often seems to be the case that the sentiment of extreme risk takers yields valuable clues to future market behavior. Option buyers are no exception.

If the volume of call options in a given period is greater

than the volume of put options, one may logically assume that option speculators as a group are expecting higher prices and are bullish on the market. On the other hand, if the volume of put options is relatively greater than that of calls, these same speculators hold a generally bearish attitude.

Option traders lose money on balance. Their judgments of the direction of individual common stock prices, and of the market as a whole, are usually wrong. Therefore, a high Put/Call Ratio (a large volume of puts relative to calls) usually precedes a period of rising prices, not falling prices as the option speculators would prefer. Conversely, a low Put/Call Ratio (indicating relatively little put buying activity and greater call buying activity) is invariably followed by declining prices instead of rising prices as the preponderance of option buyers desire.

From 1945 to 1976, the Put/Call Ratio was computed using volume in the over-the-counter options market. In 1977, the options exchanges began trading both puts and calls on 25 stocks, and from 1977 to 1982 the P/C Ratio was based on that volume. By 1983, the Ratio was expanded to use put and call volume on every stock with listed options.

To stabilize the indicator, we utilize contract volume only for those puts and calls with a striking (exercise) price within 10% of the current market price of the underlying stock. This eliminates far "in the money" options and far "out of the money" options from the tabulation.

First, a Put/Call Ratio is computed for options in which the stock price is greater than the strike price but not more than 10% above it. A second P/C Ratio is computed for options in which the stock price is below, but not more than 10% below, the exercise price. The two Ratios are then simply averaged to derive the overall Market Logic P/C Ratio.

Low readings (20% to 35%), signifying excessive call specu- lation, are bearish. High readings (above 140%), indicating excessive put speculation, are bullish. Bearish readings tend to be a bit early relative to market turns, but bullish readings frequently coincide to the very day with market troughs.

The Market Logic Put/Call Ratio is one of the most sensitive and valuable of all market indicators now in use.

*Option Activity Ratio:* A derivative statistic of the put and call data is the so-called Option Activity Ratio (OAR) calculated by dividing total put and call volume by NYSE volume. A high OAR is bearish for it signals the excessive option speculation that frequently accompanies market tops. A low OAR is bullish for the opposite reason: if there is a dearth of speculation, the market should be depressed and near a major trough. Recently the indicator has lost its usefulness. The sharp decline in over-the-counter option business during the last few years has thrown the OAR into a severe downtrend, rendering interpretation next to impossible. Several more years' development of the registered option exchanges will be required to furnish sufficient data to construct the OAR anew.

# 24 Stock Margin Debt

Stock margin debt is the aggregate amount of money owed to New York Stock Exchange member firms by customers who have borrowed money in margin accounts to help finance stock purchases. The series is calculated as of the final trading day of each month by the NYSE and released to the public approximately two to three weeks following that date.

Margin account traders have traditionally been considered to be sophisticated Wall Street traders. The characterization is not strictly accurate. In the aggregate margin traders are always most overextended at market tops when they should be less willing to carry large margin debt balances. Similarly, at important market troughs, when they should be heavily invested in common stocks, their margin account balances are invariably quite low, indicating an erroneous feeling of pessimism on the market trend.

Just as importantly, these speculators exert a very profound impact on the course of market trends. When stock margin debt is rapidly expanding margin speculators are aggressively buying on balance and stock prices work their way higher from the force of their activity. When stock margin debt decreases, representing net selling by margin speculators, stock prices are generally driven lower.

Margin debt trends are closely related to the prevailing initial margin requirement established by the Federal Reserve System. The margin requirement defines in percentage terms the minimum down payment of cash which must be put up by an investor when buying common stocks. The balance of the purchase price may be borrowed from other sources. When the margin requirement (which has historically ranged from as low as 40% to as high as 100%) is reduced, speculators need put up less of their own money to buy stocks. This added inducement to purchase equities naturally has a bullish impact on stock prices. When the margin requirement is increased, traders find that they must use more of their own funds to make new stock commitments and can borrow less. A given amount of their own money earmarked for the market by margin speculators is then incapable of purchasing as many shares of common stock, a phenomenon which has a relatively bearish effect on the market.

Stock margin debt has been reported monthly for over four decades. Until 1970 the series was entitled "debit balances." In June of that year the New York Stock Exchange revised its definition of the statistic and commenced calculation of the new series, "stock margin debt." The latter has been backdated through June 1964.

As stock prices and trading volume have increased through the years, stock margin debt (and debit balances before it) has also naturally exhibited a long uptrend. The level of debt at any given time is therefore somewhat irrelevant. The best ways to provide current perspective are to analyze trends or changes in the series rather than its level. For example, a comparison of the most recently reported monthly stock margin debt figure with an average of the monthly readings over the past twelve months (an exponential moving average is best) has proved to be a successful market timing indicator. If the current level of margin debt is above the twelve month average, the series is deemed to be in an uptrend, margin traders are buying, and stock prices should continue upward. By the same line of reasoning, sell signals are rendered when the current monthly reading is below the twelve month average. This is evidence of stock liquidation by margin traders, a phenomenon which usually spurs prices downward.

This timing system has been tested over the past 35 years and has an excellent record. Following a long bullish rise from the bull market low in 1942, a sell signal was flashed in 1946. A downtrend in the market averages rapidly ensued. As illustrated in Figure 8, stock margin debt continued in a downtrend until 1947, at which time it leveled off, signalling a sideways moving market. It finally turned up in 1949 just prior to the commencement of the great bull market of the 1950s and 1960s. Throughout the last two and a half decades the indicator has mapped market trends in a superlative fashion. The important tops of 1956, 1959, 1961, 1966,

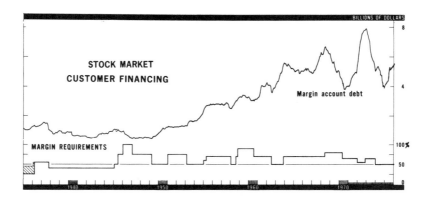

FIGURE 8.    Stock Margin Debt (monthly) and Initial Common Stock Margin Requirements (effective dates); 1935 - 1975.

1968, and 1973 were all accompanied or preceded by turns in stock margin debt. Similarly, the troughs established in 1957, 1960, 1962, 1966, 1970, and 1974 were accompanied by upturns in the debt series. Table 30 presents a summary of the forecasting results of this indicator since 1942.

TABLE 30

STOCK MARGIN DEBT
AND MARKET PERFORMANCE (1942-1975)

| Trend of Stock Margin Debt | Probability That A Bull Market Is In Progress | Probability That A Bear Market Is In Progress |
|---|---|---|
| Up | 85% | 15% |
| Down | 41% | 59% |
| 34-Year Average | 70% | 30% |

When the indicator is in an uptrend, the odds are almost six to one that a bull market is in progress. While the indicator's definition of bear markets is somewhat less precise, when the debt series is in a downtrend the odds on the existence of a bear market almost double from the 30% long term norm to 59%.

In conclusion, the stock margin debt trend is an excellent long term market indicator. When analyzed in conjunction with the trend of credit balances (see following chapters), the product is one of the best trend following indicators in existence.

When margin speculators borrow money from brokerage firms to finance their trading activity, the brokers themselves must draw upon alternative sources for the needed funds. One of these is credit balances (cash) carried by other customers in brokerage accounts. What brokers cannot supply from this source they must borrow from commercial banks. The total volume of these bank borrowings by all brokerage firms is termed "Brokers' Loans," a series which has been used as a market forecasting tool by a number of analysts.   However, as it is largely dependent upon the debt and credit balance series themselves, it really contains no additional predictive power.

# 25 Credit Balances

Customers' net credit balances are the aggregate amount of cash carried by stock market investors in cash and margin accounts with New York Stock Exchange member brokerage firms. The series is calculated as of the last day of each month by the NYSE and is released to the public approximately two to three weeks thereafter.

Credit balances are usually considered to be a measure of the stock market sentiment of unsophisticated, small investors since larger, more intelligent, market participants would seldom, if ever, allow their cash balances to lie idle with brokerage firms earning no interest.   Rising credit balances indicate that these relatively uninformed investors are building up their cash reserves by selling stock.   Such bearishness is likely to be accompanied by rising stock prices.   On the other hand, when stock prices are falling, unsophisticated small investors use their idle cash balances to buy stock on the decline.   More frequently than not the market will continue to decline.

Although they are wrong on trends, ultimately these amateurish investors are proved right.   Because they sell as stock prices are moving up, they hold the maximum amount of cash at precisely the proper time — near major market peaks.   Similarly, by buying on market declines, they are usually low on cash and relatively fully invested near impor-

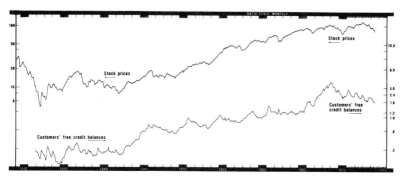

FIGURE 9.    Customers' Free Credit Balances (monthly) and Standard & Poor's Composite Index (quarterly); 1930 - 1974.

tant troughs, again a most intelligent policy. Where these investors are wrong is during sustained trends, and here is where the series has value as a forecasting indicator.

Figure 9 presents a 40 year chart of credit balances. Note how the series traced the great bull market of 1942-1946 during which time the Standard & Poor's Composite Index gained over 150%. The volume of credit balances then peaked just before the 1946-1949 decline before once again commencing an uptrend. During the next two decades the series generally accompanied the market's up and down trends, occasionally even leading cyclical turns. The record, although far from perfect, is good. More recently credit balances established a major peak just as the market topped out in late 1968. The series then established an important low concomitant with the important 1974 market trough.

One excellent method of forecasting with the credit balance series is to average the monthly readings over about one year, and then compare the current level with that average (the same technique that has proven useful for stock margin debt). If the current figure is above the average, credit balances are deemed to be in an uptrend and stock prices should rise. If the current reading is beneath the average, credit balances are, by definition, in a downtrend and stock prices are likely to continue heading lower. Table 31 shows the 34 year record of this indicator.

TABLE 31

CREDIT BALANCES AND MARKET PERFORMANCE (1942-1975)

| Trend of Credit Balances | Probability That A Bull Market Is In Progress | Probability That A Bear Market Is In Progress |
|---|---|---|
| Up | 85% | 15% |
| Down | 51% | 49% |
| 34 Year Average | 70% | 30% |

The trend in credit balances is one of the better long term market indicators available.  Although it is not as good an indicator as stock margin debt, the two work best when they are used together.

# 26 The Stock Margin Debt Credit Balance Indicator

The stock margin debt and credit balance indicators have a synergism that multiplies their usefulness when used jointly.

Table 32 reveals the composite record of the two indicators.  For both the debt and credit series, the trend is considered bullishly up when the most recent monthly reading is above the average reading of the past twelve months.  The trend is considered down and bearish when the current reading is below the twelve month moving average.  An exponential moving average has been used.

TABLE 32

MARGIN DEBT, CREDIT BALANCES,
AND MARKET PERFORMANCE (1942-1975)

| Trend of Stock Margin Debt | Trend of Credit Balances | Probability That A Bull Market Is In Progress | Probability That A Bear Market Is In Progress |
|---|---|---|---|
| Down | Down | 29% | 71% |
| Down | Up | 57% | 43% |
| Up | Down | 69% | 31% |
| Up | Up | 95% | 5% |
| 34-Year Average | | 70% | 30% |

During the past 34 years bull markets have been in progress 70% of the time (about 24 years), while bear markets prevailed the remaining 30% (or 10 years). However, when the trend of each indicator was graded "down," the odds that a bull market was in progress sank to only 29%. Just as dramatic, when stock margin debt and credit balances were both in uptrends, a bull market was in progress 95% of the time and a bear market extant only 5% of the time, 19 to 1 odds in favor of the bulls. The two intermediate cases, wherein one of the series was advancing and the other was declining, revealed closer to average results, suggesting a relatively neutral position on the combined indicator.

The Stock Margin Debt/Credit Balance Indicator is such a superb measure of important cyclical market trends that it deserves a role in integrated market forecasting systems.

# 27 The Speculation Indexes

As with most things done to excess, too much speculation can be potentially dangerous. Speculation in the stock market is no exception. Major bull markets emerge out of a mood of depression, a lack of confidence, extreme conservatism, and a relative absence of speculation. As an uptrend gains momentum, newcomers jump into the market and bid stock prices higher and higher. Confidence improves, conservatism dwindles, and speculative fires glow again. For a time the new speculation is healthy; eventually it becomes overdone. By the time everybody in the country is reading the stock pages in the morning paper and searching for, even demanding, the next "sure fire winner," it is a safe bet that the bull market has over-reached itself and a bear market is about to commence.

One of the best measures of market speculation, as well as one of the more significant indicators of future market performance, is the ratio of American Stock Exchange to New York Stock Exchange volume. Developed in the 1960s by the *Indicator Digest* advisory service, the "Speculation Index," as it is popularly called, has a half century record of prophetic market calls.

A high Speculation Index indicates relatively greater volume on the more speculative Amex — normally a dangerous portent for the market. A low ratio signifies a dearth of speculative activity — a very positive sign, as it suggests that investors are ignoring the Amex cats and dogs and are concentrating their action in the higher quality NYSE issues.

The simple one week Speculation Index readings fluctuate erratically. This problem can be largely eliminated by smoothing the index over several weeks; a 15 week moving average appears to be close to optimal. Historically the smoothed ratio has ranged between extremes of about 10% and 60%. The long term average reading is close to 30%.

Major bullish signals most recently emanated from the Speculation Index between 1974 and 1976 when the ratio hovered continuously in the 10% to 15% range. In fact, only two periods in history have witnessed such extremely favorable readings (see Figure 10). The first was in the early 1920s, while the second coincided with the end of the great market crash in 1932. The two periods ushered in eras of decidedly different socio-economic behavior (the Roaring

'20s versus the Depressing '30s), but remarkably similar stock market performances.

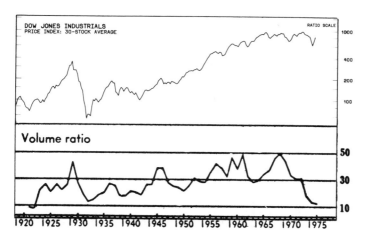

FIGURE 10.   Speculation Index — Annual ratio of Amex to NYSE volume and Dow Jones Industrial Average (quarterly); 1921 - 1975.

The great 1921-1929 bull market saw prices, as measured by the Dow Jones Industrial Average, increase by almost 500%, equivalent to the Dow advancing from its 1974 low of 578 to about 3450. Almost as dramatic, yet often obscured behind the grim facade of the 1930s erected by historians, is the 1932-1937 bull market which powered the Dow to a 370% increase, equivalent to a move to about 2700 in the average from its 1974 low.

More recently significant market troughs in 1942, 1949, 1953, 1957, 1962, 1966, 1970, and 1974 were all accompanied by relatively depressed readings in the Speculation Index. While the indicator did not always pinpoint the market lows, it did serve as an excellent measure of overdone pessimism in the market, following which sizeable bull markets regularly ensued.

The Speculation Index is even more renowned for its sell

signals. As noted from the annual plots in Figure 10, well defined peaks in the ratio of Amex to NYSE volume were established in 1929, 1937, 1946, 1956, 1959, 1961, and 1968, all excellent selling points. The market top in 1961 is of special significance. In retrospect the ensuing 1962 crash can be seen to have reflected only an excess of speculative sentiment and not a fundamentally unsound condition in the nation's economy. The indicator's bearishness was all the more important for its uniqueness.

The index does suffer from an unfortunate flaw in construction. In its basic form, no adjustment is made for changes in the relative number of stocks or quantity of shares listed on the two exchanges. Obviously, trading volume is highly dependent on the number of listed companies and the number of shares they have outstanding.

If the American Stock Exchange were to list new stocks at a much faster rate than the New York Stock Exchange, the volume ratio would inevitably exhibit a secular uptrend (or a downtrend if the Amex expanded less rapidly than the NYSE). The bias may be largely eliminated by expressing the weekly dollar volume of shares traded on each exchange as a percentage of the total dollar value of common stock listed for trading. Multiplying each exchange ratio by 52 converts the weekly percentages to an annual basis, which can be called Volume Turnover Ratios, or VTR's. A "Volume Turnover Speculation Index" can then be derived by dividing the Amex VTR by the NYSE VTR. Interpretation of this improved indicator is basically the same as for the traditional Speculation Index.

Extensive daily or weekly historical data for testing the new ratio is not readily available, although it has been presented in the *Media General Financial Weekly* from 1973 through 1976. Annual data can be obtained from the New York and American Stock Exchanges. The *Financial Weekly* data has the virtue of excluding preferred stocks which impart a small amount of additional bias in the traditional ratio. Several more years of accumulated data will be required before current "Volume Turnover Speculation Index" readings can be properly placed in historical perspective. In the meantime market technicians would be well advised to follow both indicators.

# 28 Corporate Indicator #1: Secondary Offerings

A secondary offering, or distribution, is the sale of a block of stock to the public by an existing stockholder or group of stockholders.

The sale of a secondary is handled off the exchange floor by one or more underwriters. The offering price is fixed but is usually near the current market price of the stock. In most cases the offering is too large to be efficiently handled in the normal course of everyday trading of the stock on the exchange floor.  The ordinary intent of the sellers in a secondary is to dispose of the block at a price above that which could be obtained if the stock were offered piecemeal in the regular auction market.

A secondary is generally considered bearish for a stock. There are two principal reasons for this. First, the sale of the shares by large stockholders who are often in unique positions to know of the internal affairs of the company bespeaks little for the company's prospects.  Second, the offering in effect adds to the supply of stock in the marketplace and at the same time absorbs investment funds which might otherwise be used to bid for existing supplies. The potential buying power available to bid for the publicly held stock is thus diminished, and this diminution of demand, along with the coincident increase in public supply, is likely to have the effect of sending the market price lower.

What is true for individual stocks is, by extension, true for the market as a whole.  A large number of secondaries is bearish for the market because it signifies a lack of confidence in future economic prospects by large shareholders in many companies, and because it adversely alters the market supply — demand relationship.

A below average number of secondaries is bullish for it not only connotes confidence by large shareholders unwilling to part with their stock, but also reduces the relative supply of shares.

The aggregate *dollar volume* of secondary offerings is an extremely erratic series, as one or two exceptionally large distributions can easily dominate the total in any given week. The *number* of offerings has been a generally more reliable and less biased indicator.

When the number of secondaries increases to, say, ten or more per week (not a hard and fast limit due to the secularly increasing number of offerings), the investment groups making the offerings are likely to be taking advantage of excessively high prices for their stocks. In all likelihood such a condition is reflected in the prices of most other stocks as well, and the market is probably overvalued. In 1972, for example, the market was confronted with a virtual torrent of secondary offerings. The excessively high prices which induced these offerings and the resultant diversion of investment funds to the offered stocks and away from the rest of the market, eventually contributed to the greatest crash since the 1930s.

An average of one or two secondary offerings per week is usually bullish. In 1974 the number of offerings dried up to virtually nil, signalling a major zone of undervaluation for the market.

*Barron's* has reported the number and volume of secondary offerings since the late 1950s on a weekly basis. At the present time this is the only reliable source of data, as S.E.C. compilations are published with too great a delay.

# 29 Corporate Indicator #2: New Stock Offerings

"New stock offerings" are the dollar amount of new corporate offerings of common stock to the public. The indicator is very similar in concept to "secondary offerings."

Companies sell stock to the public primarily when they need capital for expansion and related purposes. This usually occurs when business prospects are bright and when companies view their stocks as generously priced by the market. New stock offerings soar when stock prices are riding a wave of enthusiasm and when the market will be most receptive. As the conditions for this most naturally exist near major cyclical tops, a high volume of offerings is bearish. The new source of supply introduced into the market's supply-demand equation also has the effect of diverting investment funds away from other stocks, thus exerting downward pressure on prices.

On the other hand, low levels of stock offerings often coincide with good buying points. When stock prices are extremely depressed, the volume of new offerings is invariably either extremely small or non-existent. Like everyone else, corporations are loath to sell new stock to the public when they cannot receive a good price for it.

As the nation's economy has grown, the volume of new stock offerings has expanded along with it, resulting in a long term uptrend within the series. To draw valid market forecasting conclusions, this trend should be eliminated. The task may be accomplished quite easily by dividing the dollar amount of offerings by the U. S. Gross National Product. Constantly expressing the dollar volume of new common stock financing in terms of the economy's dollar rate of output in effect detrends the indicator.

The resultant Stock Offerings/GNP Ratio normally

fluctuates in an annualized weekly range of zero to 0.50%. Within these "limits" the series is quite erratic from week to week and should be averaged over ten to twenty weeks.

The smoothed ratio has a very good record of market calls. Since World War II, exceptionally low (bullish) readings occurred in 1942, 1943, and 1963. Somewhat less extreme, but still significant, readings were registered in 1949, 1957, and 1974. Very high (bearish) extremes occurred in early 1946 and in late 1972. Moderately bearish readings were observed in 1951, 1959, and early 1969.

On the whole, this is an excellent record. The Stock Offerings/GNP Ratio is a new indicator and it deserves incorporation into larger systems of market forecasting indicators, especially those focusing on long-term trends.

The volume of new stock offerings is reported on the "Market Laboratory" page of each issue of *Barron's.* Gross National Product is reported by the federal government on a quarterly basis and is published in all financial newspapers. GNP data may also be obtained from a monthly government publication entitled "Economic Indicators," recently priced at $24 per year. Subscriptions may be entered by writing: Superintendent of Documents, U.S. Government Printing Office, Washington, D.C. 20402.

# 30 Corporate Indicator #3:
## Stock Splits

The number of companies declaring stock splits and dividends is another interesting and novel indicator of speculation — but the speculation of the companies whose stocks are traded on Wall Street, not the speculative sentiment of Wall Streeters themselves.

One of the most enduring myths on the Street is that stock splits are usually followed by dynamic upside price movements. Several excellent academic studies have demonstrated the fallacy of this argument vis-a-vis individual stocks. The analyses have proven that price behavior of common stocks following declaration of stock splits does not deviate significantly from the average returns of all other stocks.

Related to market fluctuations, what was a myth becomes a lie, for stock splits are actually a contrary market indicator. When stock split declarations fill the financial pages, it is usually a sign that *all* stocks are overpriced and will decline.

Although comprehensive weekly or monthly historical data is not readily available, Table 33 reveals the number of

TABLE 33

STOCK DISTRIBUTIONS BY NYSE LISTED COMPANIES
OF AT LEAST 25%

| Year | Number of Splits | Year | Number of Splits | Year | Number of Splits |
|------|------------------|------|------------------|------|------------------|
| 1927 | 28 | 1944 | 11 | 1961 | 66 |
| 1928 | 22 | 1945 | 39 | 1962 | 70 |
| 1929 | 40 | 1946 | 75 | 1963 | 64 |
| 1930 | 15 | 1947 | 46 | 1964 | 104 |
| 1931 | 2 | 1948 | 26 | 1965 | 115 |
| 1932 | 0 | 1949 | 21 | 1966 | 140 |
| 1933 | 1 | 1950 | 49 | 1967 | 92 |
| 1934 | 7 | 1951 | 55 | 1968 | 147 |
| 1935 | 4 | 1952 | 37 | 1969 | 150 |
| 1936 | 11 | 1953 | 25 | 1970 | 39 |
| 1937 | 19 | 1954 | 43 | 1971 | 70 |
| 1938 | 6 | 1955 | 89 | 1972 | 117 |
| 1939 | 3 | 1956 | 97 | 1973 | 77 |
| 1940 | 2 | 1957 | 44 | 1974 | 37 |
| 1941 | 3 | 1958 | 14 | 1975 | 55 |
| 1942 | 0 | 1959 | 103 | | |
| 1943 | 3 | 1960 | 75 | | |

stock distributions (splits and dividends) of at least 25% made by NYSE listed companies in each year since 1927. Given the annual nature of the data, it is difficult to derive a precise market timing system from the series. Still, a cursory analysis does indicate that the number of stock distributions would have been of assistance in identifying periods of over-done conservatism and undervaluation, as well as excessive speculation and overvaluation.

For example, 1932 and 1942 were the only years in which nary a single company split its stock by at least 25%  Not coincidentally, those years marked two of the greatest buying points in the 20th century.  Other cyclical lows in stock splits during the last fifty years accompanied the excellent buying points of 1949, 1953, 1958, 1963, 1967, 1970, and 1974.

The year 1929 witnessed a definite peak in stock splits, as did the ebullient years of 1936, 1946, 1951, 1956, 1959, 1966, 1969, and 1972.  All of these years save 1951 marked propitious times to bail out of common stocks.

There are two plausible explanations for the predictive success of this indicator.  First, companies normally use stock splits as a means of decreasing the price of their common stock to a level which makes purchase of it easier for smaller investors.   A high price is a natural precondition and, by definition, stock prices are higher around market peaks than they are near bottoms.  At cyclical troughs, the market's own action has lowered the prices of common stocks and no artificial action need be taken by company managements to bring prices down to more purchasable levels.

Second, company officers and directors are by no means immune to periodic speculative binges.  They, too, can get carried away with rising profits and rising stock prices.  Their frequent ownership of significant quantities of their com-pany's common stock, and their concomitant financial stake in its welfare, doesn't improve their objectivity.  They tend to declare stock splits just when economic conditions seem rosiest (the observed fact that most stock distributions are either accompanied or followed by increases in cash divi-dends bears this out), and when the stocks themselves are likely to be just peaking out.  In contrast, when earnings and prices are falling and depressed, company managements are reluctant to declare stock distributions.  First, the investing public would likely view as pure gimmickry any split attempts at such times, and second, managements are usually more concerned with reinvigorating their company (and saving their jobs) than with manipulating the stock market. That, of course, is the best time to buy their stock. What is true for individual stocks is, by extension, true as well for the market and an absence of stock splits marks a good time to buy all stocks.

The declaration of a stock distribution often precedes the split itself by several weeks. To minimize the effect of lags at market turning points, an index of stock splits should be based on the declaration, rather than the effective, split date. A check of the daily "Dividend News" column in the *Wall Street Journal* or the weekly "Speaking of Dividends" feature in *Barron's* would appear to be the best sources of current data. Past and future data should be viewed in the light of the secularly increasing number of common stocks listed on the New York Stock Exchange.

# 31 Market Bellwethers

Market analysts have long searched for a stock or group of stocks which might logically be expected to lead the rest of the market. If such a bellwether exists, it follows that by monitoring that stock or group the future price behavior of the entire market might well be foreseen.

Many stocks have been suggested as possible bellwether candidates — among them DuPont, Merrill Lynch, and Fairchild Camera. However, the only bellwether stock which has been systematically examined for predictive accuracy over many decades is General Motors.

*General Motors Bellwether.* As originally developed, the GM Bellwether Indicator stipulates that when General Motors' common stock does not fall to a new low within a four month period the market should move higher. If

General Motors fails to establish a new cyclical high within a four month period the market should trend downward. For example, the latest buy signal shown in Table 34 has its roots in GM's December 6, 1974 low. Since it failed to penetrate that low by April 6, 1975, a buy signal resulted.

TABLE 34
THE GENERAL MOTORS BELLWETHER RECORD

| Date | Signal | % Gain or Loss | Cumulative Value of $10,000 Portfolio |
|---|---|---|---|
| July 21, 1929 | Sell | + 75.5% | $ 17,552 |
| Oct. 30, 1932 | Buy | + 166.4% | $ 46,758 |
| Mar. 9, 1937 | Sell | + 33.1% | $ 62,245 |
| July 31, 1938 | Buy | + 4.2% | $ 64,859 |
| Mar. 12, 1939 | Sell | + 39.9% | $ 90,764 |
| Apr. 18, 1942 | Buy | + 148.1% | $ 225,185 |
| May 29, 1946 | Sell | + 15.6% | $ 260,269 |
| July 16, 1948 | Buy | + 192.5% | $ 761,288 |
| Mar. 14, 1956 | Sell | + 10.1% | $ 838,483 |
| Apr. 18, 1958 | Buy | + 34.6% | $ 1,128,598 |
| Nov. 9, 1959 | Sell | − 12.0% | $ 993,166 |
| Apr. 23, 1961 | Buy | + 5.4% | $ 1,046,797 |
| Apr. 13, 1962 | Sell | + 19.7% | $ 1,252,807 |
| Oct. 26, 1962 | Buy | + 43.0% | $ 1,791,513 |
| Mar. 2, 1964 | Sell | − 20.4% | $ 1,426,941 |
| Apr. 29, 1967 | Buy | − 0.5% | $ 1,419,805 |
| Jan. 29, 1968 | Sell | − 4.6% | $ 1,354,353 |
| July 29, 1968 | Buy | + 1.0% | $ 1,367,896 |
| Feb. 24, 1969 | Sell | + 15.5% | $ 1,580,057 |
| Oct. 26, 1970 | Buy | + 19.5% | $ 1,888,168 |
| Aug. 30, 1971 | Sell | − 7.8% | $ 1,739,947 |
| Mar. 13, 1972 | Buy | + 3.1% | $ 1,793,885 |
| Aug. 7, 1972 | Sell | − 6.9% | $ 1,670,645 |
| Jan. 21, 1973 | Buy | − 8.5% | $ 1,528,641 |
| May 11, 1973 | Sell | + 14.0% | $ 1,743,262 |
| Apr. 15, 1974 | Buy | − 9.8% | $ 1,570,679 |
| July 14, 1974 | Sell | + 4.1% | $ 1,634,919 |
| Apr. 6, 1975 | Buy | + 28.3% | $ 2,098,025 |
| Aug. 6, 1976 | Sell | | |

The rationale behind the indicator is that as the largest industrial company in the world, what is good for General

Motors is good for the market. Accordingly, trends in the price of GM should be the precursor of similar action in all common stocks, as other companies benefit from or are hurt by the same economic forces which affect General Motors.

The GM Bellwether's first measured signal, a very propitious sell, was on July 21, 1929, indicating that General Motors' common stock made a high four months earlier on March 21, 1929, but failed to penetrate that level on the upside by the signal date. General Motors continued in a downtrend until June 30, 1932, at which time the stock set a new low. Failing to establish yet another new low within the ensuing four months resulted in a buy signal on October 30.

By buying and selling short in accordance with the GM Bellwether's signals during the last 47 years, an initial $10,000 invested in Standard & Poor's Composite Index would have grown to $2,098,025 (ignoring commissions), a compounded return of 12.0% per annum.

By comparison, a strategy of simply buying and holding would have returned 2.3% per year, plus an annual dividend return of about another 4.0%, so after commissions the GM Bellwether made a significant net contribution to profitability. The indicator had an especially good record from 1929 through the early 1960s.

In the 14 years since 1962 the record has been very poor. The yearly rate of return for the GM Bellwether trading strategy has been only about 1% (and an actual loss after commission costs) versus a total annual return of over eight times that rate for a strategy of simply buying in 1962 and holding on through 1976. Why has the indicator's usefulness lessened in recent years? The structural weakness of the GM Bellwether theory is the assumption that the existence of a new four month high or low is an adequate forecast of future price actions. A more important reason may be that although General Motors Corporation has long been a bellwether of the U. S. economy, in the '20s and '30s it was also a speculative favorite on Wall Street. As such, it tended to attract short term trading funds and perhaps even the interest of "smart money" investment pools.

In other words it was a particularly sensitive indicator of the speculative supply and demand forces which usually control the psychological ups and downs of Wall Street. Today, the stock no longer fills this role; General Motors more often has a home in the relatively stodgy portfolios of bank trusts, pension funds and the like.

The GM Bellwether ranks with the Dow Theory as an historical curiosity. It is fun to follow, but it hardly rates as a rational basis for a profitable market strategy.

*Merrill Lynch Bellwether.* Because Merrill Lynch is the largest brokerage firm in the nation, its stock is thought to accurately mirror the outlook for the entire market, leading some commentators to select it as a bellwether of future market direction. Evidence in support of this thesis is sparse. Merrill Lynch has been listed on the New York Stock Exchange since July 27, 1971, and sufficient data has not been accumulated to render a valid judgment on the merits of the stock as a market indicator.

Using what meager data is available, an examination of recent turning points in the broad market (as measured by the unweighted Combined Total Return Index of all NYSE and Amex listed stocks) and ML common suggests that the

TABLE 35

### THE MERRILL LYNCH BELLWETHER RECORD

| Event | Combined TR Index Turning Point | Merrill Lynch Turning Point | Conclusion: Merrill Lynch is. . . |
|-------|---------------------------------|-----------------------------|-----------------------------------|
| Peak   | Mar.  9, 1972  | Mar. 24, 1972 | 15 Days Late |
| Trough | Oct. 16, 1972  | Oct. 17, 1972 | 1 Day Late   |
| Peak   | Dec.  8, 1972  | Dec. 11, 1972 | 3 Days Late  |
| Trough | June 25, 1973  | July  9, 1973 | 14 Days Late |
| Peak   | Oct. 12, 1973  | Oct. 12, 1973 | Coincident   |
| Trough | Sep. 13, 1974  | Sep. 16, 1974 | 3 Days Late  |
| Peak   | July 15, 1975  | July 23, 1975 | 8 Days Late  |
| Trough | Sep. 17, 1975  | Dec. 22, 1975 | 96 Days Late |
|        |                | Median        | 8 Days Late  |

stock's predictive ability may be somewhat exaggerated.

As indicated in Table 35, not a single Merrill Lynch turning point has yet preceded an intermediate turning point in the broad market. It would be more appropriate to conclude that the broad market is a leading indicator of Merrill Lynch, not the other way around.

*Other Bellwether Stocks.* Of course, *some* stocks have to lead each market turn, so some analysts' favorite bellwether will always be seen in the light of hindsight to have correctly called a cycle. It is unlikely that forecasting the market can ever really be this easy.

# 32 Utility Stocks: A Real Bellwether?

Utility stocks are so sensitive to interest rates that bond and money market developments are often reflected in the Dow Jones Utility Average long before they exert any influence on the stock market generally. For this reason, utility stocks are frequently a useful leading indicator of general market trends.

There are several reasons for the interdependence between utility stock prices and interest rates. First, owing to their customarily high dividend yield, utility stocks are often treated as a substitute for bonds, whose price fluctuations are almost totally dependent on interest rate changes. Second, most utilities have large amounts of debt in their capital structure, on which they must pay interest. The amounts of such payments are critical to their profitability. Third, the utilities are dependent upon easy availability of funds in the capital markets to finance the expansion on which their long term profitability depends. Given this dependence of all common stock valuation on interest rates, it is not surprising that utility stocks frequently change trend ahead of the general market.

Although over 150 utility stocks are listed on the New York Stock Exchange (the largest single industry group), the 15 stock Dow Jones Utility Average (DJUA) serves as a useful proxy for market forecasting purposes.

The results of a simple test on the last 35 years of data reveal that if the DJUA declined during just a single week, the chance that the general market would rise in the following six months was about 60%. If the DJUA rose during a week, the probability of a subsequent market rise increased to 76%. Statistically, the difference is highly significant, as the average probability of a market rise over any six month period is about 66%.

In other words, the mere knowledge of a DJUA advance or decline in one week provided information on the future trend direction of the market. Of course, an examination of week to week changes is extremely crude and signals are subject to "whipsaws" (constant reversals).

One useful refinement is to compare the current DJUA with the level of 15 weeks earlier. If the present reading is higher, utility stocks may be classified as in an uptrend and the stock market should follow upward as well. If the current DJUA is lower, a downtrend is established and the broad market should follow the utilities lower. Since the utility average has a greater chance of embarking upon a sustained trend over a 15 week period than in a single week, buy and sell signals are less frequent and whipsawing is reduced (although it is not completely eliminated). Used in conjunction with a large array of other market indicators (such as in an econometric model), this analytical technique can contribute to an overall favorable prediction record.

Another system of analysis that has proven effective entails a comparison of the current DJUA reading with the average weekly value of the index over the past year. Depending upon whether the present reading is above or below the one year average, the market's climate is deemed to be bullish or bearish. This method tracks market trends extremely well and is even less subject to whipsaws, although

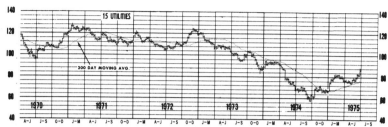

FIGURE 11. Dow Jones Utility Average — Weekly price range and 200 day simple moving average; April 1970 - July 1975.

it is not as sensitive in picking up market turning points as the two previously described techniques.

Figure 11 shows the Dow Jones Utility Average during the first half of this decade. Note that the late 1972 high failed to surmount the previous peak established in 1971, thereby warning of an impending bear market. The utility average then commenced a severe and sustained downtrend for the life of the 1973-1974 bear market before bottoming out in September 1974, two and a half months prior to the Dow Jones Industrial Average trough. Utility stocks then traveled an upward course throughout the following year, leaving little doubt as to the validity of the new bull market.

The utility stock average provides a unique, money sensitive measure of investor sentiment. It is a valuable leading indicator of the market's future trend — a real bellwether.

# 33 The Classic Indicators of Market Breadth

Market breadth analysis is based upon simple counts of the number of stocks going up or down in price or establishing new price highs or lows. Such indicators probably seem especially crude to you in this era of high speed computer technology which is capable of so much more than merely counting pluses and minuses. However, the breadth measures have a very large following, in part because they have been on the investment scene for so many decades.

When most stocks are participating in a general price advance, the market is said to have good breadth. If the blue chip averages, such as the Dow Jones Industrials, are advancing but the majority of stocks are declining, the market has bad breadth. (Forgive the puns; they are ancient and well established.) To a large degree the forecasting value of the breadth indicators is overrated, although in some forms, primarily trend following, they do impart useful information.

*Advance/Decline Line.* The Advance/Decline Line (or A/D Line) is the simplest of all breadth measures. It is calculated by subtracting the number of stocks which decline in price each week from the number which advance and accumulating the weekly differences. (The A/D Line can also be calculated on a daily basis.) When more stocks are advancing than declining, the A/D Line moves upward, while a majority of issues falling in price causes the line to trend downward. To facilitate historical comparability, it is advisable to slightly alter this basic calculation. The following method should be used: (1) each week divide the difference of advances minus declines by the total number of issues changing in price; (2) accumulate the weekly ratio readings. The result improves the standard Advance/Decline Line because the net number of advances or declines is constantly expressed in terms of the number of issues traded, and the series achieves a measure of historical comparability. Without this adjustment the A/D Line is biased by the long term increase in the number of issues traded.

When this improved Advance/Decline Line is in an established uptrend, the odds are that stocks are in a bull market. When the improved A/D Line is in a downtrend, the probability of a major downtrend is greater. The only problem is, What constitutes an "established" up or downtrend in the A/D Line?

Table 36 presents the record of an indicator which has a relatively simple definition of established trend. An uptrend is defined as the current weekly Advance/Decline Line reading above the average A/D Line reading of the last 52 weeks. A downtrend is defined as the current Advance/Decline Line reading below its one year average. The test result on this simple indicator reveals a high degree of accuracy and suggests that the Advance/Decline Line is a superb market tool for trend following purposes.

TABLE 36

ADVANCE/DECLINE LINE AND MARKET TRENDS (1941-1975)

| Trend of Advance/Decline Line | Probability That A Bull Market Is In Progress | Probability That A Bear Market Is In Progress |
|---|---|---|
| Up | 91% | 9% |
| Down | 33% | 67% |
| 35-Year Average | 68% | 32% |

*Disparity Index.* A disparity index compares relative price trends of two stock market averages. Frequently used disparity indexes include comparisons of the relative performances of low priced stocks with high quality issues, glamour stocks versus the broad market, and growth stocks versus cyclical issues. (The latter is called the Dual Market Principle by its creators, Kenneth Smilen and Kenneth Safian.)

The most common comparison is between a prominent index of blue chips, such as the 30 stock Dow Jones Industrial Average, and a more broadly based measure, such as the Advance/Decline Line.

Important changes in market trend are theoretically signaled when these two indexes diverge — when one rises and the other falls or when one rises or falls faster than the other. When a divergence occurs, the Advance/Decline Line is believed to more accurately presage the future because it reflects the action of the broad market rather than a small

FIGURE 12. Disparity Index — Bearish divergence between daily Advance/Decline Line and Dow Jones Industrial Average; January 1961 - January 1962.

sample of blue chip issues.

Figure 12 demonstrates the principle of divergence. Prior to the 1962 bear market the Advance/Decline Line turned down well in advance of the major market averages. As the Dow Jones Industrials and S&P 500 proceeded upward to new highs during the last eight months of 1961, the declining A/D Line showed that most stocks had already started down. By the end of 1961 it became apparent that a significant disparity between the broad market and the Dow had developed and that a further downward movement might well be imminent. The ensuing market crash is now history. (Unfortunately, the Disparity Index followed up this spectacular success with a clear cut sell signal in 1964 right in the middle of a protracted bull market.)

In the late 1940s the Advance/Decline Line also led the

market averages at a major cyclical turn. Between 1946 and 1949 the Dow Jones Industrial Average meandered through a relatively narrow trading range, establishing a series of successively lower troughs. The Advance/Decline Line simultaneously trended upward, making a succession of higher troughs. By mid-1949 it was apparent that the broad market had developed substantial upward momentum and that a major advance might well ensue. In retrospect 1949 proved to be the base from which a 19 year super bull market emerged.

While the Disparity Index has provided many timely and profitable signals, it is far from infallible. The length of lead warning time is highly variable, ranging up to as long as one and a half years, which is the equivalent of no warning at all.

Technicians should note, too, that the Disparity Index is better at forecasting market tops than market bottoms. The 1946-1949 experience is actually the index's only leading buy signal in the last 50 years. In large part this is accounted for by a long term downward bias in the Advance/Decline Line making uptrends difficult to achieve. (For example, the A/D Line is much lower today than it was twenty years ago.) The downward bias produces frequent periods of negative divergence, with the A/D Line moving lower and the DJIA trending higher. This recurrence of sell signals permits Disparity Index adherents to believe the index rarely fails to call a bear market. This is true. But it also calls about twice as many as actually occur.

To the extent that the theory of disparity is valid and to the extent that the Advance/Decline Line accurately reflects the broad market despite an intrinsic downward bias, *any fairly* constructed index of broad market behavior should also top out before the Dow and presage extended bear market declines. This has indeed frequently occurred. Following the 1970 market low, all major price and capitalization weighted indexes trended upward to a January 1973 peak, but the New York Stock Exchange Total Return Index, the best broadly based and continuously calculated market index available, peaked ten months earlier in March 1972, coincident with the Advance/Decline Line. A similar divergence occurred in 1928-1929. Computerized studies of market behavior in the 1920s show that properly constructed, unweighted market averages peaked out in 1928 along with the Advance/Decline Line, many months prior to the commencement of the Great Crash in the autumn of 1929.

To summarize, the classic A/D Line Disparity Index is a mediocre indicator of important market tops subject to a serious statistical bias and requiring much subjective interpretation. In this case the underlying theory is better than the indicator and deserving of more study. Almost all research to date has focused on the Advance/Decline Line in preference to any other broadly based market index, primarily because the former is the only measure for which extensive historical data is available on a daily or weekly basis. Future research and real time use of the Disparity Index should either adjust the Advance/Decline Line to eliminate its intrinsic bias or concentrate on the relationship of pairs of properly and equivalently constructed stock indexes.

*Highs and Lows.* These elementary statistics signify the number of stocks on the NYSE or Amex which have established a new high or low price for the year during the most recent day (or week). Market analysts have long held that when more stocks are making new highs than are making new lows, the market is in a primary uptrend and further advances should ensue. If new lows predominate, a bearish market climate is said to exist. While there is some truth to this basic hypothesis, the forecasting value of highs and lows has been greatly exaggerated. The high-low data does not really yield any information on the market's trend beyond that which can be derived from other indicators.

Part of the difficulty with the high-low data rests in the unevenness of its calculation. The determination of whether a stock establishes a new high or low is based upon data which is contained in most financial newspapers; namely, whether the stock has reached a new high or low price for the calendar year to date. The problem with this calculation is that as the year progresses and as individual stocks establish wider and wider price ranges, it becomes increasingly more difficult to establish a new high or low for the year. Most calculations are begun in about mid-March of each year. If at the end of March a stock trades outside its range of the first three months of the year, it has made a new high (or low as the case may be) based on the *three* month range. By December the range is calculated over a *twelve* month period, and in early March of the following year the high-low base stretches over *fourteen* months. Then in mid-March the base period abruptly reverts back to two and a half months, drastically altering the implications of different high-low breadth readings.

The changing base problem (which is sufficient by itself to render the raw data almost useless) can be eliminated by calculating the number of new highs or lows on a constant 52 week moving basis; that is, always comparing current price with the range of prices over the latest 52 weeks. A new 52 week high or low is established if the current price is outside the 52 week high-low range. At this writing the only regularly published source of such data is the *Media General Financial Weekly*. Their statistics have been calculated over just the last three years and a sufficient historical record does not yet exist from which to draw statistically valid conclusions.

Using the standard data since 1941, the author has tested literally hundreds of high-low indicators. Very few yielded significant forecasting results. The avenues of research which have been pursued include the difference between highs and lows, the high-low difference relative to the number of issues traded, independent analyses of the number of new highs and number of new lows at various market stages (such as extremes at bear market troughs), comparisons of NYSE and Amex high and low data, sophisticated "linear" and "curvilinear" systems, and many more. Almost without exception they reveal the high-low data to be practically devoid of market forecasting power.

What little useful information can be culled from the data (primarily trend following) is also contained in less statistically reprehensible and superior price and trend following predictive indicators.

# 34 Negative and Positive Volume Indexes

The Negative Volume Index (NVI) measures the trend of stock prices during periods of declining market volume. The theory underlying the indicator is that trading by unsophisticated investors occurs predominantly on days of exuberantly rising volume, whereas informed buying and selling (i.e., "smart money" activity) usually occurs during quieter periods of declining volume. The direction the market assumes on days of negative volume changes supposedly reflects accumulation (buying) or distribution (selling) of stock by those who are in the know.

The indicator can be calculated on a daily or weekly basis. In the past Negative Volume Indexes have *always* been constructed using advance-decline data, with the Advance/Decline Line being accumulated only for days in which volume is below that of the previous day. On days of positive volume changes the index is held constant.

There is no good reason for this fixation on the A/D Line. In truth, a Negative Volume Index can be calculated with *any* market index — the Dow Jones Industrial Average, the S&P 500, or even "unweighted" market measures. In view of the fundamental disadvantages of the A/D Line (discussed in the preceding chapter), a Negative Volume Index calculated on the basis of some market price index should be preferred. Somehow this point has escaped the attention of technicians to date.

Starting with a base index level, say, 100.00, a quantity

equal to the percent change in a market index is added to the NVI only in those periods in which volume has fallen relative to the preceding period. If volume has risen, the NVI value is not changed. Table 37 illustrates the computation with the Dow Jones Industrial Average. For example, on January 7,

TABLE 37

NEGATIVE VOLUME INDEX: EXAMPLE

| Date (1976) | NYSE Volume (mil. shares) | Volume Change | DJI % Change | Negative Volume Index |
|---|---|---|---|---|
| January  7 | 33.17 | . . . . | | 100.00 |
| January  8 | 29.03 | Down | +  1.03% | 101.03 |
| January  9 | 26.51 | Down | +  0.35% | 101.38 |
| January 12 | 30.44 | Up | | 101.38 |
| January 13 | 34.53 | Up | | 101.38 |
| January 14 | 30.34 | Down | +  1.83% | 103.24 |
| January 15 | 38.45 | Up | | 103.24 |
| January 16 | 25.94 | Down | +  0.55% | 103.81 |
| January 19 | 29.45 | Up | | 103.81 |
| January 20 | 36.69 | Up | | 103.81 |
| January 21 | 34.47 | Down | −  0.38% | 103.41 |

1976, New York Stock Exchange volume was 33 million shares. On January 8, volume declined to 29 million shares. Since the daily volume change was negative, the Negative Volume Index was adjusted by an amount equal to the percent change in the Dow. As it turned out the average rose 1.03% (in this case, about nine points). Since the Negative Volume Index previously read 100.00, the new reading would be 101.03 (1.0103 x 100.00). The Negative Volume Index revealed that on this day sophisticated investors were buying stocks and pushing prices higher on the volume decline, a bullish syndrome. The syndrome was repeated the next day, January 9.

On January 12 NYSE volume showed a daily increase, so the Negative Volume Index remained unchanged for the day regardless of which way prices moved.

Once a Negative Volume Index has been calculated, the

next step is to derive a system of ascertaining buy and sell signals. Although it is possible to draw in trendlines or to note "support" and "resistance" areas, such methods are relatively crude and unsophisticated and entail much guesswork.

A more refined technique, which computer testing has proven successful, averages the daily (or weekly) index readings over the past year and then relates the current reading to the one year average. If the current NVI figure is above its one year average the Negative Volume Index is, by definition, in an uptrend, smart money has been buying, and stock prices should head higher. If the current reading is below the one year average, the NVI is in a downtrend, smart money has been selling, and the market is likely to head lower.

The experience of the last thirty five years is that when the weekly NVI is graded bullish by this technique, the odds are better than 95 in 100 in favor of a major bull market (see Table 38). When the current NVI is below its long-term average, the odds are somewhat more than 50-50 in favor of a bear market. The primary value of the Negative Volume Index, then, is as a bull market indicator.

TABLE 38

NVI AND MARKET PERFORMANCE (1941-1975)

| Trend of Negative Volume Index (NVI) | Probability That A Bull Market Is In Progress | Probability That A Bear Market Is In Progress |
|---|---|---|
| Up | 96% | 4% |
| Down | 47% | 53% |
| 35-Year Average | 70% | 30% |

The NVI has exhibited a downward trend over the years, a result of the normal phenomena of price advances on increasing volume and price declines on decreasing volume. (The Negative Volume Index rises only when prices go against the norm and increase on decreasing volume.) This downward propensity is partially responsible for the NVI's less than dramatic success as a bear market indicator. As bullish upward trending NVI's are difficult to achieve, buy signals, when they occur, have a high degree of accuracy. A bearish, downward trending NVI is more common, and its sell signals, being more frequent and less discriminating, are also less reliable.

In sum, the Negative Volume Index is an excellent indicator of the primary market trend. More particularly, it is one of the best bull market prediction indicators in existence.

The Negative Volume Index's opposite number is the Positive Volume Index (or PVI), which measures market changes only on days, or weeks, that NYSE volume has increased from the preceding period. Just as the NVI has a downward trend bias over long periods of time, the PVI generally moves upward.

Using the same signal derivation technique as that described for the NVI, when the current PVI reading is above its one year average, the odds on a bull market are four in five and the chances of a bear market are only one in five (see Table 39). When the current PVI is in a downtrend — below its average reading of the past year — the odds on a bull market are less than half as good, only 33%, and the chances of a bear market triple to 67%. While the Positive Volume

TABLE 39

PVI AND MARKET PERFORMANCE (1941-1975)

| Trend of Positive Volume Index (PVI) | Probability That A Bull Market Is In Progress | Probability That A Bear Market Is In Progress |
|---|---|---|
| Up | 79% | 21% |
| Down | 33% | 67% |
| 35-Year Average | 70% | 30% |

Index has forecasting ability, any value to be gained from the index can also be gained from the A/D Line and NVI themselves. The PVI has *no additional* forecasting value.

# 35 The "Going Nowhere" Indicators

When once asked his current opinion of the market, J. P. Morgan allegedly responded with a now classic answer: "It will fluctuate." Most investors and speculators purchase stock for that very reason; they expect prices to fluctuate — upward.

Numerous market timing systems are also based upon the concept of fluctuation. Some analysts subscribe to the idea that a trend in motion tends to continue. These technicians respect fluctuating prices, assume they will continue fluctuating in the *same* direction, and buy and sell accordingly. Other analysts hold the opposite viewpoint: that the further the market moves in one direction, the more likely it is that it has moved away from its true value and hence that it should *reverse* direction. They, too, hold that prices will continue to fluctuate — but in the opposite direction. Still other analysts, mostly academicians, insist that stocks are always fairly priced and past fluctuations have no relevance to the future. Thus there is a great market for ideas on a fluctuating market.

But what of a market which does nothing, which fluctuates very little if at all; a market which is "going nowhere?" Can any useful information be derived from that? The Going Nowhere Indicators say "Yes."

*Unchanged Issues Index.* This index is based upon the number of issues which trade but remain unchanged in price on a given day or week. The number of advancing, declining, and unchanged stocks on the New York and American Stock Exchanges is reported in almost all general and financial news periodicals.  The Unchanged Issues Index is calculated by dividing the number of issues which are unchanged in price by the total number of stocks traded.  The ratio is normally expressed in percentage form.  A typical reading might be 15%, although the index has ranged from as little as 5% to upwards of 25%.  Low readings are considered bullish and high readings bearish.

The rationale underlying the indicator is the tendency of stock prices to bottom very quickly, but to form tops over extended periods of time.  The last few days and weeks of important declines are usually extremely sharp and so are the first several days and weeks of ensuing recoveries.  In contrast top formations frequently stretch over an extended period of time.  The market often goes nowhere for several weeks or months.

The point of these observations is that during weeks when prices are fluctuating rapidly, either a great many stocks advance or a great many decline;  few remain unchanged.  Thus the Unchanged Issues Index tends to be low when price fluctuations are greatest . . . near market bottoms.

When broad top formations are developing, the market stagnates with neither advancing nor declining issues gaining the upper hand for an extended period of time.  Naturally the number of issues remaining unchanged in price on these weeks is high.

Although the indicator has value as a long term market forecasting tool, it is also useful in timing shorter term swings.  On this basis, the indicator is better calculated on a daily than on a weekly basis.  A moderate degree of smoothing to eliminate random fluctuations, say a five or ten day moving average, aids in interpretation.

*Absolute Breadth Index.*  It is possible to construct an approximately comparable indicator by subtracting the difference between the number of advancing and declining stocks with the sign of the resultant statistic ignored.  In this absolute advance-decline differential, 1200 advances and 600 declines would be absolutely equivalent to 1200 declines and

600 advances. When the absolute differential is high, price changes are large and frequent, the number of stagnating issues is usually low, and the market is probably nearer a bottom than a top. A low absolute advance-decline differential, with relatively small and infrequent price changes, indicates the market is probably approaching a top area.

A highly reliable forecasting tool based on this phenomenon can be calculated on a weekly basis by dividing the absolute value of advances minus declines (ignoring the sign, plus or minus, of the differential), by the total number of issues traded. The resultant Absolute Breadth Index (ABI), averaged over ten weeks, normally reads about 25%. Readings above 40% are highly bullish and values below 15% usually precede periods of far below average, and frequently negative, market returns. The complete record over various holding periods based on the last twenty years of data appears in Table 40.

TABLE  40

ABI AND MARKET PERFORMANCE (1956-1975)

| Absolute Breadth Index (ABI) | S&P 500 Index 3 Mo. Later | S&P 500 Index 6 Mo. Later | S&P 500 Index 12 Mo. Later |
|---|---|---|---|
| Under 15% | − 0.3% | − 1.3% | 0.0% |
| 15% to 40% | + 1.5% | + 2.9% | + 5.0% |
| Over 40% | + 4.0% | + 5.0% | + 13.2% |
| 20-Year Average | + 1.5% | + 2.8% | + 4.8% |

The Absolute Breadth Index and the Unchanged Issues Index measure roughly equivalent phenomena. Both are excellent derivatives of the "Going Nowhere" Indicator.

# 36 Most Active
## Stocks

The price behavior of the stocks most heavily traded on the New York Stock Exchange can occasionally provide useful insights into the internal condition of the market. These stocks, popularly termed the "most active issues," are the subject of several indicators of investor sentiment.

One of the oldest of these indicators is the Active Issues Average Price Index, which is merely the average price of the stocks which have been most actively traded during each week. The indicator is based on the premise that when stock exchange activity is primarily directed toward low priced (and presumably more speculative) issues, the major market uptrend is reaching a terminal blowoff stage and stock prices should subsequently decline.

Alternatively, when the average price of the most active stocks is exceptionally high, market activity is alleged to be concentrated in issues of superior quality, and the technical condition of the market is deemed sound. Such activity occurred at opportune buying points in mid-1957, mid-1962, and in the fall of 1966.

While the underlying theory may have some merit, inconsistencies in the data required for practical use of the index cause more false signals than accurate ones. Part of the problem resides in the long term uptrend of average stock prices. In the 1940s the average price of NYSE listed issues ranged between $10 and $25 per share. By the end of the 1960s the average stock price was closer to $40 or $50.

This naturally raises the question, In a given market cycle, how high is high and how low is low? The problem could easily be resolved if the average price of the most active stocks could be related to the average price of all stocks on the exchange. Then a simple ratio of the two statistics would quickly reveal the *relative* price of the most active issues. Unfortunately, no continuously published record of the average NYSE stock price currently exists going back more than a few years.

The forecasting ability of the indicator is also imperiled by a statistical quirk in the data. Lacking a comparative series for the entire market, a bullish reading on the Most Active Issues Price Index is yielded by a *high* average price of the most actively traded issues. Such a reading would ideally occur at the depths of market contractions. But as all prices are, by definition, *low* at such troughs, a high average price reading on the most active issues is exceedingly difficult to obtain. Similarly, a *low* average price for the active stocks, signalling excessive speculative sentiment, should ideally occur near market tops, the very time when the average price of all stocks is, by definition, extremely *high*.

The mixing of these two phenomena makes a jumble of the indicator by tending always to throw the average price of the most active stocks onto a middle ground. Until sufficient historical data is developed on the NYSE average price,for comparative purposes, this indicator would best be avoided.

The actual price performance of the most active issues provides another line of pursuit. The active stocks list is usually considered the trading ground of large and presumably sophisticated investors such as mutual and pension funds, banks, and other institutions ("smart money," according to this theory anyway). These groups must buy and sell large blocks of stock because their investment portfolios are so huge. This in turn requires stocks that have unusually good liquidity and are actively traded; that is, the most active stocks.

The basic performance measure, then, is calculated by subtracting the number of stocks on the weekly most active list that declined in price from the number of stocks on the list that advanced. If advances exceed declines, the most active stocks are moving higher, "smart money" is deemed to be buying, and general market advances should ensue. If declining issues outnumber advancing issues, "they" are selling and the market should subsequently trend lower.    Crude, but simple.

The weekly counts may be treated in either of two ways: the first by averaging the weekly advance-decline difference over a certain period of time (say, three or five weeks), and the second by accumulating the weekly differentials into an Active Issues Advance/Decline Line.    Both series are comparable in construction to similar indicators based upon overall market breadth.

Although the reasoning appears sound, in actual practice the indicators' market prediction records leave something to be desired.    The technician will *always* do better to study *total market* advances and declines than the active issues' advances and declines.    (The problem may reside in the traditional determination of active stocks by measurement of the number of shares traded rather than the dollar value of those shares. The standard treatment allows low priced stocks, temporary speculative favorites, and merger candidates to enter, and possibly bias, the series.)

The most active issues advance-decline indicators are right less often and wrong more often than exactly comparable indicators based upon total market breadth.    While the active stocks can be of predictive value, that value is lessened in relative terms by the ability of the total market breadth indicators to render the same accurate signals, and more besides, and to yield fewer false signals as well.

# 37 Overbought/Oversold Index

The Overbought/Oversold (OB/OS) Index, also called the Advance/Decline (A/D) Ratio, is calculated by dividing the number of advancing issues on a given day by the number of stocks which declined. When the ratio of advances to declines is high, the market has been trending higher. When the ratio is low, the market has been moving down. The daily ratio is usually averaged over a period of about ten days to eliminate random fluctuations and to furnish a smooth curve for interpretational purposes.

The ten day OB/OS Index generally ranges between 0.5 and 2.0. Traditionally the market is considered overbought (too high) when the index is above 1.25 (i.e., when the number of advancing stocks is at least 25% more than the number of declining stocks). The market is considered oversold (too low) when the ratio is below 0.75 (i.e., when advancing stocks are at least 25% fewer in number than declining stocks).

Constructing more precise timing methods from the indicator is difficult. Many attempts have been made; few, if any, seem to have been successful. One notable effort was made in the late 1960s by Harvey A. Krow, who developed a trading system based upon his own observation of the ratio's historical tendencies *(Institutional Investor,* February 1968). A sell signal first required a ten day OB/OS Index above 1.25 signifying that the market had advanced substantially and might be susceptible to a downward reversal. The reversal itself was defined by an Index decline of at least 0.05 in a single one day period (for example, from 1.40 to 1.35 or below). Buy signals were furnished in precisely the opposite manner. The index must first have been in decidedly oversold territory, which Krow defined as below 0.75 in bull markets and below 0.50 in bear markets, and then jump upward by 0.05 within a single day.

Krow tested his system on market data from 1953 through 1966 and concluded that it contained a high degree of accuracy. False signals were few in number, and virtually all signals were followed by extended market moves in the desired direction. Research by this author, however, has determined that the system has failed to work well in ensuing years. It tended to furnish so many false signals that its accurate signals were rendered effectively useless. In addition, Krow's stipulation that the OB/OS Index initially be below a different level depending upon whether a bull market (0.75) or bear market (0.50) was in progress requires us to know most of the answer before we start to ask the question, a defect not untypical of many otherwise perfect market systems.

The Overbought/Oversold Index is more frequently used for specifying general areas of market turns than for precise timing. Inasmuch as the key test of an indicator is what the market does following a particular reading, on this basis the OB/OS Index is suspect. Extensive computer analysis of the index and the market reveals virtually zero predictive power. The index persists in overbought and oversold areas for periods of time as short as one day and as long as several months. For a trader interested in timing short and intermediate market moves, this range simply leaves too much room for interpretation. Thus, despite its popularity the Overbought/Oversold Index is overrated.

# 38 Short Term Trading Index

The Short Term Trading Index measures the concentration of volume in advancing and declining stocks. According to the most popular interpretation, if more volume is flowing into the average advancing stock than into the average declining stock, the situation is bullish for the market. Alternatively, a preponderance of volume in declining issues is bearish.

The calculation method shown below is slightly different

$$\text{Short Term Trading Index} = \frac{AV/A}{DV/D}$$

where, AV = Volume of Advancing Stocks, A = Number of Advancing Stocks, DV = Volume of Declining Stocks, and D = Number of Declining Stocks.

from that used by most analysts, but readers should find it more understandable and easier to calculate.

The first step is to determine the average volume per advancing stock and the average volume per declining stock on the New York Stock Exchange. Assume that on a given day 1,000 issues advance on the NYSE and those 1,000 stocks have a total trading volume (termed "up" volume) of 10 million shares. Then the average volume per advancing stock is 10,000 shares, calculated by dividing 10 million shares by 1,000 stocks. A similar calculation is made for issues which have fallen in price. If, on the same day, 500 stocks decline and those 500 issues have a total volume ("down" volume) of 5 million shares, the average volume per declining stock is also 10,000 shares (5 million shares divided by 500 stocks).

In this hypothetical situation, even though twice as many stocks advanced as declined, volume is concentrated equally in both rising and falling issues, and the Short Term Trading Index reads 1.0, a *neutral* situation.

If the average volume per advancing stock had been 20,000 shares, the rising stocks would have had twice as much average volume as the declining stocks (20,000 versus 10,000) and the Short Term Trading Index would equal 2.0. Such a reading is normally considered extremely bullish.

If the opposite situation occurred, with volume per advancing stock (10,000) only half the volume per declining stock (20,000), the ratio would read a bearish 0.50 (10,000 shares divided by 20,000). Note that the bearish reading of 0.50 is akin to the bullish reading of 2.0. Similarly, bearish extremes of 0.33, 0.25, and 0.10, respectively, are exactly the opposite of bullish readings of 3.00, 4.00 and 10.00. (A more frequently used formula is: $(A/D) / (AV/DV)$, called "MKDS" or "TRIN" on various stock quotation services. Readings below 1.0 are bullish and readings above 1.0 are bearish. The calculation method proposed above, however, is easier to grasp and intuitively more logical.)

The index has been variously applied to predictions of

market changes as short as hourly and as long as several weeks. Although the index has many adherents, it has seldom been tested rigorously, and its true predictive ability is uncertain. The trading index has the general characteristic of fluctuating with market prices; that is, it gives bullish readings when the market is rising and bearish readings when prices are declining. This characteristic is caused by the fact that volume is generally the dominant component in the index. When prices are rising, a greater than proportionate amount of total market volume is usually concentrated in advancing stocks, causing high index readings. When the market is falling, down volume is usually predominant, and low index readings ensue. In essence, then, the trading index is a price following indicator: high index readings usually accompany rising markets, and since high index readings are bullish, further rising markets are predicted, which in turn should be accompanied by further high index readings, and so on.

For market prediction purposes, the trading index can be analyzed in several ways. One is to note changes in the index toward greater or lesser bullishness or greater or lesser bearishness; or from bearish to bullish or bullish to bearish. If the daily readings are averaged over a three to five day period to eliminate short term random fluctuations, shifts from bearishness to bullishness (say, from below 0.85 to above 1.20) accompany the formation of intermediate term market troughs about 80% of the time. These buy signals are occasionally early, but are more often slightly late, averaging a lag of about two days from the actual market turning points. Sell signals, derived by a shift from bullishness to bearishness (say, by an index decline from above 1.20 to below 0.85), are also useful, though not quite as reliable as the buy indications.

A second technique is to treat the index as a contrary indicator. When it gets too bearish, a bullish market turnaround may be imminent, and vice versa.

Still another method of analysis takes into account the

tendency of the index to fluctuate with the market. In essence, this technique relates trading index readings to accompanying market changes. A bullish reading would be derived when the trading index is greater than would normally be expected to accompany a given market change. By the same token, readings would be considered bearish when they are lower than would normally be expected to accompany a given market change. Using this technique, ostensibly favorable readings would be bearish if they are not high enough, and ostensibly unfavorable readings would be bullish if they are not too low.

Needless to say, most of these methods of analysis require a good deal of subjective judgment in establishing buy and sell signal criteria. Although there are doubtless additional interpretational methods which have not yet been formalized or studied rigorously, the index seems to have limited forecasting value. Ascertainment of its full worth must await further, more comprehensive testing.

# 39 Industry Group Diffusion Index

A diffusion index is simply a calculation of the proportion of individual factors under analysis which are moving in one direction. If you examined the twelve leading economic indicators on the National Bureau of Economic Research's "Short List" and determined by some criteria that nine indicators were rising, you would have created a diffusion index with a reading of 75%. The proportion of stocks advancing in the market on a given day also constitutes a simple diffusion index.

One useful market indicator utilizing a diffusion index is based on industry group analysis. We observed earlier that good "breadth" is favorable for the market's future. That concept can be further refined to specify that if the favorable breadth is spread over a large number of industry groups, the advance is more soundly based (and more likely to continue) than if only a few industry groups are providing all the strength.    Some technicians believe that glamour stocks are particularly sensitive to impending changes in market trend and single out industry groups of high flyers for special analysis.

The author has tested a diffusion index of industry groups with above average price/earnings ratios (an objective measure of "glamour") since 1973 which has provided generally profitable market signals.  Table 41 lists each buy and sell signal date and the market change which ensued, as measured by the New York Stock Exchange Total Return Index.

TABLE 41

INDUSTRY GROUP DIFFUSION INDEX
BUY AND SELL SIGNALS

| Signal | Date | % Gain or Loss from Signal |
|---|---|---|
| Buy | July 6, 1973 | + 20.5% |
| Sell Short | October 19, 1973 | + 12.6% |
| Buy | March 1, 1974 | − 7.5% |
| Sell Short | May 3, 1974 | + 23.9% |
| Buy | October 24, 1974 | + 36.0% |
| Sell Short | May 2, 1975 | −15.7% |
| Buy | July 18, 1975 | − 4.8% |
| Sell Short | July 25, 1975 | + 3.9% |
| Buy | October 25, 1975 | + 27.6% |
| Sell Short | April 9, 1976 | |

On a compounded basis the Industry Group Diffusion Index provided a net positive return of 129% during the 2¾ year period, an annual rate of return of 35.2% (commissions and taxes excluded).

The index is based upon the computer calculated price performances of sixty major industry groups and nearly 200 sub-groups encompassing all issues listed on the New York and American Stock Exchanges.  From these groups, each one currently valued at a price/earnings multiple at least one and a half times the market average is isolated for further analysis. This set of high P/E groups effectively encompasses the more speculative stocks in the market and their price action reflects the supply and demand of speculative money. Since short and intermediate term market trends are a product of supply and demand shifts, and since the speculative activity which establishes these trends is often attracted to the high P/E groups, it follows that these groups may offer unusual insight into the supply and demand forces of the entire market.

A diffusion index is calculated weekly by determining the proportion of the current high price/earnings groups that have risen in price over the most recent three month period. When the current diffusion index reading is above the reading of five weeks previous, speculative money may be considered to be flowing into the marketplace and the broad market should follow these groups upward. When the diffusion index is contracting on a five week basis, the condition is bearish for the market as a whole.

Though by no means infallible, the index is a better than average forecaster of intermediate term market direction. Due to its trend following nature, false signals are usually reversed with small losses, and correct signals tend to result in large gains.

When used in conjunction with other short term indicators, the Industry Group Diffusion Index can provide valuable input for overall forecasts.

# 40 Daily Price Persistency

Within the last few years a number of market observers (mostly academicians) have come to the conclusion that there is no price persistency in the stock market. These observers postulate that future price changes are totally unrelated to past price changes.

While this theory (known as the Random Walk Hypothesis) has gained a growing number of adherents, the facts prove otherwise. There is a significant amount of price persistency in the market. Although virtually countless examples could be cited, an exceedingly elementary one is presented in Table 42. Based upon an analysis of 2,000 trading days between 1965 and 1972, the market, as measured by the New York Stock Exchange Total Return Index, has displayed a definite and significant tendency to follow rising days with rising days and falling days with falling days.

TABLE 42

DAILY PRICE PERSISTENCY IN THE MARKET (1965-1972)

| NYSE TR Index in Day 1 | NYSE TR Index % Change Day 2 | Probability of Rising Prices |
|---|---|---|
| Up | + 0.22% | 73% |
| Down | − 0.24% | 38% |
| 2,000 day average | + 0.03% | 58% |

The ability of the market to predict itself tomorrow solely on the basis of what it did today leads to the question, Are two consecutive up days or two consecutive down days even more significant in predicting the next day's change? Table 43 presents the answer. In this table uptrending markets

TABLE 43

TWO DAY PRICE TREND
AND MARKET PERFORMANCE (1965-1972)

| Market Changes in Day 1 and Day 2 | NYSE TR Index % Change Day 3 | Probability of Rising Prices |
|---|---|---|
| Up    - Up | + 0.21% | 74% |
| Down - Up | + 0.24% | 70% |
| Down - Down | − 0.25% | 38% |
| Up    - Down | − 0.21% | 38% |
| 2,000 day average | + 0.03% | 58% |

have been divided into two categories: whether the market has risen two days in successsion or whether the latest day's advance was preceded by a decline. Downtrending markets are also divided into two categories: whether the market has fallen twice in succession or whether the latest down day was preceded by an up day. The results show no significant difference between the subcategories, indicating that one day price persistency is all that is really significant. It appears that the longer the market moves in one direction, the greater is the probability that the next day will finally show a change in the opposite direction.

If the fact that the market rises or falls today yields significant information as to whether the market will rise or fall tomorrow, it is possible that the last few moments of today's market action may be of even greater importance. A statistic known as "tick" specifies the net number of stocks on the NYSE whose latest change in price was up or down. The tick figure at the close of each day's trading is a representative indication of whether the market closed the day on a strong or weak note. It seems logical that the last few minutes of each trading day might be especially attuned to the next day's market change.

Three independent periods encompassing several market environments (June through December 1966, January through December 1970, and July 1972 through February 1973), 540 trading days in all, have been used for testing. Table 44 presents the probability of the next day's market change being up or down given the alternative conditions of the preceding day's price being up or down or the preceding

TABLE 44

MARKET CHANGE AND FINAL TICK AS ONE DAY PREDICTORS

| Market Change on Day 1 | Probability of Rising Prices on Day 2 | Final Tick on Day 1 | Probability of Rising Prices on Day 2 |
|---|---|---|---|
| Up | 66% | Positive | 75% |
| Down | 31% | Negative | 34% |

day's closing tick figure being positive or negative.

It appears that while day to day market changes tend to be of the same sign, the closing tick figure on a given day is a somewhat better indication of what the morrow will bring, although the difference is probably not significant on a statistical basis. Overall, today's market change has been 68% correct in predicting tomorrow's change, while today's closing tick figure has been 70% correct.

When the market change and final tick in Day 1 agreed, the best results of all were derived. A rising market and a positive final tick were followed by an up market in the ensuing day 77% of the time and by a falling market only 23% of the time. When the market change and final tick were both negative, the probability of a market advance the next day was just 27% and the chance of a decline was 73%.

The trend persistencies presented here could conceivably be profitably incorporated into an overall market timing strategy by deferring new purchases if the market were expected to decline on the following day, or deferring planned sales if the market were expected to advance in the following day. More reasonably, the data indicates in a simple but enlightening manner that market trends persist. Serious investors should look to the more sophisticated market forecasting tools for basing actual buy and sell decisions.

# 41 All You Ever Wanted To Know About Moving Averages

*What Are Moving Averages?* A moving average is one of a family of averages that moves through time. Its primary purpose is to smooth out the values of adjacent statistical observations and so eliminate minor and random (irregular) fluctuations. Three types of moving averages from the family will be described in the following paragraphs.

A *simple* ten day moving average of the Dow Jones Industrials consists of successive averages of its ten most recent day's closing values. Just add up the latest ten prices and divide the total by ten. With each subsequent day, the newest closing value is incorporated into the average and the value of ten days previous is dropped so that the ten most recent periods are always measured and all others are excluded.

This simple moving average is subject to criticism on two counts. First, it assigns equal weight to each of the base observations. In a ten day average, for example, each of the ten values is counted once and has a one-tenth importance (or weight) in the average. It would seem logical that more recent observations may by their very nature be more important and should receive more weight in the average. Second, as a simple average moves through time, its point to point fluctuations are strictly dependent upon two numbers, the one being added and the one being dropped. If the new number is greater than the old one, the average of all values

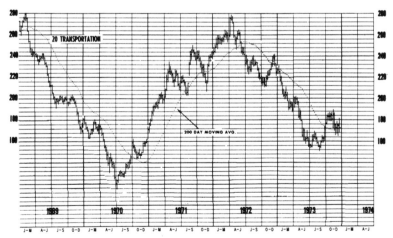

FIGURE 13.    200 Day Simple Moving Average — Dow Jones Transportation Average; January 1969 - December 1973.

will increase and so, too, will the moving average. If the current number is less than the oldest one, the average will decrease. Therefore, even though the *level* of the moving average is dependent upon all of the prices being averaged, *fluctuations* in the moving average are dependent solely upon two numbers, the one being added and the one being dropped, and the last of these is older and of questionable relevance.

A system which reduces these adverse effects is the *weighted* moving average. This system is based upon the assignment of greater weight (and hence greater importance) to more recent observations and lesser weight (and lesser importance) to older values. Table 45 presents a hypothetical ten-period weighted average. Note that the most recent

TABLE 45

EXAMPLE OF A TEN DAY WEIGHTED AVERAGE

| Day No. | Weight | x | Price | = | Weighted Price |
|---------|--------|---|-------|---|----------------|
| 1 | 1 | x | $10 | = | $10 |
| 2 | 2 | x | 12 | = | 24 |
| 3 | 3 | x | 13 | = | 39 |
| 4 | 4 | x | 15 | = | 60 |
| 5 | 5 | x | 18 | = | 90 |
| 6 | 6 | x | 22 | = | 132 |
| 7 | 7 | x | 28 | = | 196 |
| 8 | 8 | x | 32 | = | 256 |
| 9 | 9 | x | 37 | = | 333 |
| 10 | 10 | x | 40 | = | 400 |
| Totals | 55 | | $227 | = | $1,540 |

observation, Day 10, receives ten times the weight of the oldest observation, Day 1. After assigning weights to each of the ten most recent days, the weighted average is finally calculated by dividing the sum of the weighted prices by the sum of the weights and in this case the average is $28 - $1,540 divided by 55. A simple ten day average in this case would have been equal to $22.70 − $227 divided by 10. The reason for the disparity is that in the weighted method, greater importance has been systematically assigned to the more recent, and in this case higher, values in the series. (Obviously weights can be assigned in any pattern desired.) As the calculations are performed day after day, the successive weighted averages form a weighted moving average. A disadvantage of this system is that it is rather cumbersome to calculate by hand, especially for longer term moving averages, although calculation by computer simplifies the task.

A much more easily calculable alternative is an *exponential* moving average. An exponential system is based upon the assignment of a fixed weight (say 18%) to the current price, and all of the remaining weight (in this case 82%) to the previous value of the moving average itself. The proportional weight assigned to the most recent observation is frequently called a "smoothing constant." To determine the exponential smoothing constant roughly proportionate to a simple moving average of a given length, use the following easy formula:    Divide "two" by one more than the number of terms in the simple moving average you wish to duplicate. For example, to find a smoothing constant to construct an exponential moving average equivalent to a ten day simple moving average, divide two by eleven. The result, 0.18, is the smoothing constant.    Table 46 illustrates how this smoothing factor is used to construct an exponential average of the same price series which appeared in Table 45. After arbitrarily establishing the moving average as equal to the first day's price, the moving average is updated by multiplying the newest price by 0.18 and adding that to the product derived from multiplying the previous exponential moving average value by 0.82. After ten days the exponential moving average value is $25.83. That value is again greater than the simple ten day average of $22.70 because proportionately greater weight has been assigned to the more recent, and in this case higher, prices. In an exponential moving average, the weight effectively assigned to any given historical value declines as it becomes older, but it is worth noting that every day's price always has some weight in the exponential moving average.   Its weight never declines completely to zero but merely trends closer and closer to zero, while never quite reaching it.

TABLE  46

EXAMPLE OF A TEN DAY EXPONENTIAL MOVING AVERAGE

| Day No. | Price | Method of Calculation | Exponential Moving Average |
|---|---|---|---|
| 1 | $ 10 | (to start) | $ 10.00 |
| 2 | 12 | (0.18 x 12.00   +   0.82 x 10.00) | 10.36 |
| 3 | 13 | (0.18 x 13.00   +   0.82 x 10.36) | 10.84 |
| 4 | 15 | (0.18 x 15.00   +   0.82 x 10.84) | 11.58 |
| 5 | 18 | (0.18 x 18.00   +   0.82 x 11.58) | 12.74 |
| 6 | 22 | (0.18 x 22.00   +   0.82 x 12.74) | 14.41 |
| 7 | 28 | (0.18 x 28.00   +   0.82 x 14.41) | 16.85 |
| 8 | 32 | (0.18 x 32.00   +   0.82 x 16.85) | 19.58 |
| 9 | 37 | (0.18 x 37.00   +   0.82 x 19.58) | 22.72 |
| 10 | 40 | (0.18 x 40.00   +   0.82 x 22.72) | 25.83 |

An exponential moving average is similar to a weighted moving average in that more recent observations assume greater importance.   But it is much easier to calculate, requiring less time to update.

More sophisticated techniques for calculating moving averages exist, but the three outlined above are the ones most frequently applied to stock market analysis. The exponential moving average is probably the best (but least frequently used), although each method has its place.

*How Are Moving Averages Used?*    Although moving averages are useful in smoothing out irregularities in indicator series, they can also be used to create forecasting systems based on market indexes or prices of individual stocks.

The number of moving average systems which have been developed are simply too numerous to count.   Some are based upon a moving average rising or falling;   others on the relationships between two, three, or more moving averages of different lengths. Multiply the number of possible systems by the number of possible moving average lengths and multiply that by the alternatives of daily, weekly, or monthly calculation, and the multi-dimensional array of all possibilities becomes virtually limitless in size. Observe, too, that all possible systems may be computed with several types of moving averages, including, but not limited to, simple, weighted, and exponential, and other more sophisticated and complex types. The array of moving average systems is infinite.

A moving average system in practical use will be described here to demonstrate the basic trend following concept. In the late 1960s a popular market trend following system was developed based upon a ten day simple moving average of the New York Stock Exchange Composite Index. Stripped of minor requirements, buy signals were provided when the current market index went above its ten day moving average. Such an event indicated that the recent price trend was upward and, according to the trend following theory, prices should subsequently trend even higher. Sell signals were furnished in precisely the opposite manner: a downside penetration of the ten day moving average by the most recent price. This denoted a weakness in recent market prices and, again according to the theory, the market should continue still lower. One analyst even boasted that with this indicator the market "almost obeyed (his) commands," obviously an exaggerated, even misleading, statement (and one not particularly endearing to the Securities & Exchange Commission).

*Do Moving Average Systems Really Work?* In an unpublished thesis by the author, that particular ten day moving average system was rigorously tested over the period December 31, 1966 through April 30, 1970. Although several false trend indications emanated from the system's sell signals, buy signals were generally excellent, with false signals held to a minimum and most intermediate uptrends successfully identified. A study of subsequent time periods revealed less successful market prediction, especially in 1972 and 1973 when the market was extremely erratic and several whipsaws resulted in numerous transactions and little or no profit. Overall the indicator has apparently been more useful than not and produced trading profits for its adherents greater than they would have earned by just buying once and holding on. Followers of the random walk hypothesis insist that the market cannot be predicted on the basis of what is already known today; that current prices reflect all current knowledge. They maintain that such a result must either be a product of hindsight or has occurred more or less by chance. More likely, the system worked because trend following in general has historically been a valid market tool. Trends do tend to persist in the marketplace and can be used to advantage. A timing system predicated solely on a moving average indicator may not show a large profit after transaction costs. As part of a larger system of market prediction, it can nonetheless make a valuable contribution.

There are no magic numbers in trend following. Some technicians assert that a ten day moving average is not optimal, that a 5 day or 20 day or perhaps some esoteric number such as a 13 day moving average is superior. Or, on a longer term basis, some analysts might insist that a 10, 30, or 40 week moving average is best, while others suggest that perhaps some odd moving average length of say, 7 or 39 weeks, is optimal.

These analysts are dreaming. To stress again, there are no magic numbers. Some moving average lengths may have worked best in the past, but, after all, *something* had to work best in the past and by testing everything possible, how could one help but find it?

It should be a basic requirement of any moving average trend following system that practically all moving average lengths predict successfully to a greater or lesser degree. If only one or two lengths work, the odds are high that successful results were obtained by chance.

In truth virtually any moving average will be of some value

in trend following. The market does move in trends. Historical tests conducted over significantly long periods of time prove again and again that the market has a greater probability of moving higher in the future if it has moved up rather than down in the past. Neither the length nor the type of moving average seems to make too much difference.

Table 47 provides examples of the forecasting value of several widely used moving average systems which have been

TABLE 47

MOVING AVERAGE SYSTEMS AND MARKET PERFORMANCE
(WMA = Length of Moving Average in Weeks)

|  | S&P 500 Index 3 Months Later | S&P 500 Index 6 Months Later |
|---|---|---|
| Price above 10 WMA | +2.5% | +5.4% |
| Price below 10 WMA | +1.6% | +3.1% |
| Price above 30 WMA | +2.6% | +5.0% |
| Price below 30 WMA | +1.1% | +3.6% |
| 10 WMA above 30 WMA | +2.5% | +4.5% |
| 10 WMA below 30 WMA | +1.5% | +4.5% |
| Price above 10 WMA above 30 WMA | +2.9% | +5.5% |
| All other possible combinations | +1.4% | +3.4% |

tested over a recent 35 year period on the Standard & Poor's 500 Index. (All moving averages are of the "simple" type.)

In each case, a bullish configuration has led to superior market returns, but the returns have not been large enough to justify the commission expenses incurred by the numerous in and out trades required by such systems.

In conclusion, moving averages provide a useful means for determining whether a price is trending upward or downward and in differentiating between above-average and below-average future market changes. Since trends do persist, moving average analysis has a place in a comprehensive approach to market forecasting.

# 42 Volume
## Indicators

All stock price fluctuations are a direct result of changing supply and demand. Reduced to the very essence, the interaction of these two fundamental economic forces is manifested in the prices at which stock transactions are executed and in the volume of stock which changes hands at various prices. Given this basic set of facts and a wealth of historical stock price and volume data, it is not surprising that many technical analysts attempt to use historical volume information to forecast future market price changes.

After extensive testing of market data over the last 35 years, a few general tenets may be stated. Price and volume tend to move together. When one increases, the other increases; and when one falls, the other tends to decline as well. Historical examples of prices rising on falling volume, or falling on rising volume, while not rare, are the exception rather than the rule.

*Price versus Volume.* We have seen in the preceding chapter that rising prices tend to be followed by rising prices, and falling prices tend to be followed by falling prices. Increasing *volume* is also normally succeeded by rising prices, and declining volume is usually succeeded by falling prices. With these basic relationships in mind, it should come as no great surprise that a combination of rising prices and rising volume is normally the most bullish syndrome of all.

Practically every analysis of price and volume, whether measured in days, weeks, or months, reveals that concurrently rising price and volume is the most conducive to further rising prices. It follows, and this conclusion is also supported by the evidence, that a combination of falling prices and falling volume is the most bearish possible portent for future price changes.

Table 48 presents a price/volume relationship array, just one of an infinite number of such arrays that could be constructed. Volume is NYSE volume, and both past and future price changes are based on the NYSE Composite Index. The determination of whether price or volume is falling, unchanged, or rising is based upon a five day percentage change in the average daily value of each series over the most recent three trading days. Both price and volume changes are then divided into three groups which have an approximately equal number of daily readings.

TABLE 48

DAILY PRICE/VOLUME RELATIONSHIPS (1965-1972)

| Price and Volume Characteristics | NYSE Composite Five Days Later |
|---|---|
| Price: Sharply Falling | − 0.11% |
| Price: Relatively Unchanged | + 0.13% |
| Price: Rapidly Rising | + 0.27% |
| Volume: Sharply Falling | − 0.09% |
| Volume: Relatively Unchanged | + 0.07% |
| Volume: Rapidly Rising | + 0.36% |
| Price and Volume: Sharply Falling | − 0.10% |
| Price and Volume: Relatively Unchanged | + 0.25% |
| Price and Volume: Rapidly Rising | + 0.45% |

The most important conclusions to be gleaned from the table are: (1) rising price is a relatively bullish portent for future price changes and falling price is relatively bearish; (2) rising volume is even more bullish and falling volume is relatively bearish; (3) rising price accompanied by rising volume is the most bullish of all and falling price accompanied by falling volume is consistently bearish. Almost all price/volume tables created with alternative averaging and change parameters, be they in terms of days or weeks, and the author has created dozens, show similar results and lead to identical conclusions.

Although more complex non-linear price/volume relation-ships could be evolved and tested, the general conclusions stated here are probably as significant as any and state cor-rectly the general association of historical price and volume with future price.

*Buying and Selling Climaxes.* A quickening in the rate of price decline accompanied by an extraordinarily sharp rise in volume is known as a selling climax. This phenomenon has frequently occurred near the end of major bear markets. For example, in late May 1962 the Dow Jones Industrial Average completed an extended downtrend by falling 11 and 35 points on successive days, with volume increasing on each of those days. On the third day volume accelerated further while prices staged one last plunge. Finally, at mid-day the market turned around and staged a 40 point rally on still heavier volume.

Selling climaxes have also accompanied the final stages of market declines in June 1965, August 1966, and May 1970. Most such blowoffs are usually followed by a few days or weeks of rising prices followed by a further price decline to a level close to the low established by the earlier selling climax. This second low is usually accompanied by extreme pessi-mism as investors fear another protracted decline. More often than not such fears are ill-founded and the market embarks upon a new bull market trend instead.

A buying climax is defined as a slowing in the rate of price appreciation accompanied by sharply increasing volume. Classically, a buying climax occurs near a market top preced-ing a major bear market. In practice, this phenomenon is extremely difficult to identify.

*Big Blocks.* Another increasingly popular market measure is based on "large blocks," usually defined as single trades of stock consisting of at least 20,000 shares. A summary of all large block trades on the NYSE for the preceding five days is reported weekly in *Barron's*. The summary includes the name of the stock, the number of shares traded, the price at which the trade was executed, and the price of the immediately preceding trade.

Two primary indicators have been developed from this data. The first is the trend of the number of large block trades. When the series is in a rising trend, institutions and other large investors who normally trade these large lots are assumed to be increasing their interest in the market.

Presumably a rising trend is bullish and a falling trend is bearish . . . but only presumably. The hypothesis has never been fully tested because  only a few years of published historical data exists (much too little to obtain significant conclusions) and because the definition of "large blocks" has been changed from time to time (from 5,000 to 10,000 to 20,000 shares), causing inconsistencies in the trend of the series and rendering analysis extremely difficult.

The second indicator derived from the large block data is based upon what is known as "tick analysis." By observing whether the transaction price of the block is above or below the price of the previous trade in the stock, a determination of whether the buyer or the seller was more eager to consummate the trade can be made. In turn, a judgment of whether market demand or supply forces are more powerful can be deduced. The indicator itself is defined as the ratio of large block upticks to the total number of large blocks. In general, the ratio series tracks the market, rising when prices are rising and falling when prices are falling. A small amount of lead time at market turning points seems to exist. These conclusions are, however, somewhat tentative. So little historical data exists that it is next to impossible to derive statistically significant evidence from the indicator.

*Low Priced Stocks' Volume.* The ratio of the weekly volume of *Barron's* 20 Low Priced Stocks to the weekly volume of the 30 stock Dow Jones Industrial Average compares the trading activity in speculative low priced issues with that in high quality blue chip stocks. When low priced issues are being actively traded, a speculative atmosphere in the market exists. Such a condition usually coexists with periods of excessively high prices.  On the other hand, low volume in low priced issues relative to volume in blue chips is reflective of market sobriety . . . and of undervalued stock prices.  The concept does seem sound.  In practice, though, this particular indicator has exhibited numerous random trends and appears to be largely without significant predictive ability.  (In part this may be a function of *Barron's* definition of speculative low priced stocks and arbitrary changes in the index's stock components.)

*Most Active Stocks' Volume.*   *Barron's* also publishes weekly readings on the ratio of weekly volume of the twenty most active stocks on the New York Stock Exchange to total NYSE volume.  Based on a theory similar to the Low Priced Stocks Volume indicator, this measure, too, has exhibited numerous variable trends and has little, if any, forecasting value.

As a broad generality it may be concluded that rising volume is good for stock prices and falling volume is bad.  The relationship is variable and imprecise.  More detailed analysis of volume is one of the less productive forms of technical analysis.

# 43 January Barometer or Boomerang Barometer?

According to an old saying, as January goes, so goes the year.

The proof of the pudding, say the January Barometer adherents, is that from 1949 through 1975 January accurately predicted the market's direction for the entire year 24 out of 27 times, an 89% degree of accuracy.

The rationale underlying the January Barometer is simply that January uniquely begins the calendar year.  Since the financial markets are geared to a calendar year, investors tend to reassess the investment climate each January.  This

January reassessment sets the tone for the entire year.

Important socio-economic events timed to the calendar year abound. To name just a few, most corporations end their accounting periods on December 31st, providing a basis for not only their own but also Wall Street's forecasts of sales and earnings for the following year. December also marks the time of investor tax selling − of cleaning out portfolios in preparation for a rearrangement in January. Most of the nation's economic statistics are based on a calendar year as well. And, of course, nearly everyone tends to reassess his life in January (ever hear of New Year's resolutions?)

Noting these and other factors, a few analysts have compared the market's January change to its performance for the entire year during the last two or three decades. As noted above, they found an extraordinarily good relationship. January's performance really did seem to be intimately tied into the entire year.

An intensive examination of the January Barometer over the last half century discloses a couple of flaws in the analysis.

First, as January is itself part of the year, it makes no sense whatsoever to include the market return for that month within the entire year's return it is ostensibly trying to forecast, as most analysts have done. If the market rose 8% in January and 7% for the entire year, it would obviously have to have declined between February 1 and December 31, but January Barometer fans would claim their favorite indicator was right again − up in January, up for the year. It makes more sense to compare the return for January with that of the next eleven months, February through December.

On this basis the "Barometer" has been right 22 times (81%), not 24 times (89%), out of 27 years, not quite so good. And definitely not so good when one considers that since the market rose in 20 of the 27 years anyway, a simple guess on January 1 that the "market will go up this year," would have been right 20 times. Hence the January Barometer gained just two years of forecasting accuracy, and at the expense of using hindsight to develop the system. But the worst is yet to come.

Interestingly, most analysts have hesitated to show January Barometer results prior to 1949. Their reticence can be understood, because prior to that year the January Barometer accurately forecast the market's direction for the next eleven months less than half the time. In fact, the overall 50 year record, from 1926 to 1975, shows only 32 hits, a batting average of just 64%. Had one always guessed "up" for the February - December period, he would also have been right 32 times — 64%!

TABLE 49

JANUARY BAROMETER ... THE 50 YEAR RECORD

| Year | January Percent Change | Feb.-Dec. Percent Change | Year | January Percent Change | Feb.-Dec. Percent Change |
|---|---|---|---|---|---|
| 1926 | + 0.5% | − 0.2% | 1952 | + 1.6% | + 10.1% |
| 1927 | − 0.5% | + 29.4% | 1953 | − 0.7% | − 6.0% |
| 1928 | − 0.6% | + 38.6% | 1954 | + 5.1% | + 38.0% |
| 1929 | + 5.7% | −16.7% | 1955 | + 1.8% | + 24.2% |
| 1930 | + 6.3% | −32.7% | 1956 | − 3.7% | + 6.5% |
| 1931 | + 4.9% | −49.5% | 1957 | − 4.2% | −10.6% |
| 1932 | − 2.8% | −12.7% | 1958 | + 4.3% | + 32.4% |
| 1933 | + 0.7% | + 45.5% | 1959 | + 0.4% | + 8.1% |
| 1934 | + 10.6% | −15.0% | 1960 | − 7.2% | + 4.5% |
| 1935 | − 4.2% | + 47.6% | 1961 | + 6.3% | + 15.8% |
| 1936 | + 6.6% | + 20.1% | 1962 | − 3.8% | − 8.3% |
| 1937 | + 3.8% | −40.8% | 1963 | + 4.9% | + 13.3% |
| 1938 | + 1.3% | + 23.6% | 1964 | + 2.7% | + 10.0% |
| 1939 | − 6.9% | + 1.5% | 1965 | + 3.3% | + 5.6% |
| 1940 | − 3.5% | −12.2% | 1966 | + 0.5% | −13.5% |
| 1941 | − 4.8% | −13.7% | 1967 | + 7.8% | + 11.4% |
| 1942 | + 1.4% | + 10.9% | 1968 | − 4.4% | + 12.6% |
| 1943 | + 7.2% | + 11.5% | 1969 | − 0.8% | −10.6% |
| 1944 | + 1.5% | + 12.1% | 1970 | − 7.7% | + 8.4% |
| 1945 | + 1.4% | + 28.9% | 1971 | + 4.1% | + 6.5% |
| 1946 | + 7.0% | −17.6% | 1972 | + 1.8% | + 13.6% |
| 1947 | + 2.4% | − 2.3% | 1973 | − 1.7% | −15.9% |
| 1948 | − 4.0% | + 3.5% | 1974 | − 1.0% | −29.0% |
| 1949 | + 0.1% | + 10.1% | 1975 | + 12.3% | + 17.2% |
| 1950 | + 1.7% | + 19.7% | | | |
| 1951 | + 6.1% | + 9.7% | Average | + 1.3% | + 4.9% |

So, what should one conclude?

Well, based on the record, flip a coin on New Year's Eve and you will have just as good a chance of being right about the February to December market trend as if you used the January Barometer . . . and you will have your answer 31 days sooner.

# 44 The Seasonality Indicator

*Trading by the Calendar.* The January Barometer is not the only attempt at calendar year timing efforts. A surprising number of analysts also believe that a simple concentration on the months of the year can lead to seasonal profits. January, July, August, and December, for example, are sometimes considered bullish months, while February and September are viewed bearishly. Through the years some of these months have been combined to yield additional simplistic trading rules such as, "Buy on July 4th and sell on Labor Day," or "Buy on Thanksgiving and sell at New Year's and pay your Christmas bills," or "Sell at Rosh Hashana and buy back at Yom Kippur," a reference to orthodox Jews disdaining the market between these two September holidays (although why stock prices should decline and not rise during this period is unclear). And there are the famed summer and year-end rallies. Despite sporadic successes, few of these "rules" have provided consistent profits decade in and decade out. What profits would have emerged can be explained by completely different, and much shorter, seasonal patterns to be discussed on ensuing pages.

For those in search of a simple to research and easy to use seasonal rule, the best was stated a century or so ago by Mark Twain, "October," the sage observed, "is one of the peculiarly dangerous months to speculate in stocks. The others are July, January, September, April, November, May, March,

June, December, August, and February. "

It really isn't surprising that simple seasonal rules don't work well in the market. If they did, everyone would use them and quickly bid prices to the point where any profit potential would disapppear.

*Introducing the Seasonality Indicator.* If conventional seasonality indicators reflect an excessive desire for profits through simplicity and are effectively useless, is there any seasonality in the stock market worth exploiting at all? Yes, indeed! The Seasonality Indicator is potentially one of the most useful of all short term market indicators. But not surprisingly, it is a bit more complex and the profit opportunities, while ultimately enormous, are not so readily apparent.

The Seasonality Indicator consists of two primary components: Month-End and Pre-Holiday. The first hypothesizes superior stock market performance on the last trading day of each month and on the first four trading days of each month. The Pre-Holiday component hypothesizes greater than average returns on the two trading days immediately preceding a holiday market closing.

As will be discussed in the following pages, the combined use of the two seasonal components between 1928 and 1975 enabled a hypothetical commission free trading strategy to increase a portfolio from $10,000 to $1.4 million. Of course, commissions — especially today's high rates — render such a trading strategy inoperable. How, then, can you use seasonality to benefit you and increase the value of your own portfolio?

If you are buying, it pays to act before the onset of the favorable period, both to capture the extra seasonal return and to avoid paying higher prices for your stock. If you are selling, you should naturally wait until the end of a seasonally favorable period.

Assume that at any random date between 1928 and 1975 you had to raise $10,000 by selling NYSE listed common stocks. Knowing that the long term trends of the economy and stock market are upward, you might well have decided to wait until the last possible moment to enter your sell orders so as to receive the highest possible price. How profitable this postponement might have been was highly dependent on the market's seasonal pattern.

On average, if the days you deferred selling were among those identified as *least* favorable by the Seasonality Indicator, your shares would have *fallen* in value by $4 for each day you waited. On the other hand, if the days you waited had been under the favorable influence of the Month-End component of the Seasonality Indicator, your stocks would have *risen* in value $11 a day. Furthermore, if the waiting days involved were under the influence of the Pre-Holiday component of the Seasonality Indicator, your portfolio would have gained at an average rate of $18 a day. Finally, if each day you waited happened to be under the simultaneous influence of both the Month-End and Pre-Holiday seasonal components, your portfolio would have soared an extra $38 per day.

Similar gains would have been realized by buying stocks *before* the onset of seasonally favorable periods. Over the course of a few years, dozens of such profit making opportunities manifest    themselves.

If these returns do not sound sensational to you, keep in mind that they are one day returns only. On average, every time you had a transaction to make, you would have duplicated the results. Over the course of many years, these daily returns could have meant thousands of dollars in extra profits for every $10,000 in your portfolio . . . all a result of simply waiting (or not waiting) a few days here and there to execute already planned transactions.

The point of all this is that although commission expenses may render impossible a cashing in on seasonality by in and out trading, advance knowledge of these periods can be extremely valuable when you are buying or selling for other considerations.

*Month-End Seasonality.* Stocks have a marked tendency

to rise during the first four days of every month and on the last day of every month. Put together, this continuous span of five trading days constitutes the "Month-End" component of the Seasonality Indicator.

There are a number of reasons for this unusual market phenomenon, including month-end portfolio adjustments by institutions, investment of monthly stock purchase plan proceeds by mutual funds, and month-end salary draws by members of the investing public which route them into various investments.

Market technicians have made many attempts to analyze market seasonality. Unfortunately, the testing methods have been rather crude, such as counting the number of times the market has advanced or declined on a certain day of the month.

To document the month-end concept, we have analyzed every trading day starting with the end of December 1927. Let us hypothesize two investors. The first, the Seasonal investor, buys stocks (as represented by Standard & Poor's 500 Index) at the beginning of each five day month-end period, sells out at the end of the five day period, and holds cash until the next month-end period. The second investor, the Non-Seasonal investor, does precisely the opposite — he holds cash during the month-end period and is long stock during the rest of each month.

Assuming no particular significance to the month-end phenomenon, the Non-Seasonal investor actually has a tremendous advantage — for over the very long term stock prices generally advance and he is invested in stocks at least three-fourths of the time, while the Seasonal investor is invested in stocks less than one-fourth of the time. (Prior to 1952 when the security exchanges were open on Saturdays and there were even more trading days each month than currently, the Non-Seasonal investor had an even greater advantage).

Each of these two hypothetical investors is given $10,000 to start and, *assuming no commissions,* here is how they fared between the end of 1927 and December 31, 1975: the Seasonal investor's portfolio experienced an astonishing growth in value to $572,020 while the Non-Seasonal investor's portfolio shrank to a minuscule $899. The results are so dramatic and statistically significant that they are unlikely to have occurred by mere chance.

Of course, the Non-Seasonal investor had more time in which to take in the dividends but our Seasonal investor had more time in which to earn additional interest on his idle cash.

Further, the results are consistent through the years. Despite the disadvantage of holding stocks only one fourth of the time, the Seasonal investor achieved a better return in 38 of the 48 years studied.

A strategy that ignores commissions cannot be implemented in actual practice for even a no-load mutual fund would tire of an investor who buys and then redeems shares five days later on a monthly basis. (If such a fund existed, the results could be improved through the use of leverage.)

Of more interest is the practical application of the Seasonality Indicator in every day market operations. It is clear that an investor planning to sell stocks near the end of a month will, *on average,* benefit by waiting until near the end of the fourth trading day of the following month. Similarly, market participants planning to make new purchases would be well advised to get their orders in before the last trading day of the preceding month so their new investments will benefit from this seasonal pattern.

After adjustment for the length of their holding periods, the Seasonal investor has been a winner in 43 of the past 48 years. In 20 of these 48 years the Seasonal investor earned a profit while the Non-Seasonal investor was incurring a loss — but there was never a single year that the reverse situation occurred. The basic result was so universal, in both good markets and bad, that the Seasonal investor made a profit in all 30 of the bull market years and in 10 of the bear market years, while the Non-Seasonal investor managed to profit in only 20 of the bullish years and in none of the bearish ones.

Naturally this indicator won't work every single month. Good as the results are, they are not perfect. Of the 576 month-end periods since 1927, 389 (68%) showed positive performance compared with about 58% positive performance that would be expected by chance. Put another way, 32% of the month-end periods actually produced losses. Nevertheless, when used consistently over a long time span, month-end seasonality works exceptionally well and should be an integral element in any portfolio strategy.

*Pre-Holiday Seasonality.*  Imagine the entire market gain of the last half-century, from 1928 to 1975, condensed into just two years of trading!  That is the record of the Pre-Holiday component of the Seasonality Indicator.

Rigorous historical research reveals that stock prices behave in a significantly positive manner in each of the two trading days preceding a holiday market closing. Although after commissions market traders cannot earn profits from in and out trading on this pre-holiday syndrome, stock prices generally act so favorably on these days that increased profits can be obtained by incorporating this seasonal factor into a total long term investment policy. This can be accomplished by timing purchases just prior to the commencement of a pre-holiday period and making stock sales just after.

The most likely rationale for this bullish seasonal propensity is that traders wish to lighten up on the short side of their portfolios just prior to holidays. They thereby cover themselves against any unexpected good news that may be announced while the market is closed. (Historical research also reveals that on average the market performs better during the last hour of trading every day and on the last trading day of each week, probably for the same reason.)

The research results are based upon an analysis of the Standard & Poor's 500 Index daily price behavior around 419 holiday market closings from 1928 to 1975. During this period the S&P 500 advanced from 17.53 to 90.19, an increase of 414% excluding dividends. (In other words,

$10,000 invested in the Index on December 31, 1927, would have grown to $51,400 by December 31, 1975).

There have been nine holidays for which the Exchange has traditionally closed trading. These holidays, along with the cumulatively compounded percentage market gain in each of the two days just prior to the holiday closing, are shown in Table 50. (Day 1 is the first day of the two day syndrome period; Day 2 immediately precedes the holiday.)

TABLE 50

PRE-HOLIDAY SEASONALITY RECORD (1928-1975)

| Holiday | Number of Closings | Percentage Return Day 1 | Day 2 |
|---------|--------------------|-------------------------|-------|
| Washington's Birth | 47 | −  0.1% | + 12.2% |
| Good Friday | 48 | +  7.3% | + 17.8% |
| Memorial Day | 45 | −  4.7% | + 22.8% |
| Independence Day | 47 | + 13.3% | + 37.3% |
| Labor Day | 48 | + 16.8% | + 33.7% |
| Election Day | 42 | + 17.9% | +  4.6% |
| Thanksgiving | 48 | +  4.3% | +  1.1% |
| Christmas | 48 | −  7.1% | + 15.2% |
| New Year's | 46 | + 31.1% | + 19.6% |
| Total compounded | 419 | + 102.6% | + 333.3% |

Note that every pre-holiday period has been favorable when Day 1 and Day 2 results are combined, but that trading sessions just prior to Independence Day, Labor Day and New Year's have been especially favorable.

Treating all holidays in the aggregate, Day 2 is obviously the most profitable. In just 419 trading sessions the market more than quadrupled. $10,000 would have grown to $43,330, almost as much as the gain by the market during the entire 48 years. Furthermore, based on 250 trading days in a year, this growth was accomplished in the equivalent of just 1 year and 8 months. Viewed in this context the return from Day 2 provided a compounded profit of 141% per year.

To illustrate the enormity of this return, had the market been able to sustain the 141% rate of gain through the entire 48 years, an initial $10,000 investment would have grown to about $22 sextillion ($22,000,000,000,000,000,000,000).

Day 1 was not quite as profitable — the indicated compounded doubling of value in 419 trading days is equivalent to a 53% annual rate of return. Invested for 48 years at that rate of growth, $10,000 would have grown to only $6.8 trillion dollars ($6,800,000,000,000) — four times the current U S. Gross National Product — and probably enough to retire on, even after inflation.

Such returns have not, of course, been realized but are only hypothetical gains used to demonstrate the significance of the Pre-Holiday Component of the Seasonality Indicator. (These figures also illustrate how unrealistic it is for anyone to expect to consistently earn returns of 50% or 100% per annum.)

Combined Day 1 and Day 2 results yield a compounded growth of 778% in 838 trading days. That is, $10,000 would have grown to $87,800 in the holding period equivalent of just 3-1/3 years. Given the market's overall gain during the 48 years of just 414%, investments during the remaining 44-2/3 years would have suffered a loss of about 41%.

To summarize, if two hypothetical investors, the Seasonal and the Non-Seasonal, each started with an initial capital of $10,000, they would have realized the following results (assuming no commissions) by using alternative strategies:

| Strategy | Years Held | $10,000 Became |
|---|---|---|
| Seasonal Investor | 3-1/3 | $ 87,787 |
| Non-Seasonal Investor | 44-2/3 | $  5,855 |

Of course, the Non-Seasonal investor, being in the market longer, had more time in which to collect dividends, but the

## TABLE 51

### PROFITABILITY OF ALTERNATIVE INVESTMENT STRATEGIES

| Year-End | Seasonal Strategy | Non-Seasonal Strategy | Buy & Hold Strategy | Year-End | Seasonal Strategy | Non-Seasonal Strategy | Buy & Hold Strategy |
|---|---|---|---|---|---|---|---|
| 1927 | $10,000 | $10,000 | $10,000 | 1951 | $174,163 | $779 | $13,561 |
| 1928 | 11,429 | 12,153 | 13,890 | 1952 | 186,452 | 813 | 15,159 |
| 1929 | 13,703 | 8,929 | 12,236 | 1953 | 185,214 | 764 | 14,155 |
| 1930 | 13,966 | 6,266 | 8,751 | 1954 | 217,098 | 945 | 20,528 |
| 1931 | 12,872 | 3,598 | 4,632 | 1955 | 253,997 | 1,021 | 25,947 |
| 1932 | 11,239 | 3,497 | 3,930 | 1956 | 303,306 | 878 | 26,627 |
| 1933 | 19,058 | 3,023 | 5,761 | 1957 | 317,764 | 718 | 22,816 |
| 1934 | 20,251 | 2,676 | 5,419 | 1958 | 390,056 | 807 | 31,500 |
| 1935 | 22,658 | 3,381 | 7,661 | 1959 | 415,967 | 821 | 34,172 |
| 1936 | 30,344 | 3,229 | 9,800 | 1960 | 453,350 | 731 | 33,157 |
| 1937 | 30,611 | 1,966 | 6,018 | 1961 | 523,358 | 780 | 40,826 |
| 1938 | 46,281 | 1,628 | 7,535 | 1962 | 564,425 | 638 | 36,004 |
| 1939 | 49,469 | 1,440 | 7,125 | 1963 | 661,675 | 647 | 42,806 |
| 1940 | 50,819 | 1,187 | 6,035 | 1964 | 690,242 | 700 | 48,357 |
| 1941 | 56,414 | 879 | 4,957 | 1965 | 736,189 | 716 | 52,835 |
| 1942 | 67,926 | 820 | 5,573 | 1966 | 718,374 | 638 | 45,919 |
| 1943 | 74,484 | 894 | 6,658 | 1967 | 777,733 | 708 | 55,144 |
| 1944 | 78,570 | 964 | 7,576 | 1968 | 897,935 | 660 | 59,368 |
| 1945 | 94,759 | 1,045 | 9,904 | 1969 | 916,685 | 573 | 52,624 |
| 1946 | 93,248 | 936 | 8,729 | 1970 | 1,047,185 | 502 | 52,677 |
| 1947 | 107,180 | 814 | 8,729 | 1971 | 1,170,934 | 497 | 58,361 |
| 1948 | 105,498 | 822 | 8,672 | 1972 | 1,343,367 | 501 | 67,482 |
| 1949 | 113,663 | 841 | 9,562 | 1973 | 1,201,795 | 463 | 55,761 |
| 1950 | 132,296 | 880 | 11,644 | 1974 | 1,203,602 | 325 | 39,104 |
|  |  |  |  | 1975 | 1,440,716 | 357 | 51,441 |

Seasonal investor had more time in which to earn low risk interest on his idle cash.

The Pre-Holiday Seasonal strategy has been consistently profitable through history. In only three years of the 48 year test period did it lose money. Those years were 1931, 1939 and 1973 (the latter two suffered only very minor declines of about 1/2 of 1%). In all of the other 45 years, a pre-holiday trading strategy would have been profitable on balance!

*$10,000 to $1.4 Million — The Complete Seasonality Record.* The complete Seasonality Indicator consists of the two day "Pre-Holiday" and the five day "Month-End" components. Together they identify about 70 market trading days each year which have historically provided above average price appreciation.

There is some overlap between the two strategies; that is, some pre-holiday periods also fall within a month-end period. (This always occurs, for example, with the 4th of July.) Table 51 traces the overall seasonal strategy result for the combined pre-holiday and month-end periods, eliminating all overlapping. The strategy is compared with a strategy of investing only on those days not identified as favorable by the Seasonality Indicator (the "Non-Seasonal" strategy) and with a naive strategy of purchasing the market index on December 30, 1927, and simply holding it throughout the 48 year period (the "Buy & Hold" strategy).

The results of the various strategies are startlingly different. A seasonal strategy saw $10,000 grow to over $1.4 million while a $10,000 initial investment in the non-seasonal strategy shrank to a minuscule $357. It is worth noting that the portfolio based on the seasonal strategy gained value in 41 years while the non-seasonal strategy's portfolio increased in only 20 of the 48 years. The seasonal strategy also provided a percentage return superior to that of the non-seasonal strategy in 40 of the 48 years despite the fact that the seasonal strategy was only invested in the generally up-trending market about one fourth of each year. Furthermore, after adjusting for length of holding period, the seasonal strategy provided a superior annualized percentage return in 45 of the 48 years covered.

Readers interested in further exploring stock market seasonality should consult the following three sources: *Behavior of Prices on Wall Street* by Arthur Merrill, *The 1976 Stock Market Almanac* by Yale Hirsch, and "Seasonal Variations in Price Changes and Holding Period Returns of Common Stocks," a 1969 Ph.D. dissertation by Richard W. McEnally at the University of North Carolina.

# 45 The Mystery of Market Cycles and Periodicity

Observers in the physical sciences have long noted the tendency for certain phenomena to fluctuate in fixed cycles. Sun spots, for example, tend to cycle at regular intervals of approximately eleven years in length, impacting their uncertain forces, with their disputed effects, upon the earth throughout each cycle. Other observers have noted the strange propensity of the "Fibonacci" number series to persist throughout the universe. Heated debate has subsequently emerged over whether fixed cycles exist in human nature as well and, more directly to the point of issue here, whether that effect is transmitted to stock market fluctuations.

It should be stated at the outset that the subject of this discussion is not the widely known "business cycle" which appears at variable intervals of time in varying degrees of intensity. There is little doubt that such "cycles" do exist in the economic and financial worlds. Certain events naturally lead to other events, and the sequence is, to a large degree, predictable. However, it is quite another thing to extend this general proposition with the assertion that such phenomena always occur at *identical time intervals* and with *identical intensities*. Nevertheless, the latter is the established domain of the cyclic theorists. Their studies concentrate on rhythmic cycles which, by definition, impact upon their subject at fixed and predefinable points in time, or consist of fixed and predefinable degrees of magnitude or numbers of movements.

At one time or another literally hundreds of cycles have been stated to have a force on stock market fluctuations. The Foundation for the Study of Cycles published a catalog in 1964 which lists over 200 alleged stock market cycles, ranging in length from 20 hours to 89½ years. Many of the listed cycles are conveniently vague, such as an eight to eleven year cycle in industrial stock prices first noted in 1937. Others are almost impossibly precise — for example, a report of a 12.31 week cycle in the price of General Motors between 1948 and 1962.

One of the most popular stock market cycles is allegedly four years long. According to cyclic experts, stock prices reach a low point at roughly 48 month intervals, although other experts argue that the cycle is more properly measured in 52 month intervals, and still others insist that a 46 or even a 41 month interval is proper. At times the market has appeared to meet the four year cycle specification, but rarely with sufficient precision to have made a cycle-based trading rule profitable.

Another cycle which has achieved some recent popularity is the so-called Kondratieff Wave, originally suggested several decades ago by a relatively obscure Russian economist named Nikolai Dmitriyevich Kondratieff (Kon-draa-tee-ev). According to its adherents, the Kondratieff Wave, which usually spans about 50 years from beginning to end, accounts for all major swings in commodity prices (see Figure 14, page 166) and economic boom-bust cycles in capitalistic systems. By extension, its followers maintain that it accounts for many social and political events as well (e.g., political scandals — Grant, Harding, Nixon; unpopular wars — War of 1812, Civil War, World War I, Vietnam War; popular wars — War with Mexico, Spanish American War, World War II, ?; and so forth).

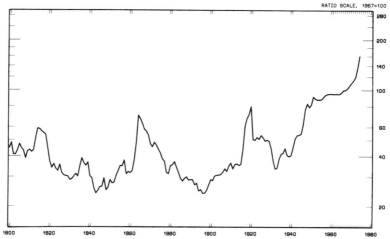

FIGURE 14.    Kondratieff Wave — Fifty year cycles in U. S. Wholesale Price Index (annually); 1800 - 1974.

Another popular cyclic theory is the Elliott Wave. Propounded by Ralph Elliott in 1939, the Elliott Wave principle states that stock prices are governed by cycles founded upon the Fibonacci series of numbers (1-2-3-5-8-13-21. . . each number in the series equalling the sum of the two numbers which precede it). The Fibonacci series was developed by Leonardo Fibonacci, a thirteenth century Italian mathematician. It was later discovered to abound in nature, accounting for the spirals in sunflower seeds and snail shells, the arrangement of leaf buds on a stem, and countless other natural phenomena. According to the Elliott Wave theory, stock prices tend to move in a predetermined number of waves consistent with the Fibonacci series. A bear market, for example, might consist of three waves, composed of two waves down surrounding one intermediate reaction wave up; or an extended bull move might consist of five waves, composed of three up, with two down moves intervening.

Note that the Elliott Wave principle is keyed to the number of price trends, not their time duration. Yet another system propounded upon that principle is the so-called

"Three Step Rule," which states that major market moves, in particular bull markets, consist of three primary and distinct upward movements. The foremost proponent of the "Three Step Rule" is noted technician Edson Gould, who maintains that although the Rule does define general market parameters, investors should be prepared for the possibility of a fourth upward move as well. (Would it not seem advisable to also be "prepared" for a fifth, sixth . . .?)

The list of cyclic examples that analysts have applied to the stock market goes on ad infinitum. The question is, Do they work?   Or, do enough of them work often enough so that they make a useful contribution to market timing?  The answer is probably no.  Numerous mathematical techniques, both simple and complex, have been developed to test for the existence of cycles within time series.  What scant evidence has emerged in support of cyclic phenomena in the stock market falls into the category of "if you try enough things, a few of them are bound to work."  Cycle advocates have never offered any rational theory as to why market moves should consist of a predetermined number of cycles or why cycles should occur at predetermined frequencies.  Until they do, it is best to bear in mind that all cycle research to date suffers from a number of fatal biases.

First, with the benefit of hindsight and subjective judgment, it is relatively easy to imagine cycles which do not really exist.  In a word, cycles are often "created" after the fact to fit observed events.  When applied to "real time," most identified cycles have broken down rather quickly.

Second, the conclusions of many market cycle studies have been derived from a measurement of only two or three sampling periods.  It goes without saying that scientific method demands that conclusions be based upon as many observations as possible.  In the case of market cycles, which rest upon rather general — not to say mysterious — laws, an even larger number of sampling periods is required.

Third, many cyclic theories provide generous exceptions to their rules.  The Three Step Rule has its "possible" fourth step. The Elliott Wave has so many exceptions they seem to outnumber the rules. And even if these theories do adequately describe some market cycles, the number of times the market deviates from them is usually so frequent as to render the entire systems suspect.

Finally, some cycles seem to be suspiciously successful. A cycle theorist, for example, might maintain the existence of 13, 17, and 25 week cycles and then label any complete market move lasting between 13 and 25 weeks as corresponding to one of the three cycles or fitting some combination or average of them. In short, cycles sometimes can't fail because their users won't let them.

Most cycles are without doubt figments of the imagination. Nevertheless, strange things exist in the universe, and the ultimate resolution of the truth of cyclic phenomena must await future study. In the meantime, if cycles have a utility, it is in reminding us that "This, too, shall pass;" that no bull market or bear market lasts forever.

# 46 Inflation and Stock Prices

Are common stocks really a good hedge against inflation? Investors have been asking that question for decades. In the 1920s noted economist and investment analyst Edgar Lawrence Smith told the public that the answer was "yes." But after the discouraging experience of the last few years, that answer deserves reexamination.

The puzzle is complicated by the fact that there appears to be not one, but two solutions. In the long run, common stocks have indeed proven to be an excellent inflation hedge. In the 20th century to date the total market return on stocks from price appreciation and dividends has averaged about 9% per year. During the same period the rate of inflation, as measured by the Consumer Price Index, averaged 2½% per annum.  Simple subtraction shows that common stocks have provided a "real" (inflation adjusted) annual rate of return of about 6½%.  There is a logical and compelling reason for this result.   If stocks did not provide inflation compensatory returns in the long run, nobody would buy them and those who held stocks would sell them. The resultantly unequal supply-demand pressures would lower stock prices to the point where the securities would ultimately be so cheap that it would finally be possible to profit from their purchase on an inflation adjusted basis.

The short run answer is quite different.  Rampant inflation appears to result in, perhaps even cause, *lower* stock prices. To cite the unfavorable recent experience, from December 1968 through September 1974, inflation accelerated sharply in the worst spiral since World War II, averaging an annual rate of over 6%.   If common stocks are a good inflation hedge, as most investors hoped, they should have risen at a rate at least as great as the inflation.  They certainly should not have fallen.  In fact, they not only declined, but declined severely.  The average NYSE stock fell 58%, even after adding in returns from dividends, a compounded rate of loss approaching 15% per annum!

This paradox, that common stocks are a good long term but a poor short term hedge against inflation, is a most interesting one.  Its resolution can contribute to an understanding of the valuation of common stocks and the causes of their fluctuations.

The intrinsic value of common stocks is determined by investors' current expectations of just two factors:   future interest rates and future dividends (or earnings).  Both factors are intimately tied to inflation.

The relationship between the rate of interest and the rate of inflation can be illustrated by an easy example:  If your neighbor asks you for a one year loan of $100 and you expect prices (inflation) to rise at a 6% annual rate, you will need to charge him more than 6% interest in order to have the same purchasing power at the end of the year as you now have plus a profit. You will need at least $106 just to purchase what currently costs you $100. Banks, businesses, and loan companies are no different; they, too, require an adequate compensation for expected inflation. Therefore, the higher the expected rate of inflation, the higher will be the market rate of interest.

In turn, increasing interest rates (caused by increasing inflation) are bearish for the stock market because alternative interest bearing securities — bonds, for example— provide increasingly attractive returns and draw speculative and investment monies toward them and away from stocks. To compete in the marketplace with these less risky securities, common stocks must also offer higher returns. The best way to obtain a higher return from any investment is to pay a lower price for it, and so common stocks fall in price. They continue falling until their potential total return from dividends and growth has risen enough to offset the increased inflation. (By similar logic, declining interest rates are bullish for stock prices.)

Thus, through its effect on the rate of interest, the rate of inflation is closely tied to the rate of return in the stock market as well.

The other essential element of stock valuation is expected future flows of dividends or earnings. It is future events which determine true current stock values because it is future earnings which will ultimately provide returns to investors. If corporations manage to keep pace with inflation-induced rising costs by holding prices up as well, they should not be hurt; nor will stock prices be adversely affected as earnings and dividends will have been held at least constant in real terms. When future earnings and dividends fail to keep pace with the rate of inflation, companies, and so investors, will be worse off. The determining factor in the ability of corporations to make appropriate inflation adjustments is the degree of stability of the inflation rate.

In the past, high rates of inflation have always been unstable and transitory, not constant. Thus it has appeared that a high rate of inflation is unfavorable. In fact, it is the basic instability of inflation which has been especially unfavorable. A constant inflation rate, regardless of whether that rate is 1%, 10%, or 100%, is actually favorable for business and bullish for the market (after it once adjusts to that rate). In a constant inflation environment, not only are interest rates also constant, but consumers and businesses alike can easily adjust budgets and prospective expenditures and revenues to the price levels which they can then easily foresee.

Note that it is the future which is important. Businesses, like all other economic institutions, are always keyed to the future. Inventory is purchased for future production and sale. Plant and equipment is built and purchased for future use. Money is borrowed to be spent in the future and to be repaid out of future revenues. Inflation affects prices, and so all future economic transactions are dependent on future prices for their profitability. In the short run corporations have shown themselves incapable of adjusting operations and profits to cope with future inflation when they are not sure how rapidly those rates of inflation will change. Unstable inflation results in uncertain inventory policies, lags in making price adjustments, confusion in capital expansion budgets, and in general adversely affects business planning.

Unstable inflation, even a sharply falling rate, also tends to confuse consumers, the all important purchasers of the goods and services which business produces. Uncertain whether future income will be sufficient to meet future expenditure requirements, consumer fears of continually accelerating or wildly fluctuating inflation rates induce them to stop spending money and to save more for later years when it will be needed to cope with uncertain prices. This in turn tends to reduce business sales, then production, then earnings, then dividends. In anticipation, the stock market falls.

When inflation is stable economic decisions can be made more easily. The uncertainty of the future is significantly reduced. Hence, in the long run corporate earnings have more than kept pace with inflation because businesses have made up in periods of moderately falling and stable prices what was lost during periods of wildly fluctuating prices.

Thus the paradox is resolved.  In the short run inflation increases interest rates and also results in business and consumer uncertainty which causes declining earnings.  Expectations regarding both factors adversely affect stock prices.  In the long run inflation and interest rates approach a middle norm making common stocks attractive relative to alternative investment mediums.   In addition, businesses are able to adjust their production and pricing schedules to provide a positive net real rate of return.  Both conditions are bullish for the market.

During periods of unstable, and especially accelerating, inflation, common stocks therefore make poor investments and should be sold.  However, in the long run common stocks are an excellent hedge against inflation.

# 47 News and the Market

On occasion you have probably picked up the morning paper, turned to the financial section, and seen a headline declaring:  "Market Rallies on Bullish Earnings Reports," or "Market Slumps on Mid-East War Jitters."  It would seem there is a specific reason behind every day's market action, or at least journalists think so.  Are such headlines accurate . . . is the market highly news oriented  . . or does this just reflect the newsmen's need to provide a reason for the next day's paper?

The role that news does play in market fluctuations is debatable.  Several studies which have been conducted solely to ascertain the effect of news on the market have reached widely varying conclusions.  Most of the analyses on this subject have been confronted with subtle biases.  Just what constitutes good or bad news for the stock market?  This is frequently a matter of subjective judgment or interpretation. For instance, is news of rapid money supply growth good because it increases financial liquidity, thereby enabling people to buy stocks?   Or is it bad because it ultimately exacerbates inflationary pressures and therein destroys investor confidence?

There is another dangerous bias involved in already knowing subsequent market performances and unconsciously using those performances as the basis for describing certain news events as good or bad. Every day's news is a mixture of good and bad. If the market rises, it will be attributed to a favorable item of news, with the next morning's market commentary often noting that traders "ignored" this or that unfavorable development.

The stock market is relatively efficient in responding rapidly to obviously significant news events and in adjusting prices to reflect updated knowledge.   In fact, it usually responds so quickly as to effectively prohibit investors from profiting on news induced price moves. To cite an admittedly extreme example, when John F. Kennedy was assassinated on November 22, 1963, the Dow Jones Industrial Average sank 21 points. Yet prices collapsed so quickly that precious few investors were able to liquidate positions between the time of the assassination news and the end of the price decline (which culminated in a closing of the Exchange). When the market subsequently reopened its doors four days later, stocks retraced their previous declines (the Dow jumped 27 points), but again did so instantaneously, thereby prohibiting the realization of trading profits.

Three factors generally determine the impact an event will have on stock prices.   First, its financial significance; that is, the degree of its ultimate impact on future earnings, dividend payouts, and the like. Obviously the more pervasive and extreme the news impact, the greater will be its effect on market prices.   Second, the extent to which the event deviates from market expectations is of the utmost importance. A fully expected event is, by definition, not news, and will not appreciably affect stock prices. But if an event is not expected to occur, or at least is not widely expected to occur, and if it changes the future earnings and dividend prospects of a stock or the market, then prices should react accordingly. Third, the more efficient the market mechanism, the quicker will be the price adjustment.

With the exception of those events which the public and market analysts have traditionally misunderstood or failed to understand at all (such as complex Federal Reserve System actions or indicators of investor psychology), or which have gone relatively unnoticed and hence unappreciated (such as corporate insider transactions), the U. S. stock market has invariably responded too quickly to allow any but the most nimble traders to profit therefrom.

In a 1967 doctoral dissertation Victor Niederhoffer examined the impact on the market of daily news events, defined in terms of banner headlines in the New York Times, from 1950 to 1966. Classifying various events in a seven-classification spectrum ranging from extremely good news to extremely bad news and examining market performance on subsequent days, Niederhoffer was able to arrive at several interesting conclusions. Extremely bad news events outnumbered extremely good news events. Bad news tended to follow bad news and good news tended to follow good news. Large price changes in either direction were substantially more likely to follow important world events than to follow randomly selected days.

There was also a tendency for price changes on days two through five following an extreme news event to react in the opposite direction from which the market moved on the first day. For example, news of 16 presidential illnesses or deaths between 1916 and 1966 invariably prompted a quick market decline. The average decline was over 1%. In every case the market rose on the ensuing day and actually gained an average of 2½% in days two through five following the event, more than compensating for the initial fall.

With few exceptions, acting on news events has rarely been

a profitable endeavor. What should be exceptionally rewarding is a correct interpretation of a news event that everyone else is interpreting wrongly. Deviation from average market performance requires a deviation from average thinking. And if investment performance is to be more rather than less profitable relative to the market, such independent thinking must be right more often than wrong. Thus, money can seldom be made in the market by simply acting with the common herd on news events. Money can be made by first, uniquely and correctly interpreting those events and, second, uniquely and correctly perceiving the real reasons underlying market fluctuations.

A well informed investor who has developed a rational set of expectations regarding the direction of the market will rarely improve his position by spur of the moment action based on the latest story off the news wires.

# 48 A Unified Theory of Market Prediction

A complex world cries out for simplicity. In the labyrinthine corridors of the stock market where no one individual can totally understand how to cope with all the difficult problems, the temptation is to discard the search for a complex solution and look instead for a simple one. This is a trap. Complex problems rarely have simple solutions. Yet simplicity is the avenue of approach many people in the investment community take. The three most common of the simplistic solutions to the stock market forecasting problem are, (1) that what has happened will continue to happen, (2) that the forecasting game cannot be won so there is no use in trying, and (3) that the market is so inefficient that virtually any system of forecasting will work. None of these approaches is wise. But in the formulation of a rational theory of market prediction, they are all instructive for they tell us what not to do. Each will be examined in turn.

First there are the extrapolators. When the market has risen for a sustained period, it always seems there is a group of commentators who believe that only further rising prices are in store. It is no accident that most forecasts of a rising market occur after the market has already risen. After the market has declined a couple hundred points, these same commentators can usually see nothing but more falling prices ahead. And after the market has meandered about within a trading range for an extended period of time, these same "analysts" rush forward with all kinds of money-making ideas of how to profit from a sideways moving market: trading ranges, too, are extrapolated into the future.

The danger of this "what has been, will be" approach is plain enough. Nothing goes on forever; all things change. Eighty years ago Mark Twain observed that the Lower Mississippi River had lost 242 of its 1,215 miles since 1722, an average of a trifle over one mile and a third per year. Using the device of statistical extrapolation, Twain playfully commented:

> "Any person can see that seven hundred and forty two years from now the Lower Mississippi will be only a mile and three quarters long, and Cairo and New Orleans will have joined their streets together, and be plodding comfortably along under a single mayor and a mutual board of aldermen."

Isn't it interesting, he went on to observe, how one can get "such wholesome returns of conjecture out of such a trifling investment of fact." As is plain from the evidence presented in the preceding chapters, successful market forecasting requires much more than simple extrapolations of past trends. A more thoughtful approach to the forecasting problem is required if a successful system of market prediction is to be developed.

Second come the "random walkers," who believe that it is impossible to consistently earn above average profits in the market except by chance. In recent years many of their published works have insisted that technical analysis is pure bunk. They have set up an elaborate array of tests to support their case. Under the guise of academic integrity they have "proven" that timing systems do not work, that superior market forecasting using publicly available information is impossible, and that the investor would do best to buy a few randomly selected stocks on a few randomly selected dates and just hold them for some randomly selected periods of time.

Although such a viewpoint is not without some value because many market myths are in real need of debunking, the random walkers have intentionally directed their wrath at the weakest targets. There is a danger in extending their conclusions outside the range of the very limited underlying studies. The random walk theorists have still to penetrate very deeply into testing stock selection techniques and they have hardly scratched the surface on market timing. As is evident from the studies presented in preceding chapters, objective analysis reveals many indicators to be superb market forecasting tools. For some reason the random walkers have chosen to overlook this evidence.

The third approach is exemplified by the bulk of established Wall Street practitioners. Countless books have been written in recent decades by "practical" Wall Streeters proposing new timing systems and commenting favorably on existing systems. If there is a common theme to these dissertations, it must be that every forecasting technique works, or at least there are none that do not work; because criticisms of established systems have been notably absent from their presentations. Simple or complex; fundamental, technical, monetary, or psychological in orientation — no matter, all forecasting systems are included on the acceptable list without discrimination. There is just as much danger to this viewpoint that everything is valid as to its opposite that nothing is.

Our analysis of market indicators uniquely differentiates

between the many indicators which are largely devoid of forecasting power and those which have been shown to possess extraordinary predictive ability.

The major remaining step is to integrate the useful indicators into an overall system of market prediction. However, before the indicators can be meaningfully integrated, it is first necessary to develop a rational theory of market behavior, setting forth the broad outlines of how the stock market pricing mechanism functions.

The theory underlying stock market fluctuations is quite elementary as economic processes go. In a continuous auction market supply and demand are always precisely equal, with even the slightest imbalance being immediately eliminated by changes in price and volume. When market commentators observe that "prices fell yesterday in a flood of panic selling," they ignore the elementary fact that every share sold is purchased by someone. Likewise, the proverbial waves of "profit taking" never really depress the market, because for each profit taking seller there is a profit seeking buyer. Similarly, there is no such thing as a "buying stampede" . . . there may be price stampedes, but every share bought has been contemporaneously sold.

Whenever the volume of shares offered for sale at existing prices increases beyond the volume for which there are waiting purchasers at current prices, the market will establish a new "equilibrium price" which is invariably lower. Prices will fall until the lower equilibrium price attracts new buyers, restoring the balance, or until the decline in price discourages sellers, decreasing the potential supply. Price is the essential element. Whenever the volume of shares for which there are buyers at current prices exceeds the number of shares offered, prices will rise, discouraging purchasers and bringing out new sellers until equilibrium is restored.

The ability to foresee and profit from future price changes in the stock market rests upon: (1) an ability to assimilate, correctly interpret, and act on available information before it is fully appreciated by most market participants and fully reflected in prices;  and (2)  an ability to measure the mood of market participants.

As to the first, most information, although *disseminated* almost instantly, is *assimilated* slowly and ultimately fully understood by a small portion of the investing public. Such information may lead to price adjustments that are drawn out over long periods of time and may not even be recognized by most investors. For example, while the first drop in interest rates is never sufficient to wipe away the gloom of a bear market, as one piece of encouraging news after another emerges, we find fear replaced with hope and a bull market in progress. To cite another example, a glamour stock selling at an astronomical price/earnings ratio does not lose 90% of its value the day the first quarterly earnings figures reflecting a decelerating rate of growth is announced;  as quarter after quarter of increasingly disappointing results are reported, the stock enters a lengthy downtrend as it returns to the realm of more prosaic issues.

Information which is obscure or difficult to comprehend is the most useful, as that is the type of information which is also most slowly assimilated by most market participants.

Take as an example of poorly understood news a bank reserve requirement reduction by the Federal Reserve Board. What fraction of the 20 million plus active investors whose hopes and fears help form stock prices instantly appreciated the bullish significance of this news buried half-way down a story on page 28 of the *Wall Street Journal* on November 14, 1974?

> "(The Federal Reserve Board) lowered to 17½% from 18% the reserve requirement on net demand deposits over $400 million . . ."

The answer is, almost no one. (The big news on that day was progress on the settlement of a coal mining strike.) As we observed in Chapter 7, this little item nonetheless probably represented the single most bullish financial event in the last 15 years.

The second essential element of successful stock market prediction is an ability to measure the mood of market participants. It is axiomatic that when everyone is bullish and has adjusted their portfolios to their bullish expectations, there are few remaining potential buyers; and conversely at the opposite market extremes — hence the success of contrary opinion.

Most investors buy stocks because they *expect* prices to advance, and most sellers are in the market because they *expect* prices to decline. Changes in these expectations are the underlying forces of all stock price movements. Sometimes dramatic news developments cause many investors' expectations to change at the same time, and as a result prices move dramatically and quickly.

Investors seem to realize as well, at least subconsciously, that the commodity involved is not their own expectations, but rather their own estimate of what everybody else's expectation will come to be. In other words, investors buy stock in the expectation that the price will advance, realizing full well that such an advance will occur only if other investors will also subsequently buy it. But these investors, too, will buy only because they expect other investors to subsequently buy, and those investors will buy because they expect still others to buy, and so on — an infinite regress. John Maynard Keynes (who propounded the system of economic theory known as Keynesianism) brilliantly illustrated this endless spiral of expectations nearly forty years ago:

> "Professional investment may be likened to those newspaper competitions in which the competitors have to pick out the six prettiest faces from a hundred photographs, the prize being awarded to the competitor whose choice most nearly corresponds to the average preferences of the competitors as a whole; so that each competitor has to pick, not those faces which he himself finds prettiest, but those which he thinks likeliest to catch the fancy of the other competitors, all of whom are looking at the problem from the same point of view. It is not a case of choosing those which, to the best of one's judgment, are really the prettiest, nor even those which aver-

age opinion genuinely thinks the prettiest. We have reached
the third degree where we devote our intelligences to anticipat-
ing what average opinion expects the average opinion to be.
And there are some, I believe, who practice the fourth, fifth,
and higher degrees."

An example of an indicator which really does nothing
more than measure the mood and expectations of a particular
group of investors is the Short Interest Ratio. Widely-known
and utilized by market technicians, but virtually ignored by
fundamentalists, the Short Interest Ratio has time and again
signaled the beginning and end of major bull markets.

Most of the stock market indicators with proven forecasting value fall into the two categories described above: indicators that the public fails to properly understand, appreciate,
and assimilate, and indicators which measure the mood and
psychology of investor groups and the market itself.

Around this theoretical framework for stock market
forecasting, we are now ready to proceed with the incredibly
complex task of integrating the useful indicators into a total
market forecasting system. The cognoscenti call this "constructing or estimating a model." Our model of the stock
market will be constructed with the help of the science
of econometrics.

# PART TWO
## ECONOMETRICS AND THE STOCK MARKET

## 49 An Introduction to Econometrics

Since before the days of the biblical prophets, men have yearned for a glimpse of the future. But *scientific* forecasting techniques are a product of the middle twentieth century. The method most widely used today was developed especially to deal with economic problems. That science — econometrics — applies mathematics and statistics to the study of economic and financial problems.

The framework econometricians erect to solve these problems is a mathematical "model" (or representation) of the system they are studying. The complex mathematical intricacies of constructing an econometric model are beyond the scope of this book, although Selected References identifies several practical texts in the field for interested readers.

*Econometrics and the "Real World."* There are few phases of life in an industrialized society which are not touched by econometrics. Econometric models have been built to describe systems as infinitely complex as the entire world's economy and as relatively simple as the pattern of homemakers' responses to soap advertising. Such models usually have one of two goals: to increase understanding of the inner workings of complicated processes (for instance, how government fiscal and monetary policies interact to affect economic activity), or to permit presently available facts to be efficiently combined into forecasts of future conditions (for instance, estimating how much new generating capacity a power company must order now to meet consumption demands a decade hence employing such variables as energy costs and population growth).   Our interest in econometrics is in the latter usage — the forecasting model.

*Econometrics and Data Processing.* The problems associated with forecasting the stock market are not unique in the field of applied economics. The validity of the forecasts provided by any econometric model is largely a function of the availability of accurate, relevant data over a reasonably long historical period.

It would be very difficult, for example, to build an *accurate* model with which to forecast next year's demand for citizens band radios . . . there is too little information on what factors govern that relatively new market and too little historical data with which to test those factors. On the other hand, a properly designed econometric model forecast of next year's demand for television sets should be quite accurate, as the market is well understood, is known to be closely tied to general economic conditions, and a substantial historical record exists upon which to base a model.

Next only in usefulness to a large body of historical data is data of great accuracy.   Models of the domestic automobile industry benefit from the availability of state registration records disclosing *exactly* how many cars are sold or scrapped each year, but models of world food production suffer from the absence of reliable data in many less developed countries.

Fortunately, historical data regarding the stock market and related indicators is available going back to the last century, and most of the available data is amazingly precise as economic time series go.   The trading volume and prices of stocks on the New York Stock Exchange on a given day in 1906 is known exactly, whereas the nation's economic output and average product prices that year are, at best, estimates formulated decades later, and revised on several occasions. There is so much accurate data available on the market that it is staggering. Probably no other field of human endeavor has maintained such complete records (and utilized them so poorly).

It was in part the availability of a great array of exceedingly accurate historical data that first led the author to believe that the stock market might be particularly amenable to the construction of a broad based econometric forecasting model. But just beginning to assimilate this information requires the resources of large scale data processing systems. Hand calculation is plainly out of the question. Without the evolution of advanced computers, detailed analysis of such voluminous historical data would be impossible.

It is worth noting at this point that computers are essentially big, dumb, *very* fast adding machines. Computers never make mistakes; people who run them do. Of course, good data and fast adding machines are only means to an end. An economic theory or an econometric model is not improved because some accurate numbers have been run through a computer. A computer merely makes it possible to solve mathematical problems so large and so complex that they would never even be attempted by hand. Skeptics are fond of noting, "garbage in, garbage out," and that is true. The fact that garbage comes out of a high speed printer at the rate of several thousand characters a second makes it no less garbage. All that a computer enables us to do is perform in a few moments, with great accuracy, mathematical calculations that would take months or even years to perform on a desk calculator with a far lower degree of accuracy.

Let us now examine some of the specific stock market forecasting problems and the benefits econometrics brings to the resolution of these problems.

*Selecting the Indicators.* In the past the question of which indicators to follow and which to ignore has been answered subjectively by each investor, perhaps more on the basis of prejudice than logic. Fundamentalists laugh openly at many technical indicators;   some technicians believe their system eliminates any need to study fundamental value;   many monetarists think, "Only money matters;" and the proponents of contrary opinion believe you need only define the public mood and then do the opposite.  Probably the only reason any two analysts ever agree is because the basic underlying choices are so few — bullish, bearish, or let's wait and see.

The computer programs used to build econometric models are specifically designed to work with a wide array of diverse forecasting indicators or "variables," selecting the best and discarding the rest.  All selection and rejection decisions are reached with mathematical objectivity, free of human bias. Although many additional refinements can ultimately be utilized, once all of the data has been assembled, the computer can make the basic indicator selection decisions in a few seconds.

*Weighting the Indicators.*   Just as important as indicator selection is the question of what weighting should be assigned to each of the forecasting indicators.  This is a question that simplistic market prediction systems are ill-equipped to answer, and the problem has been more frequently ignored than studied.  Obviously the possible combinations of indicator weights is infinite.  Does a market dividend yield of more than 6% outweigh the mutual funds being overinvested?  Is a 10% reduction in the margin requirement by the Federal Reserve more important than a downturn in the real money supply?  If specialists' short selling is low and total short sales are also ebbing, which is more significant?  Do rising short term and rising long term interest rates have *independent* significance, or should they be treated as but two aspects of a single indicator?

Despite the recent advances in mathematical forecasting techniques, far and away the most popular technique of most analysts is to assemble a composite index of six or ten of their favorite indicators, rank them on the most simplistic possible scale (bullish, neutral, bearish), add up the score, and, presto, you have something of a forecast. But this method completely skips the weighting question because it ignores the relative importance and accuracy of the individual indicators.

A direct output of econometric computer programs is an explicit statement of each indicator's relative value and optimal weighting. Actually two sets of prediction weights are furnished — one set for each indicator taken by itself and a second set for each indicator considered in conjunction with all other indicators. (As we shall come to see, these latter values are an essential ingredient of multi-indicator models.) The computer's assessment of each indicator's relative value is based simply on how closely associated changes in the indicator have been with changes in the market over the historical period being studied. This sometimes leads to the assignment of very low weights to indicators which may have been right in a majority of market cycles, but which have been badly in error at a few critical turning points. After the relative value of each indicator has been ascertained, a specific numerical weight is assigned to the indicator which will ultimately be used in market forecasts. The computer makes all these calculations with blinding speed and carries out the mathematics to any desired degree of accuracy.

*The Forecasting Window.* When dealing with a process which is continuous through time, we must also select the time frame of our forecasts. Most analysts working with crude "composite" indexes completely overlook this question. It does little good to know that an indicator is in a bearish or bullish mode unless one has an understanding of whether that mode merely applies to the next several weeks of market action or whether it has relevance to the entire coming year. Every investor is acquainted with indicators that become prematurely bullish during bear markets or prematurely bearish during bull markets. Unless a specific time frame can be associated with an indicator's forecasts, it is of marginal value at crucial turning points. It does little good to say only that this indicator is "short term" or that one is "long term." What are short and long terms? One month and one year? If so, what is six months? Or three months? Or 29 days, or two years, or any other time frame you care to specify?

A major virtue of econometrics is that it requires an explicit addressment to this problem and has the added advantage of permitting a number of time frames to be simultaneously tested against each indicator. The mathematical work involved becomes staggering, but it is all readily accomplished with a computer. And the econometric model forecasts, when they emerge, will be explicit and beyond the realm of intuition, guesswork and interpretation, the three scourges of most traditional forecasting methods.

*Summary.* We have seen that the forecasting problem consists of three essential elements:

    (a)   The selection of indicators.

    (b)   The weighting of each indicator.

    (c)   The selection of time frames for forecasting. Econometric modeling provides solutions to all three problems. Again, it is not our purpose here to explore the mathematical intricacies of this process. Rather it is sufficient to know that given all relevant and accurate historical data, we can program a computer to (a) select the best indicators, (b) assign appropriate weights to each of them, and (c) identify the time periods over which these indicators can most successfully predict the market's future course.

If we adhere closely to the theoretical requirements of the technique, the resulting forecasts will, in a strict statistical sense, be better than any other possible set of forecasts which could be derived from the data. "Better" does not always mean correct because stock price formation is an inexact process and error is unavoidable. "Better" does mean greater forecasting accuracy and a higher probability of being correct than any other forecasting technique. An extremely elementary example of how this mathematical process can be used to construct a forecast from a single indicator is provided in Chapter 50. Chapter 51 then explores the interrelationships which develop as additional predictive indicators are added to the model.

# 50 An Econometric Model of Your Own

To illustrate the process of building an econometric model, we have selected a popular indicator, the Non-Member Short Sales Ratio (NMSR), which was analyzed in detail in Chapter 17. Basically, a high ratio of non-member short sales to total short sales indicates substantial short selling by the non-exchange members and reflects their belief that stock prices will decline. Because these individuals are normally wrong in their market judgments, stock prices usually go up instead. A low Non-Member Short Sales Ratio reflects ill-founded optimism by the non-members, or at least less pessimism, and thus the market generally declines.

The relationship between this indicator and future market performance is so well perceived that many technicians follow it closely, and a plethora of trading rules has been designed to profit from its informational content. Some analysts treat a ratio below 20% as a sell signal, while others claim superior results using 16% or even 12½% as a signal level. On the bullish side a 30% ratio is often considered a valid buy signal, but some observers claim it is better to wait for 35% or 40%.

In fact this indicator contains useful information across its entire range and an econometric treatment can provide a more rational "sliding scale" of forecasts. Instead of waiting for a specific signal level to be reached, we can then draw useful forecasts from the indicator at any level. To accomplish this we construct a very elementary, one variable, econometric model. (A full scale econometric model often has dozens or even hundreds of variables.)

First we assemble weekly data on the Non-Member Short

Sales Ratio for the past thirty years together with observations of the changes in a market index such as the Dow Jones Industrial Average during the one year period following each of those weeks. Our computer program will then provide us with a calculation of the historical relationship between each weekly reading on the indicator and every ensuing one year change in the market index.

The underlying mathematical calculations on the more than 1,500 pairs of numbers would take several weeks to perform by hand, but a large computer does it in slightly over two seconds. The answer provided by the computer consists basically of the mathematical correlation between the average level of the Non-Member Short Sales Ratio over the last ten weeks (i.e., a ten week moving average) and the change in the Dow Jones Industrial Average over the coming year. In our model, we are provided with the following answer: If the NMSR is equal to 20%, the DJIA is not expected to make any upside or downside progress at all during the ensuing twelve months. For each 1% increase in the ten week average NMSR above 20%, we can expect the DJIA to rise 1.1% in the coming year. Conversely, the DJIA will decline 1.1% for each percentage point the NMSR is below 20%.

Table 52 provides three examples, along with a worksheet from which you may predict next year's Dow at any given

TABLE 52

NON-MEMBER SHORT SALES RATIO ECONOMETRIC MODEL

|  | Examples | | | Worksheet |
|---|---|---|---|---|
| Latest 10 Week Avg. NMSR | 14% | 20% | 40% | ( ) |
| Minus Neutral NMSR | −20% | −20% | −20% | −20% |
| Equals | − 6% | 0% | 20% | ( ) |
| Multiplied by 1.1 | x 1.1 | x 1.1 | x 1.1 | x 1.1 |
| Equals % Change Forecast | − 6.6% | 0% | 22% | ( ) |
| Multiplied by Current DJIA | x1000 | x1000 | x1000 | x( ) |
| Equals Point Chg. Forecast | − 66 | 0 | + 220 | ( ) |
| DJIA One Year Hence | 934 | 1000 | 1220 | ( ) |

time. The examples assume that today's DJIA is equal to 1000. (Of course, when you use this model the DJIA will doubtless stand at some other level, which you need merely substitute for 1000.) Given the three alternative sample Non-Member Short Sales Ratio readings of 14%, 20%, and 40%, the model predicts a Dow Jones Industrial Average one year hence of 934, 1000, and 1220. To reiterate, the only new data you need supply to the formula for real time use is today's DJIA and the latest ten week average value of the Non-Member Short Sales Ratio.

During the last 30 years, this model alone has been able to predict up to 30% of the variations in all one year market fluctuations, a superb record. (100% would mean that *every* one year market change is forecast with *perfect* accuracy.) Of course, a one indicator model is a vast simplification from models utilizing several dozen indicators. Predictions emanating from this model, therefore, should certainly not override the forecasts of more complex multi-indicator models.

One more advantage of an econometric treatment is now apparent − a forecast is provided at every indicator level. *Degrees* of bullishness and bearishness are handled efficiently, and when the indicator is neutral and "not saying anything," the forecast is neutral as well. One major problem with the crude method of using a specific signal level for the indicator, such as a 15% "sell" criteria, is that the level has been selected with the benefit of hindsight; the next time the market may top out with the indicator at 15.1%, 16%, or some higher level, missing a sell signal altogether. Then, too, if 15% is penetrated and is bearish, what are 14%, 13%, even 10% readings, if they are not more bearish? The signal method ignores this problem; the econometric method acknowledges it and assigns a proper forecast to each event. On all accounts the econometric model provides a superior forecasting treatment.

# 51 Multiple Indicator Models

If only one indicator is used to forecast a stock market index, there is but a single relationship to be analyzed; namely, the association between the indicator and the market index. However, if two indicators, A and B, are used to forecast the market, *three* interrelationships must be studied: A versus the market index; B versus the market index; and, just as importantly, *A versus B*. The reason for the latter is the possibility of significant correlation or overlap between the two indicators.

For example, if both A and B are quite similar as, for instance, the Short Interest Ratio and the Non-Member Short Sales Ratio seem to be, in effect they constitute just one indicator, not two. It would clearly be inappropriate to assign each of the indicators weight in a prediction model fully reflective of their own independent predictive powers because their combined contribution to the forecasting model would then be twice its proper total. On the other hand, if the two indicators, A and B, are largely independent of one another, as for example, the Non-Member Short Sales Ratio is independent of the trend of money supply, then each could be assigned its full weight without biasing the predictive contribution of the other. It is this potential interdependence between indicators which necessitates a study of indicator interrelationships within the framework of a forecasting model.

As each new indicator is added to the model, the number of potential interrelationships required for study increases at a nearly geometric rate. Thus the two indicator – A and B – model required the study of three interrelationships. If yet a third indicator, C, is added to the analysis, the total number of interrelationships doubles to six; the obvious three:

1. A versus the market
2. B versus the market
3. C versus the market

and just as important, the *indicator* interrelationships:

4. A versus B
5. A versus C
6. B versus C

By the time a 50 indicator forecasting model is reached, a total of 1,275 variable interrelationships must be analyzed over perhaps a thousand or more separate time intervals . . . requiring literally millions of calculations. The complexity of the problem increases more rapidly than the number of indicators.

An intrinsic element of the econometric technique is a sophisticated analysis of *every* indicator interrelationship. When the model is completed, the relative weights of all the forecasting indicators will have been adjusted for any duplication or overlapping. Interestingly enough, the technique is so powerful that it not only analyzes every one of the pairwise indicator relationships, but also studies all indicators together in a multitudinous mind-boggling array, adjusting for overlapping between groups of indicators as well as individual indicators.

The author has designed a number of econometric models to estimate market averages over specific time intervals. The econometric modeling technique, however, is so adaptable that it permits us to do more than simply estimate a future market average. It is possible, for instance, to construct a model that will tell us whether we are presently in a bull market or a bear market. The next chapter describes one such model.

# 52 The Major Trend Model

The Major Trend Model (illustrated below) is an econometric model which synthesizes more than a dozen indicators particularly well suited to defining whether a bull market or a bear market is in progress. The greatest value of the Major Trend Model is its ability to detect the transition from bull to bear or from bear to bull very close to major cyclical turning points.

The indicators used in this model incorporate information encompassing over 25 different factors. Nearly 44% of the total weighting in the model is given to psychological indicators which measure the mood of various investor groups. Another 13% of total weight is given to money supply and other monetary conditions. Of the balance, 6% measures basic market fundamentals and the remaining factors are trend following in nature.

Values of .50 or greater in the model suggest that a bull market is in progress, while readings below .50 signify that a bear market exists. There are no downside or upside limits to the model forecasts but values below zero are considered extremely bearish and values above 1.00 are overwhelmingly bullish.

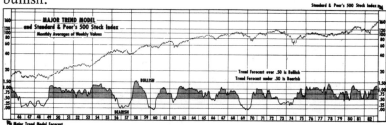

FIGURE 15. Major Trend Model — Monthly averages of weekly econometric estimates and Standard & Poor's Composite Index (monthly range of weekly average prices)

Unlike trend following "composite indexes" that are invariably most bearish at market bottoms and most bullish at market tops, the Major Trend Model's econometric treatment of a wide variety of factors generates forecasts which become decreasingly bearish as market bottoms approach and which also back away from extremely bullish positions prior to market tops.

The model may also be viewed as a probabilistic estimate of whether or not a bull market in fact exists. A reading of .81, therefore, is roughly equivalent to an 81% probability that a bull market is under way. Of course, since the Trend Model can extend below 0.00 or above 1.00 and because true probabilities are always bounded by these limits, this method of interpretation is not accurate in the strictest mathematical sense. However, it is so close to the fact that it is safe to treat it as such. Readings below 0.00 can be considered equal to 0.00 for probability purposes, and readings above 1.00 can similarly be treated as equal to 1.00. In point of fact readings above 1.00 have always occurred in bull markets and readings below 0.00 have never failed to properly indicate bear markets. Over the very long term the model will average readings of about 0.65 because that is the proportion of the time bull markets have historically prevailed.

Although an overall market policy should be based on a synthesis of all the econometric models, the on-off nature of the Major Trend Model makes it particularly adaptable to an "ex-post" simulation of comparing it with a naive market policy of buying and holding.

For example, an initial investment of $10,000 on August 30, 1945, would have grown to $78,000 by year end 1975 if it had been continually invested in Standard & Poor's 500 Index until April 30, 1964 and thereafter invested in the broad market as represented by the NYSE Total Return Index (April 30, 1964 marks the commencement of data availability for the TR Index).

Over the same 30 year period, $10,000 would have grown to $508,000 if it had been invested in long purchases whenever the Major Trend Model rose above .60 and then switched into short sales on a downside penetration of .40. (These limits are used because the model is rarely in error when it yields a reading below .40 or above .60.)

It is fairly simple to demonstrate excellent "ex-post" performance with any system if enough commission-free trades and complicated rules are imposed. It is very unusual for a scientifically and objectively derived model such as this to provide such a large return with a simple buy/sell rule and a minimum number of transactions. (In fact, there were only seven round trips over the 30 year period.) Although a more arbitrary choice of buy and sell points together with the imposition of additional trading rules will very substantially improve the historical results, these simple criteria are far more likely to prove reliable in the future.

The Major Trend Model is not designed to detect anything short of major market reversals. For example, it remained bullish during the entire period from July 22, 1949 through May 25, 1956. Over those seven years, the Standard & Poor's 500 Index tripled from 14.89 to 44.63, the longest uninterrupted bull movement of the post-war era.

Similarly, after moving to a properly bullish mode in September 1962, the model turned bearish in early 1966, coincident with the market top of that year. Note that the model stayed bullish throughout the June 1965 correction, which, in retrospect, proved to be quite mild, however shocking it was at the time. The model was also completely unfazed by the early 1968 correction and remained continuously bullish from October 1966 until the next major peak in March 1969.

The Major Trend Model provides an objective answer to the most elementary question facing every investor: Is this a good time to hold stocks? When the answer is "yes," as it is most of the time, we must turn our attention to selecting stocks — which is the subject of Part Three.

# PART THREE
## STOCK SELECTION THEORIES

## 53 Stock Selection: An Overview

While it is possible to "buy the market" by purchasing mutual funds or diversified portfolios of common stocks, for most investors the portfolio construction process ultimately comes down to the selection of individual securities.

There are two primary approaches to stock selection: fundamental and technical. The former is concerned with analysis of the company itself and deriving estimates of net worth per share, current assets, future earnings and dividends, and related measures of value. In contrast, technical analysis is devoted to studies of supply and demand for a company's stock and to those statistics which are related to price and volume. It is safe to assume that at least 90% of all stock research in this country is based upon a fundamental approach with a tiny minority of investors concerned exclusively with the technical approach.

In the final analysis there is no real substitute for a comprehensive understanding of a company and a correct assessment of its prospects. The ability to uncover inside information or to accurately forecast a company's future earnings is an invaluable asset, although interestingly enough, of questionable legality. The stream of future earnings and dividends constitutes what a stock is ultimately worth to its investors. When these earnings and dividends are estimated precisely, true value is defined. All that remains is to purchase those stocks priced beneath their true value and to sell them when they become priced in excess of that value. But few individual investors can afford to devote the time and money required for such value analyses, and those that can, find the value estimation task exceedingly difficult, if not impossible.

Tens of millions of dollars are spent on Wall Street each year in efforts to estimate company values and to make investment decisions therefrom. To judge from the historical portfolio experiences of those large investors (e.g., mutual funds, pension funds, bank trust departments) who have been most able to devote the necessary effort to analyzing fundamentals, it must be extremely difficult to estimate true value. Very few of these fundamentalists have been able to *consistently* derive better than average investment results, and in recent years most have under-performed the market.

There is a good reason for this. Aside from occasional tidbits of inside information (which the Securities and Exchange Commission is vigorously trying to eliminate), most fundamental analysts have access to and analyze the same information. Such basic measures as debt/equity ratios, current assets ratios, historical sales and earnings growth rates, dividend payout ratios, yields, price/ earnings ratios, and the like are commonplace and overused. In most cases any predictive value they might have is incorporated into current stock prices so rapidly as to eliminate their usefulness. If any of these measures do have some residual value, it is probably only at the bullish extreme. Companies which appear to be exceptionally undervalued might be isolated for further analysis and then purchased if the undervaluation is confirmed by other factors: subjective or objective, fundamental or technical.

A full treatment of fundamental company analysis is outside the scope of this book. Readers interested in pursuing the subject in depth should consult Graham & Dodd's *Security Analysis,* generally considered to be the "bible" of fundamentalism. Although it contains a few rather misleading formulae, it does cover its subject with extreme thoroughness and ought to be read by any beginning student of fundamental analysis.

However, the experience of the book's principal author, Benjamin Graham, provides a classic example of the pitfalls which can plague fundamental analysts. Graham was touted in two best selling "Adam Smith" books as the Dean of Security Analysts due to Graham's own phenomenal investment successes. In 1976 a rather interesting story emerged. It seems that the biggest winner in his portfolio, and the secret of its spectacular performance since 1948, was an insurance company named GEICO, which Graham bought in a private transaction at 21 cents per share. GEICO soared to over $50 per share in the span of 25 years. In 1975, with Graham still holding positions, GEICO revealed that unbeknown to the savvy fundamentalists, it was losing tens of millions of dollars per quarter and was threatened with bankruptcy. The stock plunged as low as $2 a share.

Turning to technical stock analysis, we have noted its disdain for the company and concentration instead on the common stock itself. While the essence of fundamental analysis is the determination of value and the purchase or sale of stocks whose price deviates from value, technical analysis is based upon two very different premises. First, that subjective estimates of value are simply too imprecise, and are thus effectively irrelevant. Second, that future price fluctuations may be predicted through analyses of historical price movements, supply and demand relationships, and other factors which impact directly upon price.

Stock price changes can be considered to be caused by two phenomena. One is a properly recognized change in value. This, as noted, is within the realm of fundamental analysis but is so difficult to measure that it may be eliminated from further consideration.

The second factor is a more or less erroneous change in investors' perceptions of value. Since value is based upon what will occur in the future (future earnings, future dividends), it would seem at first glance that with each passing moment the marketplace should logically develop a newer and keener perception of it. But in fact an infinite future always lies ahead and value always retains its basic elusiveness: it never becomes easier to estimate merely with the passage of time. Now, if price is rarely the equal of true value, but just moves around it in long and short term trends, it follows that price may as often be drifting away from value as toward it. Thus, in some instances the ability of investors to correctly perceive value is worsening, not improving. One of the roles of technical analysis is to identify the existence of such periods and to identify those investor groups who are more likely to be right or who are more likely to be wrong in correctly equating price to value. Following those who are usually right and doing the opposite of those who are generally wrong can be most profitable.

Then, too, investors are creatures of emotion. They remember the price they paid for a stock and this can influence their decisions of when and at what price to sell it.

Investors also tend to allow themselves to be caught up in the market atmosphere of the moment, be it greed, panic, fear, or even apathy. All those fundamentalists looking at the same factors at the same time tend to move prices to extremes. Thus prices tend to move in trends, and trend following (one of the basic precepts of technical analysis), has a valid theoretical basis. One reason for great sustained bull market trends is doubtless the plethora of optimistic earnings reports which emerge after an economic upswing is well in progress. Investors tend to jump aboard those issues exhibiting the greatest "fundamental" improvement and bid them up to greater extremes. Such situations offer profit opportunities to technicians trading with prevailing price trends. At the same time they ultimately spell doom, both for the fundamentalists who bought stocks at the high and for the not inconsiderable number of technicians who bought earlier for purely technical reasons but then "fell in love" with the fundamentals at the peak. (The true technician throws in the towel when prices begin to fall. Fundamentalists just think stocks are cheaper and are therefore better buys than ever.) By the time the fundamental news turns sour and the reasons for the decline are widely understood, the process is usually ready to reverse itself. A similar situation, then, works during bear markets as well.

Thus, technical indicators are frequently useful in the timing process. There is indeed an abundance of technical stock selection systems. Of course, not all of them work all of the time. (Some, frankly, don't work at all.)

A caveat worth remembering at this point is that *something* always works best. If what works best doesn't have a sound theoretical and practical basis, it is probably meaningless. Unfortunately, computers make it easy to test everything and find the something that worked best in the past.

An undoubtedly apocryphal story tells of a computer study based upon an analysis of almost every available fundamental fact regarding every NYSE and Amex stock in search of the one ultimate most profitable stock trading method. The computer is finally supposed to have said, "Buy and hold stocks of companies with names ending in the letter X." The study, you see, was made in the heyday of Syntex and Xerox.

Another very important consideration is that different market environments dictate different stock selection strategies . For example, the purchase of stocks priced far below book value per share was very profitable in the 1940s and 1950s. But during the soaring '60s such systems became relatively unprofitable and new issues, conglomerates and glamour stocks caught on. Relative strength analysis also has its place, but it is a useful tool only during certain phases of the market cycle.

It would be unfair and misleading to assert that any one stock selection system is always the right one or the wrong one.  No one ever said that speculation and investment was easy.  In the final analysis, an integrated market timing and stock selection system should be incorporated into an overall portfolio strategy.

# 54 Prices and Earnings:
## Buy Low, Sell High

*Price/Earnings Ratio.*  A Price/Earnings (P/E) Ratio is the most basic of all financial statistics;  so basic, P/E Ratios on all NYSE stocks are published daily in most newspaper stock listings.  A P/E Ratio is calculated by dividing the current stock price by the latest twelve months' earnings per share.

All other things equal, it is preferable to purchase a stock with a low P/E Ratio as it is undervalued relative to a stock with a higher P/E Ratio.  Of course "all other things" are rarely equal.  No two companies are identical, and even if two or more companies were substantially similar, the calculation of earnings can vary greatly from company to company as a result of different accounting procedures.

Numerous studies have been conducted to ascertain whether there is some predictive information in Price/Earnings Ratios which can be used to select better performing common stocks.  Most of these studies have compared current P/E Ratios with relatively short term (up to one year) future stock performance and the research results have been quite varied.  In part, the result from each study has been a function of the market environment in which the tests were conducted.

More value from P/E Ratios appears to rest in longer term stock price prediction.  One classic study in this area was performed by S. Francis Nicholson *(Financial Analysts Journal,* July-August 1960).  Nicholson calculated Price/Earnings Ratios at five year intervals for 100 common stocks, predominately industrial issues of high quality.  At each measuring period Nicholson divided the 100 stocks into five groups ranging from the 20 lowest P/E Ratio stocks to the 20 highest. The investment results which accrued to each group in each of the four non-overlapping five year holding periods from 1939 to 1959 are presented in Table 53.

## TABLE 53

### P/E RATIOS AND STOCK PERFORMANCE

| P/E Ratio Group (20 Stocks Each) | 1939- 1944 | 1944- 1949 | 1949- 1954 | 1954- 1959 | Geometric Average | Annual Rate of Return |
|---|---|---|---|---|---|---|
| 1  Lowest | 48% | 56% | 188% | 123% | 96% | 14.4% |
| 2  Next Lowest | 16% | 37% | 91% | 95% | 56% | 9.3% |
| 3  Middle | −5% | 36% | 122% | 88% | 52% | 8.7% |
| 4  Next Highest | −4% | 26% | 84% | 79% | 41% | 7.1% |
| 5  Highest | 5% | 33% | 51% | 115% | 46% | 7.9% |
| Avg.   100 stocks | 12% | 38% | 107% | 100% | 59% | 9.7% |

Nicholson's method of calculating the P/E ratios is somewhat suspect (see original article for details), and his 100 stock sample slightly outperformed the market in each five year period, but the overall results are illuminating and probably overcome any inherent biases. Note especially the relative performances among the five P/E groups.

The lowest P/E group outperformed every other group in each five year holding period. Its average five year return was 96%, an annual compounded rate of 14.4%. This rate of return is substantially in excess of the other groups which between them averaged only an 8.5% annual rate of gain. The table also indicates a generally downward trend in returns as one moves higher on the Price/Earnings Ratio spectrum. However, the one-fifth of all stocks with the highest P/E ratios did tend to provide some small improvement in performance relative to Group 4 (perhaps a result of countervailing relative strength forces).

Studies conducted subsequent to Nicholson's, notably those by Paul F. Miller, *et al.* *(The Commercial & Financial Chronicle*, September 20, 1966) and James D. McWilliams *(Financial Analysts Journal*, May-June, 1966) tend to confirm his results.   Miller's study measured annual returns for the period 1948-1964, while McWilliams' research covered the period 1953-1964, again using yearly returns.   In each case significantly superior performance was furnished by low P/E stocks and relatively inferior performance emanated from high P/E issues.

In all three of the cited studies a subtle selection bias may have influenced the results.   Each study omitted from its analysis issues which did not survive the performance measurement period.   To the extent that such omitted stocks were low P/E issues which went bankrupt, the actual average performances of all low P/E stocks may be inferior to those estimated.   However, high P/E stocks can also go bankrupt — sometimes a high P/E denotes abnormally low earnings, not an abnormally high price.   Stocks can also leave the scene because of merger.   Since low P/E issues are more likely to be acquired than high P/E stocks, the deletion of merged stocks (and their generally excellent performance) from the study probably downwardly biased the measured performance of the low P/E group in the study.

It is also possible that these studies might be biased as a consequence of the time periods used.   Had results been measured through the speculative years of the late 1960s when "glamour" and "performance" usurped value in the minds of many investors, the relative performances of the various P/E groups might have been mixed or even reversed. Indeed, these studies fell into disrepute soon after they were published because the ensuing market environment was more conducive to a "performance" approach than to a "value" approach.   Nevertheless, the more recent experience of the early 1970s would seem to suggest a regression to the market characteristics of the 1940s, '50s, and early '60s.   If so, a low P/E selection system might work once again.   In any event, the experience of the soaring '60s, even if contrary to the earlier experience, would not necessarily invalidate the primary study results. It would merely define the type of market environment in which the system might be used most successfully.

As a long term stock selection tool, P/E ratios may be extremely useful in identifying issues capable of providing well above average returns. Uncertainty in the short run notwithstanding, in the long run, according to the old adage, value will out.

*Earnings Growth.* The major problem with Price/Earnings Ratios is that they are strictly a function of history. They are calculated with historical earnings and historical (one instant ago) prices. What is past may well be prologue, but then again it may not. What really counts is the relationship of current stock price to *future earnings* (which might be termed P/FE). Future earnings, in turn, are dependent upon the future earnings growth rate of the company.

There is no question that investors who can accurately predict the earnings growth of individual companies will be able to successfully predict common stock price changes as well. Starting from a given base, the faster a company is able to increase earnings, the greater future earnings will be and the more the common stock should be worth.

The problem is to predict future earnings growth accurately. Obviously, the best way is to analyze company prospects. But half of Wall Street is working on the same problem, so arriving at a "better" earnings estimate than everyone else, strictly on the basis of fundamental analysis, is extremely difficult. An investor who tries will be competing with analysts who spend every minute of every working day studying a single industry or a handful of companies.

If fundamental analysis is out, the next question is, Can future earnings growth rates be predicted from past growth rates? If so, stocks of companies which currently show high earnings growth rates or which have reported earnings above their historical norm should be unusually good buys. Furthermore, such a system would certainly be a time saver, for *anyone* can calculate historical growth rates over the last one, three, five, or ten years accurately and easily. So easily it makes one wonder if such calculations could possibly be of any value.

The subject of earnings growth persistency has been investigated very thoroughly in recent years, and most studies have concluded that past earnings growth rates are of little value in determining future growth rates. Year to year earnings growth rates for individual companies show almost no correlation although there is a very slight tendency for an earnings gain in one year to be followed by *lower* earnings in the next, and vice versa. Over the longer term, say five years or more, earnings changes do show a tendency toward persistence. Again, though, the degree of this relationship is very small.

In other words, the results of extensive testing reveal that it is not only impossible to accurately predict future earnings growth rates on the basis of past growth rates, but it is also extremely difficult to even predict the direction of earnings changes. It is doubtful that such simple techniques as extrapolating past earnings growth rates into the future or generating derivative statistics can ever lead to superior stock selection.

The only characteristic of earnings growth rates which does seem predictable is volatility. Companies which experience very volatile earnings changes in one period (such as automobile manufacturers, steel companies, etc.) usually show highly volatile earnings in the next period as well. Companies which have relatively stable earnings changes in some years (such as utilities) are likely to have similarly stable changes in ensuing years.

Another approach is to study earnings *estimates* rather than simply earnings themselves. When companies report earnings above the consensus estimate of market analysts, their stocks usually move higher. Similarly, when analysts upgrade their estimates of future earnings growth, more investors are induced to purchase the stocks and prices also rise.    A potentially profitable technique to exploit this characteristic might be to follow several analysts' earnings estimates on a regular basis, purchasing those stocks for which analysts are upgrading their estimates and selling those issues for which analysts are forced to downgrade their earnings projections.    Such a strategy is conditional in part on the ability of the investor to jump into or out of those stocks before the market fully assimilates the new information.    It is also dependent on the investor's view of the market's view of the analyst's ability to correctly or incorrectly view the company in question.    In short, this technique has probably reached Keynes's fabled 4th degree of investor expectations (Chapter 48).

# 55 Chart Patterns: Windmills of the Mind?

According to the "random walk theory," stock prices do not have a memory.    Historical price changes cannot be used to successfully predict price changes which follow.    Market technicians hold a contrary view; they believe that historical price changes are closely related to future changes and that the latter can, in part, at least, be predicted from the former. A special class of technician is the chartist, so called because he uses charts of historical price behavior to assist in forecasting the future.

With recent advances in data processing technology, it is now quite easy to program computers to recognize and flag certain stock price patterns.    However, many technicians still prefer to rely on the intuition and interpretation inherent in analysis of pictoral representations of historical price fluctuations.    Although there are many types of charts, two have achieved great popularity (or notoriety) — bar charts and point and figure charts.

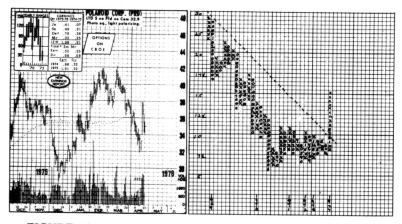

FIGURE 16. Bar Chart —
Polaroid, daily price range
and volume; 10/75 - 4/76.

FIGURE 17. Point and Figure
Chart — Scope Industries, 3
point price reversal; 1969 - 1974.

*Bar Charts.* A bar chart (example in Figure 16) is drawn in
two dimensions, price and time. Depending upon the time
interval being analyzed, a single bar may represent a day's,
week's, month's, or even a year's price behavior of a stock (or
market index). Each period's price action is described on the
vertical bar in terms of three points. The top of the bar
represents the highest price at which the stock traded during
the period. The bottom of the bar is the lowest price at
which the stock traded. Finally, a horizontal tick mark on
the bar is sometimes used to denote the stock's closing price
at the end of the period.

While one bar in and of itself does not provide a great deal
of historical information, several dozen bars begin to provide
a perspective of price behavior, and certain patterns begin to
emerge. In the exhibit, Polaroid's price behavior is plotted
on a daily basis for seven recent months and on an annual
basis for ten recent years using bar charting techniques.
Skilled chartists would identify virtually every move as
corresponding to some particular pattern.

Most bar charts present volume on the same time scale.

This opens the way to identifying patterns in trading activity as well as interrelationships between the price patterns and the volume patterns. However, lest you gain the impression that volume is as important as price to chartists, we will move on to another form of charting that dispenses not only with volume, but with time as well.

*Point and Figure Charts.* Next to bar charts the most popular charting technique is point and figure (P&F), which uses columns of X's and 0's to represent rising and falling prices respectively (example in Figure 17). Although the price scale of a P&F chart can be identical to a bar chart, its horizontal dimension is radically different. When a stock price moves higher, its upward path is denoted by a vertical series of X's. When the price reverses and starts downward, the chartist moves over one column to the right and denotes the declining trend by a directly downward series of 0's. Each square on the chart might denote $1 per share, in which case a straightaway move from $20 to $45 would be reflected in 25 X's, and a subsequent decline from $45 to $30 would be recorded by 15 0's in the adjacent column to the right.

Note that time is irrelevant to a point and figure chartist. Regardless of whether a stock's price move from $20 to $45 encompassed one day or an entire year, if it had no intervening reversals, that upward course would be marked by a single, continuous vertical series of X's. Indeed, to prevent too much horizontal movement, P&F chartists commonly hold a trend intact until a minimum reversal occurs, say, 3 or 5 points. The exact size of the required reversal depends on the price and volatility of the stock or market index being plotted.

Like bar chartists, point and figure experts insist that patterns and definite trends emerge on their charts after sufficient historical data has been entered.

We shall now proceed to analyze a few of the more popular chart patterns.

*The Volume Breakout Signal.* The popular "volume breakout" bar chart pattern is formed by an extended downward or sideways price trend on low or declining trading volume and then a sudden upward price spurt with a concomitant large increase in volume. Normally volume increases to a rate several times the previous average activity level. Following the volume breakout the stock price should continue to rise and thus the formation is considered extremely bullish.

Chartists are always encouraged by an upside breakout in prices. Such behavior frequently connotes a penetration through a resistance price; that is, a price which when met on previous occasions has brought new supplies of stock into the market, depressing the price again and again. Once a stock has broken through the resistance point, demand has conquered supply and the price can frequently move much higher. If volume increases simultaneously with the price breakout, it is yet further evidence that new and vigorous demand for the stock has entered the marketplace. In other words, the price gain at such times is caused not only by a drying up of selling pressure, but by genuine new buying interest as well. The two elements frequently act together to propel the price still higher.

Figure 18 presents an example of a volume breakout

FIGURE 18. Volume Breakout — Diamond Shamrock weekly price range and volume, with weighted moving averages.

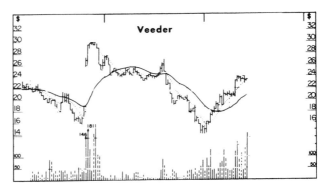

FIGURE 19. Volume Breakout — Veeder Industries, weekly price range and volume with weighted moving averages.

formation in Diamond Shamrock. In April 1975, following an extended period of relatively quiet trading activity and a sideways moving price, Diamond Shamrock suddenly broke out to the upside on a tremendous volume surge. The breakout also happened to coincide with the bullish penetration of a major long term price downtrend line and stock purchases made on the volume breakout signal or in the days immediately thereafter were ultimately rewarded with excellent further price advances.

The volume breakout pattern is not infallible. The volume breakout for Veeder in late 1974 (see Figure 19), was followed by only a very minor subsequent gain before the stock price reversed direction and began falling rapidly. Trading activity had been very light in Veeder during the months preceding the signal and the stock price had been in a decidedly downward trend. When the breakout came on exceptionally high volume, VR gapped upward several points. Speculators purchasing immediately after the breakout signal, however, succeeded only in buying at the ultimate top.

*Gaping Gaps.* One of the most intriguing of all bar chart patterns is the gap. A downward gap occurs when the high price of a stock on a given trading day is beneath its low price of the previous day. This forms a space, or a gap, on the chart. An upward gap is formed when the low price of a stock on a given trading day is above the stock's high price on the preceding day. Although chartists have identified several different gap formations, analysts differ in the degree of importance they assign to gaps in general and to specific types of gaps in particular.

One type of gap is the "breakaway." It occurs when a stock breaks out of a relatively horizontal price pattern with a gap. Another type of gap, a runaway, occurs in the midst of an extended price move, forming in the same direction as the prevailing price trend. Yet a third type is an exhaustion gap, which occurs after an extended price move in one direction and is followed by a reversal, or at least a termination, of the prevailing price trend. Since subsequent price performance is critical to its definition, an exhaustion gap cannot be absolutely identified until well after the fact.

A particularly interesting gap is called an island reversal. It is formed when prices gap in one direction, trade in a range away from the gap, and then reverse direction, gapping once again at the identical spot the original gap occurred. The island reversal gap frequently signals an extended price move in the direction of the second gap. Figure 16 (page 207) pictures an island reversal gap in Polaroid. PRD gapped downward at $34 in December 1975, then gapped upward at the same price in January 1976. This action formed a price "island" below $34, and signaled (in this case correctly) the possibility of a subsequent retracement back to the $41 price which initiated the previous downward trend.

Any gap which fails to qualify under one of the preceding labels is usually called an area, or a common, gap. This serves to tie things up in a relatively neat package by giving a name, and hence an aura of scientific mystique, to all possibilities.

Some chartists believe that gaps must eventually be "closed" (the stock trading again over the same price range as the gap). If true, the hypothesis carries important implications.

Once a gap occurs the price should subsequently reverse and cover that area. However, there are literally thousands of gaps in market indexes and individual stocks which have never been closed . . . and likely never will. As one authority has noted, "If you will think the matter over for a moment, you will see that the probability (of) a gap being closed applies just as well to a stock's returning to any price range at which it has once traded, gap or no gap." (Edwards and Magee, *Technical Analysis of Stock Trends*, 1966.) If true, there is no reason to believe any gaps impart any predictive information.

While some gaps may have significance at times, there are generous exceptions to the gap rules. A gap of only one-eighth of a point, for example, merely represents the minimum permitted price change in most stocks, and is therefore insignificant. Even larger gaps are not unusual, and hence are of little importance, in high priced and highly volatile stocks. Stocks which are relatively inactive tend to gap when even small or medium sized orders are entered, and the frequent gaps which result are seldom of importance. When a stock goes ex-dividend, its price is automatically reduced by the amount of the dividend and this, too, can cause a gap of no special significance. Finally, while gaps occurring on a daily chart are based upon the relationship of high and low prices for two successive days, there are numerous gaps which occur *during* a single day's trading which do not show up on a chart at all even though their significance may be far greater.

Gaps may have occasional technical significance just as any chart pattern may have *occasional* significance. The many exceptions to the gap rules suggest that any chartist attempting to utilize gaps in stock selection and timing must of necessity exercise a great deal of subjective judgment.

In conclusion, gaps are not any more useful than any other chart pattern, perhaps just a bit more fun.

*Other Chart Patterns:*    Because there is a potentially infinite number of price patterns that a stock can trace, chartists have identified (devised) a virtually infinite number of chart patterns to correspond to them. These patterns are known by such esoteric names as head and shoulders, reverse head and shoulders, single, double, and triple tops and bottoms, flags, pennants, spikes, saucers, triangles, rectangles, lines, breakouts, consolidations, blowoffs; in short, a name for everything and everything with a name. One respected chartist, James Dines, seeks out "Prussian helmet formations," which appear similar to your everyday head and shoulders, only surmounted by a spike formation. There are even "false" signals so that the misses, too, can retrospectively be called successful patterns (in name, anyway).

*The Value of Charting.* Whether or not these patterns have predictive value has been debated for years. One study conducted by Robert Levy attempted to define by computer some three dozen popular chart patterns and measure subsequent price performance. The results revealed that in most instances prices trended in the *opposite* direction from that which chartists would have predicted on the basis of the price patterns alone. Chartists rushed to their own defense claiming that no computer program could accurately define the patterns which they deem significant. In most cases this is true because every chartist seems to have his own interpretation of a given pattern. And besides, Levy's result, even if absolutely legitimate, does not invalidate charting; it merely tips it upside down! Every chart pattern *has* to work as either a buy *or* a sell indicator.

Interpretation is the element of charting which makes it so intriguing. Many people turn to charting because it seems to be a precise method of locating buy and sell points for individual stocks. They believe, or hope, that there are certain laws stocks will follow in the majority of instances and that they might take advantage of these laws to make profits. With respect to charts, at least, nothing could be further from the truth. Despite the specific chart pattern names, despite the incontrovertible historical factuality of lines drawn on graph paper, despite the tremendous aura of precision . . . the essence of charting is not objective analysis; it is subjective interpretation. As a result, it is probably impossible to prove or disprove the ultimate predictive power of any charting system. Buying a stock because you like its chart pattern, or buying a stock because you like its balance sheet are both exercises in ego — one is granting himself a superior ability to see that which is desirable, be it in a chart or a financial statement. Just as one man will judge a beauty contest on face and another on figure (and who can say which is right?), so will some investors choose chart patterns over balance sheets.

There is an old adage on the Street that says, "There are no rich chartists." A few chartists may disagree, insisting that charting really does work. But if so, they have done a blessed poor job of proving their case.

# 56 Trend Lines and SRL's: Terminological Inexactitude

Trend lines constitute a very important element of charting theory. A trend line is drawn on a price chart by connecting two points. An uptrend line connects two or more interim low prices with a straight line. A downtrend line connects two or more price peaks in a downward direction. Short, intermediate, and long term price trends can be so delineated.

To further clarify prevailing trends, chartists like to construct channels. A channel requires two trend lines drawn parallel to each other, one on each side of the price figures plotted on the chart, so that the two lines encompass the historical price fluctuations. According to theory, a stock is expected to remain within its channel.

Virtually all trend lines have a deep-seated significance to chartists. "A trend in motion tends to continue," is a commonly heard phrase. Stock prices are expected to hold above uptrend lines and stay below downtrend lines. Hence a trend line defines a resistance point which should induce a price reversal when it is met.  On the other hand, if a trend line is broken − that is, if the price moves through it − a more extended move in the new direction is normally expected.  Thus trend lines yield buy and sell signals as well as simply marking price trends.  A chartist holding a stock would place a stop order just below a significant uptrend line and would liquidate his position if the trend line is broken.  Or he might instate a long position in a stock which breaks out above a downtrend line.

There are several anti-trend line arguments.  Most trend lines must be drawn with the use of hindsight.  Thus, although they appear to possess predictive significance, they are often merely after the fact abstractions.  Even such an elementary factor as the type of scale used on the chart to measure prices causes confusion.  For example, a stock chart plotted on an arithmetic scale (where equal *point* intervals such as 10-20-30-40 assume identical amounts of space) will provide significantly different trend lines than charts drawn on a log price scale (where equivalent *percent* price moves such as 10-20, 20-40, 40-80, etc. require identical space).  In many cases the choice of a chart's scale will determine whether the conclusion is that the stock should be bought or that it should be sold.  The variability of the horizontal time dimension on the chart (as it is different between bar and point and figure charts) compounds the confusion.  How can all of the multitudinous trend lines be correct?  If one is correct, the others would seem, by definition, to be wrong.  And, for that matter, why should any one trend line ever work (except by chance)?  What are its magical, even mystical, powers?  Why, for example, should any stock ever be required to advance or decline at a constant arithmetic or geometric rate?  These questions have never been answered.

In and out trading signals based upon trend line penetrations are also frequently so late that percentage profits are quite small, or non-existent.  Finally, while it may be true that trends do *tend* to continue, it is a fact that they *always* end.  Thus, every trend line is finally broken and must be considered not to have held . . . in other words, to have failed. Trend line analysis, at its very best, must be considered an extremely inexact science. If trend lines have any useful role to play at all, it is not in precise timing but rather in providing a general price perspective; to add illumination to the chart picture of historical performance.

Speed resistance lines (SRL's) are a more recent charting phenomenon. Popularized by noted market technician Edson Gould, the SRL theory has attracted a growing constituency. But if trend line drawing is an inexact science, speed resistance lines can only be considered inexact art!

There are two basic speed resistance lines, the one-third and the two-thirds. To determine a two-thirds upward SRL, calculate the number of points from the beginning of a price move to the most recent top. Take two-thirds of this figure and add it to the beginning price. Then plot that point directly below the recent high and connect it with the initial price by drawing a straight line. According to SRL theory, the stock or market index being measured should hold at the two-thirds speed resistance line on any downward reaction. If the price perchance breaks below the line, it should proceed further downward to meet the one-third speed resistance line which is calculated in a similar fashion but is drawn with a rate of price change that is equal to one-third of the entire price move rather than two-thirds. If the two-thirds line is broken, the one-third line should hold. If the one-third line also fails to hold a new trend is signaled and the stock price should continue in its downward direction. Of course, the same system is then applied in reverse to identify, measure, and analyze price downtrends.

For example, Figure 20 presents a chart of the unweighted NYSE Total Return Index from 1964 through 1970. The October 1966 - December 1968 bull move extended from 112 to 230 on the index, a total of 118 points. Speed resistance lines would be calculated in *December 1968* as follows: Two-thirds of 118 points is 79 points, and 79 plus the beginning price of 112 is equal to 191. Thus, the two-thirds SRL

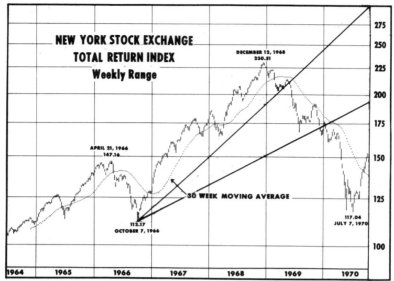

FIGURE 20.   One-Third and Two-Thirds Speed Resistance Lines —
NYSE Total Return Index; May 1964 - December 1970.

is drawn connecting the October 1966 low at 112 with a
point directly below the December 1968 high at 191. The
one-third line connects the beginning price of 112 with 151
(112 + one-third of the 118 total point gain). In this particular case the early 1968 reaction stopped short of the two-
thirds line and the subsequent 1968-1970 bear market penetrated both the two-thirds and one-third speed resistance
lines.

While all of this may sound very precise, the Speed Resistance Line theory is subject to criticism on several counts.
Why, for example, do chartists use one-third and two-thirds
SRL rates? Why not use one-fourth speed resistance lines or
fifth, sixth or even tenth SRL's? (In fact, one chartist recently did suggest that whenever a one-third speed resistance line
is violated, the next support will be a one-fourth speed
resistance line; remember, *something* always has to work
best!) To say that the market is somehow magically keyed to
one-third movements defies credibility and calls for a proof

at the least; at the most it is simply ridiculous.

The unfortunate fact of the matter is that no SRL theorists have ever presented a logical and coherent explanation of the power of their lines. They do go to great lengths to demonstrate the technique's legitimacy by pointing to case histories. But their examples just raise more questions. For, suspiciously, the SRL adherent seems to have an explanation for everything. Following a price advance, if a stock does not decline to its two-thirds line, it is merely considered a minor reaction, not worth worrying about, and the theory is vindicated. If the stock declines to the two-thirds line and reverses, the theory is vindicated. If it penetrates the two-thirds line but declines to the one-third line and reverses, the theory is vindicated. If the stock price declines to some point between the two-thirds and one-third lines, the SRL theorist would say that the combined power of both lines halted the decline and the theory is vindicated. Finally, if all SRL's fail to hold, the theorist would maintain that the system was once again vindicated because the penetration signaled a new trend direction regardless of how far that new trend might proceed.

But, really! The market always has to do something, SRL or no SRL! The explanation of everything is simply an explanation of nothing.

As if they have not created enough advantages for themselves, to further help support the efficacy of their system, SRL adherents usually make liberal use of price quotations. They might use a daily closing price or a weekly closing price or even intra-day or intra-week highs, or intra-day or intra-week lows. Anything, so long as it hits, or comes within a fathom of, a Speed Resistance Line. Or they can, and sometimes do, use the lines in reverse so that resistance lines become support lines instead. Of course, if all else fails, they can, in hindsight, pick and choose the market index or stocks that best fit the actual results.

To reiterate, no adherent of speed resistance lines has yet explained why they "work." The usual explanation is:

"Because they do." That is not good enough. In fact, speed resistance lines have no proven predictive power whatsoever. Anyone using them is either deluding himself, or is naive, or both. Any success in the market he may realize as a direct result of that usage can only be ascribed to random performance or blind luck.

Do not miscomprehend the message, however. Stock prices do move in trends and future price behavior can frequently be predicted with greater than random accuracy. Successful prediction simply requires the use of more sophisticated techniques than drawing lines on charts.

# 57 On-Balance Volume, Tick Volume, and Money Flows

When technicians wish to appear mystical and better informed than everyone else, they frequently talk in terms of "accumulation" or "distribution." Whether a stock or the market is undergoing accumulation or distribution, they assert, holds the key to future price changes.

For example, if a stock fluctuates within a relatively narrow price range for a period of time and then suddenly moves much higher, a technician might state retrospectively that the stock had been under accumulation. Had the stock broken out to the downside, it would be said to have been under distribution. The characterizations seem strange because during the time the stock was meandering about within its trading range, it is obvious that just as much buying as selling occurred (buying *always* equals selling) and so just as much stock was accumulated as distributed. Accumulation and distribution supposedly measure the extent, if any, to which the stock moves into or out of "strong" or "weak" hands; that is, whether those investors who took positions in the stock during the period of the trading range intend to hold for an extended period of time (strong hands) or whether they will sell out following the smallest gains or losses (weak hands).

*On-Balance Volume.*    One technique for measuring accumulation and distribution is on-balance volume (OBV), first developed by Joseph Granville (*Granville's New Key to Stock Market Profits*).    The on-balance volume system is based upon the assumption that volume trends lead price trends.    Table 54 presents the On-Balance Volume system of measuring supply and demand as applied to a hypothetical stock, initially priced at $30, trading through two subsequent days.

TABLE 54

ON-BALANCE VOLUME: EXAMPLE 1

| Day | Price | Price Change | Volume | On-Balance Volume | Cumulative On-Balance Volume |
|---|---|---|---|---|---|
| Friday | $30 | | | | 0 |
| Monday | 32 | + 2 | 10,000 | + 10,000 | + 10,000 |
| Tuesday | 30 | − 2 | 4,000 | − 4,000 | + 6,000 |

Each day's on-balance volume figure equals the volume for the day with the appended plus or minus sign signifying whether the stock rose or fell on the day.

The cumulative on-balance volume series is calculated by adding successive daily OBV figures.    The total is increased when the stock gains in price and is decreased when the stock falls.    If cumulative on-balance volume is positive, the stock is under accumulation, and if cumulative OBV is negative, the stock is being distributed.    In each case the stock price should follow the lead of volume − in theory, at least.

In Example 1 the stock rose two points on Monday on a volume of 10,000 shares, and so the cumulative on-balance volume rose from zero to +10,000.    On Tuesday the price declined two points, returning to its initial price of $30 on a volume of 4,000 shares. Since the price change was negative, all of the volume for that day was subtracted from the previously accumulated OBV total, reducing it to 6,000 shares. Although an OBV proponent would normally require much more than two or three days of data, reduced to its essence this hypothetical example reflects a bullish situation. Although the price of the stock finally closed at its beginning level, it had a net +6,000 shares of on-balance volume. According to the theory, volume leads price, so future price changes should "catch up" with volume by being positive on balance.

Contrast this with the opposite case wherein the volume registered on Monday and Tuesday is reversed (Example 2, Table 55).

TABLE 55

ON-BALANCE VOLUME: EXAMPLE 2

| Day | Price | Price Change | Volume | On-Balance Volume | Cumulative On-Balance Volume |
|-----|-------|--------------|--------|-------------------|------------------------------|
| Friday | $30 | | | | 0 |
| Monday | 32 | + 2 | 4,000 | + 4,000 | + 4,000 |
| Tuesday | 30 | − 2 | 10,000 | − 10,000 | − 6,000 |

In this second example, on-balance volume accumulated to a net negative sum during a period when price remained the same. The OBV technician would normally expect price declines to follow.

Note that the magnitude of a price change is irrelevant in the standard on-balance volume calculation. The examples have assumed two point changes each day, but either one could as easily have been an eighth of a point or ten points. In assigning the proper sign to the on-balance volume, it is only the direction of the price change that counts, not its magnitude.

*Money Flow.* Lest you think that on-balance volume is the holy grail of stock timing, be advised that there is a set of alternative theories which frequently lead to diametrically opposite conclusions from those drawn from OBV.

These theories center around a concept called "money flow." One of the simplest methods of quantifying money flow is to multiply daily volume by dollar price change prior to accumulating the daily readings. Another variant is to multiply volume by closing stock price. The common theme of OBV and each of these money flow methods is that the *more* volume used to produce any given price change, the greater, and more significant, is the reading.

The most interesting money flow variant, however, is based upon a system originally popularized by Jesse Livermore, the renowned Wall Street speculator of the 1920s. This variant holds that the *less* volume required to produce a given price change, the more significant is the reading. This is a precisely *opposite* theory to that underlying the other methods.

According to legend, Livermore would conduct rather expensive experiments with individual stocks to determine the sensitivity of supply and demand pressures. He might, for example, accumulate 10,000 shares of a $30 stock, pushing it up to $32 in the process. He would then proceed to sell the 10,000 shares. If, as in our first OBV illustration (Table 54), the stock declined to $30 merely by the time he had sold 4,000 shares, it would be apparent that it was "easier" (required fewer shares) to push the price down than up. Even though the OBV technique would show a bullish accumulation of 6,000 shares, Livermore would maintain that the situation was bearish because the stock price had a downward bias. By similar logic, the bearish OBV illustration in Table 55 would be considered bullish by the Livermore theory.

To quantify this money flow method, simply divide each day's price change by share volume to determine the amount of price change *per unit of volume.* Then accumulate the daily quotients. Given a trading volume of say, 10,000 shares, a gain of two points would be deemed twice as bullish as a gain of one point, while a two point decline would be twice as bearish as a one point drop. Table 56 presents a hypothet-

TABLE 56

MONEY FLOW EXAMPLE

| Day | Price | Price Change | Volume (ths. shrs.) | Money Flow: Price Chg. ÷ Vol. | Cumulative Money Flow |
|---|---|---|---|---|---|
| Friday | $30 | — | — | — | 0 |
| Monday | 31 | + 1 | 10 | + 0.10 | + 0.10 |
| Tuesday | 33 | + 2 | 10 | + 0.20 | + 0.30 |
| Wednesday | 30 | − 3 | 5 | − 0.60 | − 0.30 |

ical illustration. Note that the Tuesday money flow of +0.20 (equivalent to a 20 cent price gain per each 1,000 shares of volume) was twice as bullish as Monday's +0.10 reading because the price change on an equal volume was twice as great (+2 points versus +1). The simple on-balance volume technique described earlier would have counted each day equally bullish.

After a sharp Wednesday decline the stock price had made no net progress for the week. The on-balance volume technique would have shown a bullish net *accumulation* of 15,000 shares (10,000 + 10,000 − 5,000). In contrast, the money flow method shows a net *distribution* of −0.30. (The Wednesday money flow was disastrous with a small 5,000 share volume resulting in a 3 point collapse.)

*Tick Volume.* Several refinements can be made in all of the preceding methods. One of the most popular, but also one of the most difficult to calculate due to the lack of readily available data, is "tick" volume.

The OBV and money flow systems measure price and volume fluctuations no more frequently than daily and have been criticized for not penetrating deeply enough into the micro-economics of securities trading. Some years ago pioneering technical analyst Donald Worden hypothesized that it would be more logical to measure supply and demand on a trade by trade basis.

Daily price changes almost always consist of many

small changes caused by many individual trades. If analyzed independently, these trades might yield significantly different conclusions. Some would have resulted in price gains ("up ticks"), and others in price declines ("down ticks"). While a stock might go up two points on a given day, thus normally casting all of that day's volume into the plus category, it is conceivable that most of the volume might have occurred on down ticks and trades resulting in rising prices might have been accompanied by relatively light volume.

In other words, tick volume aficionados perform the same calculations on an *every transaction basis* as OBV and money flow technicians perform on a *once a day basis*. Special variants of the tick volume method analyze large transactions only; say, greater than 100, 1,000, or even 10,000 shares.

The pros and cons of the tick volume approach are very much the same as those which apply to on-balance volume and money flow. Tick volume merely carries the calculation a step deeper into the intricacies of supply and demand. Having done so, it may be calculated and interpreted in either the OBV or money flow manners.

*Critique.* A problem inherent in all of these techniques in their popular forms is that they are very "stock dependent," rendering inter-security comparisons extremely difficult, if not impossible. Comparisons are vital, of course, to the task of selecting a stock, or set of stocks, which is most opportune for current purchase or sale. Large companies with many shares outstanding and heavy trading volume show wider OBV, money flow, and tick volume swings than stocks with very low volume. The money flow method, which gives extra weight to large price changes, poses another problem. Here, higher priced stocks, which are more likely to show large dollar price changes, experience wider money flow changes than very low priced stocks which fluctuate more narrowly in price.

The latter problem can best be resolved by substituting percentage price changes for dollar price changes. This puts every stock on a relatively equal price change basis. The former problem of unequal trading activity is more difficult to resolve. One remedy is to first relate a stock's trading volume to the number of shares the company has outstanding. Another is to scale all stocks by relating each stock's OBV, money flow, or tick readings to themselves; that is, express each current reading in terms of the average readings in the days, weeks, or months which preceded it.

Finally, although the illustrations have generally made use of the cumulative concept, with successive OBV, money flow, or tick readings added up on a continuous accumulating score, such an analytical method is not required. Individual, non-cumulative, daily readings can be analyzed independently or, alternatively, averages of recent days' or weeks' readings can be computed. Whichever method is used, the important point is that the final volume readings are ultimately to be compared with the stock price to detect divergence between the two and hence accumulation or distribution of the stock. The volume series is universally held to lead price.

Unfortunately none of these methods have been rigorously tested in a scientific manner, and it is impossible to state definitely how reliable they are. The fact that a few of the techniques can lead to diametrically opposite conclusions and may be mutually incompatible is suspicious in and of itself.

Examples of individual stock successes can, of course, be easily constructed, and analysts wishing to present a case in support of their favorite technique are quick to offer instances which conform to their preconceived notions of proper behavior. Nevertheless, until conscientiously performed studies have been conducted to adequately test each of the various techniques and their underlying theories, all of them should be approached with extreme caution — which is to say that, at this point, there is no compelling reason to use any of them in an integrated stock selection system.

# 58 Relative Strength: Buy High, Sell Higher

While preceding chapters have been somewhat critical of chart reading, trend lines, and speed resistance analysis, do not be misled. The random walk hypothesis notwithstanding, individual stocks and the market as a whole do tend to move in trends. Investor psychology is ill-conditioned to price individual securities at their fair values. It tends to be caught up in the news of the moment and seems to be self-propelling as well, so that prices frequently move far beyond any reasonable estimate of intrinsic value. At the end of bull markets prices are usually far above any measure of fair values, while at bear market extremes prices are invariably well below intrinsic values.

Chart and trendline analysis is grounded partially on highly subjective, crude, and largely inefficient measurements of price trends. The easy availability of computer facilities makes it possible to be far more objective and precise in trend measurement and to rigorously test stock and market timing systems. One of the best tested systems is relative strength. In its most general sense, the relative strength theory states that stocks which have been strong relative to all other stocks should continue to be relatively stronger in the future, and securities which have been relatively weak tend to continue to be relatively weaker. Note that in this general form it is not absolute price strength or weakness which counts, but rather relative strength or weakness. For example, a security may be advancing in price but because most other security prices are advancing at a much faster rate, the stock may be weak relative to the market, even though it is strong in an absolute sense.

The relative strength theory is mutually incompatible with the random walk hypothesis, which says simply that past prices contain no information that can be of any use whatsoever in forecasting future prices. Many active market participants seem to believe in and practice some variant of the relative strength theory, while most academic observers of the stock market accept the random walk hypothesis. The degree of disagreement between these groups is illustrated by examining the relative strength work of Robert A. Levy, a successful fund manager and computer researcher, in the light of criticism leveled at his work by the academic establishment.

Levy summarized his most important research conclusions in the November 1967 issue of the *Financial Analysts Journal* ("Random Walks: Reality or Myth"). His study was based upon an analysis of weekly closing prices of 200 NYSE common stocks for the 260 week period beginning October 25, 1960 and ending October 15, 1965. Each week the 200 stocks were ranked on the basis of their relative price performance of the preceding 26 weeks (specifically, the extent to which the current price was above or below the average price of the last 26 weeks). Levy then experimented with various portfolio strategies based on different strength ranks.

For example, one simulated portfolio purchased stocks which, on a given week, were ranked in the top 10% of the 200 issues on the basis of price strength. These stocks were held in the portfolio until they fell out of the top 80% at which time they were sold. For the five year time period under study, this simulated portfolio provided an annual rate of return of 20.0%, after 2% round trip commission costs. By restricting new purchases to only those stocks in the top 5% of relative strength ranks, performance was improved significantly. One simulation based on this buy criterion and a sell criterion which liquidated securities when they fell out of the top 70% of the weekly relative strength ranking, returned 26.1% per annum, nearly 2½ times the return that would have been achieved by a portfolio composed of stocks selected at random.

By factoring in additional requirements on stock volatility,

Levy conducted simulations returning as much as 30% per annum. Some of these simulated returns were accompanied by significantly greater portfolio risk. However, by constructing portfolios partly of strong stocks and partly of relatively riskless bonds, the overall portfolio risk was reduced, while returns continued at rates well above those which would have been achieved by random selection techniques.

In an article accompanying Levy's, Michael C. Jensen posed strong objections to Levy's conclusions ("Random Walks: Reality or Myth — Comment," *Financial Analysts Journal,* November 1967). Jensen stated that Levy's research was biased on several counts including assumptions of the returns accruing to the comparative random portfolio, treatment of risk, certain problems of sampling error and selection bias, and assumptions regarding available transaction prices. Jensen's criticisms failed to override Levy's primary conclusion that relative strength was a successful prediction device. However, Jensen later went on to more extensively test the system. In a research study conducted with George A. Bennington (*Journal of Finance,* May 1970), the identical selection methods were tested over seven five-year holding periods, 1931-1935, 1936-1940, . . . 1961-1965. Jensen found that in several of the early test periods, especially during the 1930s and 1940s, Levy's relative strength system did not perform as well as a simple buy and hold strategy (although it did "work" in later years). Strangely enough Jensen's results did not even approximate Levy's in the roughly equivalent 1961-1965 holding period, a finding which suggests that one of the studies is somewhat suspect.

Nevertheless, Jensen's findings, even if accurate, do not necessarily invalidate the relative strength hypothesis. To some extent his results merely define the type of market environment in which it is likely to be more or less profitable. It is probably not coincidence, for example, that in Jensen's tests the relative strength system performed most poorly during the 1930s and 1940s, a period characterized by extremely oversold and "value" oriented markets. In succeeding decades more emphasis was placed on performance as stocks first drew even with and then surpassed classic standards of fair value.

Levy also presented evidence (confirmed by the author's own extensive studies) that relative strength performs best in a rising market and that during and following periods of general market weakness, strategies other than purchasing relatively strong stocks are optimal.  At major bear market troughs, for example, relatively weak stocks tend to bounce up fastest, while stocks which have failed to decline much in the preceding bear market are often stodgy issues which rarely provide outstanding profits in any kind of market.

In addition, relatively weak stocks tend to outperform the

## TABLE 57

### RELATIVE STRENGTH AND AMEX STOCKS (1963-1971)

| Strength Group | Average Future 3 Month Return | Annual Rate of Return | Volatility (Risk) Measure |
|---|---|---|---|
| 1 | +6.0% | +26.5% | 29.8% |
| 2 | +5.6% | +24.3% | 28.0% |
| 3 | +5.0% | +21.8% | 27.6% |
| 4 | +4.3% | +18.6% | 27.1% |
| 5 | +3.7% | +15.8% | 28.7% |

market near year-ends after they have been subjected to unusually heavy selling pressure by investors realizing capital losses for tax purposes.

Relative strength is therefore a valid stock selection tool less than half the time.  Any study which analyzes the relative strength system over all types of markets is biased against the method before it even gets started.  Recognition of this factor makes most relative strength study results even better than they appear in first light.

Table 57 presents some very basic results from a weekly strength study conducted by the author on all Amex listed common stocks between September 1963 and June 1971. Over 320,000 weekly price observations were considered in all. Each week all of the stocks were ranked and divided into five equal groups ranging from strongest to weakest (1-5) on the basis of relative price strength. Each quintile represents over 64,000 observations. Relative price strength was measured by means of a "Strength Rating," calculated for each stock as follows: First, each week the average price of the stock over the current and 29 preceding weeks was calculated — a 30 week average price. Second, the Strength Rating was computed by dividing the current 30 week average price by the comparable 30 week average price of 13 weeks earlier. The ratio effectively provides a *rating* of long term price *strength,* (i.e., a "Strength Rating"). The results clearly show that the stronger the stock, the better the subsequent three month price performance (comparable returns were obtained for stock holding periods other than three months), and with no significant increase in volatility of return (the academicians' favorite measure of risk). Superior returns were obtained by establishing additional, and more complex, strength criteria and by confining the analysis to market environments particularly conducive to the success of relative strength. However, the results presented here are basic and well grounded in theory and demonstrate again the efficacy of a relative strength stock selection system. Aside from the overall market atmosphere, the only important caveat which need be applied to the relative strength system is a check on unusual causes of observed price strength, such as tender offers, which might induce a one-time price strength boost.

The validity of relative strength has been confirmed in numerous other studies and there is reason to believe that the finest works in this field remain unpublished. In sum, relative strength is a profitable, time tested stock selection technique worthy of incorporation into an overall portfolio strategy.

# 59 Weak Stocks: When Are They a Buy?

Relative strength is certainly one of the most well studied theories of technical analysis. But it is also true that for every stock that is relatively strong, there is one that is relatively weak. When should these weak issues be purchased?

Stocks which have experienced a relatively weak price performance do occasionally make exceptionally good buys. One reason is that issues which have declined significantly are often priced far below their true value. Although "value" is admittedly an elusive and difficult to define concept, an extremely low price/value ratio is evidence that a stock will at some time recover to a more normal price. As investors overdo pessimism as much as they overdo optimism, it follows that any deterioration in value can be overrun by an excessive deterioration in price.

Another reason for the occasional superiority of weak stocks is the simple mathematical fact that the further a stock falls, the more room there is for subsequent recovery. (Note that the converse is not true. That is, it would be fallacious to state that the further a stock falls the less room there is for further price decline. Regardless of how much a stock has fallen, it can always decline an additional 100%.) For example, if a $4 stock moves to $8 it increases 100%. But if the stock first drops in half to $2, a subsequent move to $8 will be a 300% gain; and if it first falls in half again to $1, the move to $8 will constitute a 700% gain.

In addition to these two general qualities, there are two times in particular that excellent purchase opportunities emerge for weak stocks, one timed to cyclical market swings, the other to seasonal patterns.

The first is near major cyclical market lows. Stocks which have declined the most during severe and extended market reactions often rebound fastest in ensuing price recoveries. The reason is that they are usually the most oversold issues in the market. Investors are often uncertain whether these companies will ever be able to recover from their recession-induced losses. The marketplace is thus faced with the alternative of pricing these companies at a minuscule liquidating value, or pricing them at a value which would reflect their future earnings capability if they managed to recover. Since the probabilities of these two events are often unclear, pervasive bear market pessimism usually prevails and investors assign a much lower value to individual stocks than is warranted. Consequently, the weakest stocks are likely to make exceptionally good recovery buys.

The second particularly propitious time to buy weak stocks is at year-end. From late November through mid-December investors frequently sell stocks to realize capital losses for income tax purposes. Naturally the stocks which are most prone to this type of selling are those which have declined the most during the previous year. Therefore, from about December 15 through December 23 (i.e., up to within one week prior to the end of the calendar year – losses must be realized by this time for tax purposes), purchases of exceptionally weak stocks are often highly rewarding.

During major bull market years, such as 1967, 1968, and 1975, relatively few stocks decline in price, and tax loss selling is not a significant factor. However, when the averages decline sharply such as they did in 1966, 1969, 1973, and 1974, issues which have declined the most encounter unusual tax loss selling pressure. As tax conscious investors rush to sell them during the last few weeks of the year, the stocks become even further depressed. This selling is not as much a reflection upon the merits of the companies as investments in their own right, as it is a function of the end of most individuals' tax year.

Table 58 reveals the results of such a purchase strategy from 1964 through 1971. Compilations for 1966, 1967, and 1968 were made by Larry E. Shaffer in an unpublished academic thesis. (The 1969 experience is not included due to the overwhelming number of extremely weak stocks rendering calculation extremely difficult.) The strategy is based upon purchase of issues which made new yearly lows around December 15-20 on the New York Stock Exchange. Investment performance is measured over the subsequent two month period, which appears to be the length of time required for these issues to regain normal valuation levels.

TABLE 58

YEAR-END WEAK STOCK TRADING STRATEGY

| Holding Period | --- Weak Stocks --- | | S&P 500 |
| | Number | % Change | Percent Change |
| --- | --- | --- | --- |
| Dec. 21, 1964 - Feb. 19, 1965 | 69 | + 8.0% | + 2.2% |
| Dec. 20, 1965 - Feb. 18, 1966 | 60 | + 0.4% | + 0.8% |
| Dec. 15, 1966 - Feb. 15, 1967 | 45 | + 18.0% | + 8.1% |
| Dec. 15, 1967 - Feb. 15, 1968 | 45 | + 7.4% | − 5.0% |
| Dec. 15, 1968 - Feb. 15, 1969 | 24 | + 5.0% | − 3.7% |
| Dec. 21, 1970 - Feb. 16, 1971 | 15 | + 45.9% | + 9.7% |
| Dec. 20, 1971 - Feb. 15, 1972 | 17 | + 11.2% | + 3.4% |
| Geometric Average Rate of Return | | + 12.9% | + 2 .1% |
| Annualized Compounded Rate of Return | | + 107.1% | + 13.2% |

Although the weak stocks did not always outperform the market around year-end, the exceptions usually occurred following years in which the market rose significantly and tax loss selling was not a factor.   After major bear market declines the very weakest stocks usually achieved exceptional gains from mid-December through mid-February, invariably outpacing the market, and occasionally rising even when the market fell.

The best of all worlds, then, is the purchase of weak stocks at a year-end which happens to precisely coincide with the end of a major bear market depression. Then the advantages of both bear market and tax selling weakness can be gained. Such events occurred in 1966, 1970, and 1974.

The 1974 experience is not presented in the table. However, a representative sampling of extremely weak issues purchased in mid-December 1974, following the 2½ year bear market and coinciding with the major cyclical trough, would have performed superbly in the ensuing few months. Based upon the author's observations, an associate decided to test this theory and purchased a diversified portfolio of nearly fifty stocks exhibiting extreme relative weakness in the last half of December. Within ten weeks his portfolio had doubled in value. 1974 may have been a once in a lifetime opportunity in terms of the coincidence of a severe bear market terminating at the same time tax selling was at its peak, but nevertheless this experience is a dramatic answer to academicians who ask for proof that technical theories work. The market also rallied, though at a much lesser rate; the Standard & Poor's 500 Index, for example, appreciated only about 25%.

Following years of especially severe declines there also seems to be a general tendency for the market itself to rally from mid-December into the first month or two of the new year (e.g., 1966, 1969, 1973, and 1974). In part this may be caused by an abnormal depression of prices throughout the entire market induced by year-end tax selling pressures.

Several implications can be drawn from the foregoing analysis. First, the purchase of relatively strong stocks does not always constitute the best strategy. For two months of almost every year weak stocks outperform strong stocks, and the syndrome is repeated coming off major market bottoms.

Second, tax selling should seldom be done for its own sake. Too often, highly profitable price moves are missed for the sake of withholding a few dollars from the Internal Revenue Service. Given the demonstrably superior seasonal returns of weak stocks, however, an excellent tax selling strategy can be evolved. To avoid the crowd and realize superior overall returns, investors should sell depressed issues to realize tax losses around mid-November, *before* the stocks become further depressed by the normal December rush of tax selling. Investors should then repurchase the stocks in mid to late December, after the required 31 day waiting period, and just in time to catch their interim low prices. The stocks will then receive the benefit of late December and early January buying by value conscious investors *and* the subsequent buying by tax loss sellers when they enter the market to repurchase their securities.

Finally, as with every stock selection technique, care must be exercised in its implementation and other factors, such as the market cycle position, must be considered in conjunction with the basic system in order to bring forth its greatest value.

# 60 The Insiders: America's Most Knowledgeable Investors

Every investor wants inside information. To know ahead of the marketplace what a company (and its stock) is going to do is a sure route to financial success. To prevent manipulative abuses the Securities and Exchange Commission has placed impressive legal obstacles in the paths of investors desiring to obtain such information. At this writing the Securities and Exchange Commission and the New York Stock Exchange both have actions pending against the investment advisor who discovered and exposed the Equity Funding Corporation scandal. The watch dogs of Wall Street maintain that when an advisor discovers such significant news, he has no right to use it for his own profit or for the profit of his clients, but must instead make the information public so all investors will be equally informed. Despite these hurdles, several academic studies have demonstrated that it is still possible to use "inside information" − obtained, of all places, from the S.E.C. and the stock exchanges themselves.

"Insiders" are defined as company officers, directors, and large stockholders. They are all required by law to report details of every transaction they make in the securities of their own company soon after the actual executions.

Approximately one or two months later a complete record of these transactions is published in the S.E.C.'s "Official Summary of Security Transactions and Holdings." Based on publicly known data contained in the "Official Summary," several research studies have shown that, on the average, stocks which have had heavy insider buying provide significantly above average returns. Stocks exhibiting heavy insider selling tend to subsequently underperform the market.

The classic study on insider activity was conducted at Portland State University by Professor Shannon Pratt and Charles DeVere. Pratt and DeVere studied 52,000 insider transactions made in about 800 NYSE listed stocks between 1960 and 1966. All trades were reported in the S.E.C.'s "Official Summary." After some experimentation, an insider buy signal was defined as the open market purchase of common stock by at least three company insiders within one month. The buying activity had to be unanimous — there could be no insiders selling the stock. An insider sell signal was defined with the same criteria: three or more insiders selling the stock within a month and none buying. Repeat buy and sell signals within six months of an original signal were ignored. In all, 211 insider buy signals and 272 insider sell signals were generated in the seven year period. Price performance of the insider buy and sell stock groups following the signals is graphically illustrated in Figure 21.

Note that from the very first month of the signal, stocks with heavy insider buying significantly outperformed stocks with heavy insider selling. Although about two months generally elapse between the time of the actual insider transactions and the time the public finally gains knowledge of the trades in the "Official Summary," there apparently is still ample opportunity to profit from the information. Only a small proportion of the total difference in subsequent investment return was realized in the first two months following the original signal. Even allowing for the two month reporting lag (which, in the case of listed stocks, can be reduced by analyzing the information directly from the exchanges'

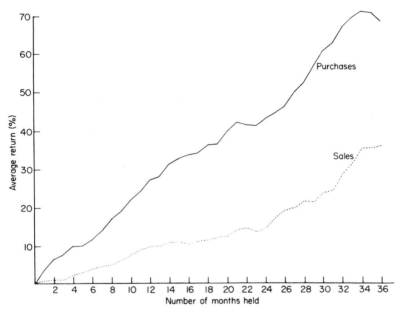

FIGURE 21. Insider Signals — Average cumulative investment performance (price return plus dividends) of insider buy and sell signal stocks, 1 to 36 month holding periods.

records), the spread between price performance of stocks with insider buying and insider selling widened for 2½ years, an amazingly long time period. By that time the buy group had returned 59.2% and the sell group only 27.1%. The month by month change in accumulated return seems incredibly consistent for a long period after the insider signal. On an annual rate of return basis, the optimal holding period appeared to be about twelve months following public receipt of the insider data. At that point the buy group returned 24.0% and the sell group only 9.9%. Furthermore, the extra returns furnished by the buy group were achieved without incurring greater risk (volatility) in the portfolio.

Thus the study provides incontrovertible evidence that stocks with insider buying tend to dramatically outperform the market.  It is worth noting, however, that stocks with insider selling did not fall in price; they merely appreciated at a below average rate.  In bull markets, stocks with heavy insider buying tended to furnish above average returns, while stocks with insider selling also advanced, but at a lesser rate than that of the market.  In major bear markets, stocks with insider selling suffered far worse declines than average, while issues exhibiting insider buying also declined, but at a rate somewhat less than that of the market.  Thus, the optimal strategy would appear to be to purchase stocks with insider buying in bull markets and to sell short stocks with insider selling in bear markets.

Since the first appearance of this study, it has been replicated in different time periods and with Amex as well as NYSE issues.  The original results have been uniformly confirmed, and no reputable studies have *ever* shown insider information to be valueless.  The "system" has attracted wide notice and numerous private and institutional investors now use it in their security selection processes.  Given such widespread usage, it would not be surprising if the system suffers in the future as traders rush to buy stocks which exhibit insider buying activity and push their prices up to such an extent as to eliminate their prospective extra returns.  Some companies may even encourage insider buying, hoping to influence analysts.  Timeliness and interpretation is, in other words, increasingly important.

The best future performance will also undoubtedly require establishing more exacting criteria for use of the insider data.  For example, one might specify a larger number of insiders for a buy or sell signal (i.e., greater than three), or eliminate from consideration especially large companies which have many officers and directors ("insiders") and whose resultingly frequent buy and sell signals may not be too meaningful.  Other elements to consider might include the consistency of insider buying or selling activity through time, the size of the insider trades (small, insignificant transactions might be excluded), and the use of the insider data in conjunction with other fundamental and technical factors.

Still, until proved otherwise, this publicly available inside information system is one of the best of all technical methods. It disproves the so-called efficient market hypothesis out of hand. It *is* possible to profit from publicly available information.

(Note: The author is editor of *The Insiders*, an investment advisory service providing comprehensive coverage of insider trading activities. Emphasizing timeliness of data reporting and extensive computer-aided analysis, *The Insiders* identifies stocks with especially significant activity and assigns an "Insider Rating" to every listed stock based on the number of insiders buying and selling, the size, recency, and price of their transactions, the insiders' position in the company, and other pertinent information. A complimentary copy of *The Insiders* may be obtained by writing to the author at 3471 North Federal Highway, Fort Lauderdale, Florida 33306.)

# 61 Volatility Analysis

Practically all stock selection techniques are designed to identify issues that will rise faster than average in bull markets or hold up better than average in bear markets. Unfortunately, few stocks possess *both* attributes. Stocks that outperform the market on the upside tend to fall most rapidly in a general decline, while those that lag behind an advance tend to suffer less in a collapse.

Just as we have seen that price trends seem to persist under certain conditions, the tendency of a specific stock or group of stocks to exhibit above average volatility also persists over time. But while all price trends ultimately come to an end, the volatility characteristics of most stocks persist for years or even decades. Hence volatility can, in and of itself, be an especially useful stock selection criterion.

When the market is expected to rise, diversified portfolios

of stocks with a history of highly volatile price swings will almost certainly outperform the market averages. Random walk theorists hasten to attribute these above average returns to the additional risk inherent in volatile stocks. They claim that on a "risk adjusted basis," such portfolios will provide only average returns. Their concept is easily proven (to their own satisfaction, at least) by defining risk as volatility — hence they contend that higher returns accruing to portfolios of volatile stocks are directly attributable to higher risk and do not represent superior stock selection.

Investors interested in making money rather than debating semantics might well argue that the only risk they fear is the risk of loss, and that kind of risk is low in a rising market. On the other hand, in a falling market almost every diversified portfolio will lose money and an investor who expects a decline should be out of stocks altogether, not merely switching to supposedly lower risk (i.e. less volatile) stocks that will just lose money for him more slowly.

Thus, to the extent that investments are confined to periods of generally rising prices, highly volatile stocks are superior investments and can provide above average returns on a far more consistent basis than most other stock selection techniques.

*Beta Volatility.* "Volatility" can be measured in many ways. One crude method is to calculate each stock's average daily or weekly price change (ignoring the sign, up or down, of those changes) over the past year or two. A far more sophisticated approach is to correlate a stock's daily or weekly percent price changes with the daily or weekly percent price changes of a broad based market index (e.g., Standard & Poor's 500 Index). This type of relative volatility is called a "Beta" statistic and is derived from a complex mathematical calculation, usually made by computer.

A Beta tells not just how volatile a stock has been, but how volatile it has been *relative to the market.* An extremely useful characteristic of Beta statistics is that they are so stable through time that it is relatively unimportant whether they are calculated from daily, weekly, or monthly data, or whether the historical base used in the calculation is one, two, or even five years in length.

A Beta of 1.00 means that, on average, a stock has traditionally matched the market's swings, moving just as rapidly as the averages on both the upside and downside, a Beta greater than 1.00 reflects above average volatility, and a Beta less than 1.00 indicates below average volatility. A Beta that is actually less than zero — a negative Beta — is typical of issues that move contrary to the general market, going down in bull markets and rising in bear markets. (Gold mining stocks often have negative Betas.)

Betas have been so widely used in recent years that they have become available at low cost to most investors. They have been widely studied and numerous historical analyses have proven that portfolios of stocks with high Betas will continue to exhibit the characteristic of high volatility in the future. It is worth noting, however, that Betas do have a tendency to drift back towards 1.00. Volatile portfolios selected on the basis of Beta alone will therefore never be quite as volatile as expected, although the Beta volatility estimate will still be very good.

*Square Root Volatility.* Low priced stocks are more volatile than high priced stocks. A formal statement of that assertion is the Square Root Rule which hypothesizes that the magnitude of a stock's price move is directly related to the price of the stock: the lower the price of the stock the more volatile it is, and, the higher the price of the stock the less volatile it is.

Specifically, the Square Root Rule states that given a certain market advance all stocks change in price by adding a constant amount to the square root of their beginning prices. For example, if the average priced stock advances from $25 to $36, the square root of the average price has moved from 5 (the square root of 25) to 6 (the square root of 36), or up 1 point. In accordance with the Square Root Rule, we would then expect all other stocks to add 1 point to the square root of their prices.

Hence, a $4 stock (whose square root is 2) should advance to $9 (the square root of 9 is 3), and a $100 stock (whose square root is 10) should advance to 121 (the square root of 121 is 11). Table 59 summarizes the results.

TABLE 59 – SQUARE ROOT VOLATILITY

| Starting Price | Ending Price | Percent Change |
|---|---|---|
| $   4 | $    9 | +  125% |
| $   25 | $   36 | +   44% |
| $  100 | $  121 | +   21% |

Note that although each stock adds 1 point to the square root of its beginning price the percentage changes in actual price are dramatically different. The lower the price of the stock the greater is its percentage advance and the higher the price of the stock the less is its percentage advance.

In a declining market, when all stocks should *lose* the same number of points from the square root of their beginning prices, we would expect the lower priced stocks to decline more rapidly and the higher priced issues to decline at a somewhat lesser rate. Unlike the Beta statistic the Square Root Volatility for a stock is always positive: All stocks are always expected to move in the same direction, albeit in different magnitudes, as the market. As a measure of expected performance for a single stock, this is, of course, somewhat unrealistic since all stocks do not always move in the same direction as the market. However, like the Beta statistic, as the portfolio becomes more broadly diversified Square Root Volatility becomes a better measure of expected percentage change. For very large portfolios it is extremely accurate. Indeed, the author's research reveals that Square Root Volatility is usually superior to Beta as an estimator of future expected return, even though Betas are much better known and more widely used.

*Conclusion.* Used independently or jointly, the Beta and Square Root Volatility measures are valuable and highly functional stock selection tools. Most investors would improve their overall performance if they refined their market timing techniques and simply resorted to holding highly volatile securities during bull markets.

# 62 Liquidity: Good or Bad?

Liquidity, or marketability, is the very reason for the existence of a securities market. In any kind of a capitalistic system, one of the major tasks is to raise capital for business startup, growth, and expansion. Most individuals would never subscribe to new security issues if they could not be assured that a market exists in which they could sell the securities if and when they so desire. A public trading market for stocks and bonds satisfies that need. Reduced to its essence, that is the sole economic function of public trading markets.

Liquidity represents the ability to buy or sell shares of a security at a quoted market price. If it is necessary to move a price substantially in order to obtain or liquidate positions, then the security is illiquid. Conversely, if a large position may be bought or sold at a given price, or within a relatively small range of prices, the security is graded high in liquidity.

Positions in liquid securities may be purchased at a lower average price and sold for a higher average price than positions in illiquid securities. Thus, highly liquid securities are more valuable than those possessing a low degree of liquidity. For example, all other things equal, highly liquid stocks such as IBM, General Motors, and AT&T should be afforded a higher valuation in the market than companies which otherwise offer equivalent risk and reward prospects but inferior degrees of liquidity. Securities with poorer liquidity must offer a prospectively greater return to make up for the extra cost involved in buying and selling them. An efficient market therefore prices illiquid securities so that they yield higher than average returns; an end effectively achieved by initially pricing them lower.

The degree of liquidity in a security may be judged by several measures. The most common is the spread between the bid and asked prices. Normally, the larger the bid-asked spread, the lower the degree of liquidity. The purchase price of a stock is initially a function of two variables: First, the price which would be paid given perfect liquidity, and second, the amount which must be paid in excess of the perfect liquidity price; in effect, the amount by which the price must be bid upward in order to obtain the position.

For example, a 3% bid-asked spread of 50-51½ (usually requiring purchase at $51.50, but sale at only $50.00) reflects very poor liquidity, whereas a 0.5% bid-asked spread of 50-50¼ represents a security with a highly liquid trading market. Listed stocks generally have narrower bid-asked spreads, and thus better liquidity, than over-the-counter issues.

As a rule, the greater the number of shares outstanding, or the greater the total dollar value of those shares, the better is the liquidity because the security has a potentially broader following. At any given time more shares are likely to be ordered for purchase and more shares are likely to be offered for sale. It is obviously easier to obtain or liquidate a security position when that security is actively traded than when it is necessary to search for prospective sellers or buyers. To the extent that outstanding shares might be *closely held* — that is, withheld from trading in the marketplace by their owners — the lesser is the total number of shares which, in effect, are serving to enhance liquidity. Thus, floating supply, the total number of shares outstanding minus the number of shares closely held, is often a good proxy for the degree of liquidity in the marketplace. The greater the floating supply, the better the liquidity.

Another measure of liquidity is the relatively new concept of *liquidity betas*. Liquidity betas define the number of dollars of volume that has historically been required to move a stock up or down 1%. The higher a stock's liquidity beta, the greater is the number of shares that have been transacted in the stock without moving the price significantly and therefore the more liquid the stock has been. The working assumption is that the liquidity beta will persist into the future.

There are no hard and fast rules on how much liquidity is required in a given portfolio. The need for liquidity resides in the possibility that some or all portfolio positions might be sold in the future. If it is unlikely that portfolio positions will need to be liquidated, then the liquidity requirement is low, and its role in stock selection should be minimal. However, if there is a high probability that funds may be withdrawn from the portfolio, then either the entire portfolio should be generally liquid or certain portions of it should be highly liquid.

Most institutional investors seek high liquidity, even though few have an obvious need for it. Pension funds, for example, are rarely faced with large cash withdrawals necessitating the sale of portfolio holdings to raise cash. Therefore, the entire fund portfolio need not be liquid. In fact, to the extent that a largely non-liquid position would provide higher returns, it would be most appropriate for such an institution. On the other hand, a small mutual fund probably requires high liquidity so that it can be prepared for the possibility of a few large redemptions.

The need for portfolio liquidity, then, is a function of the unique requirements of its owner. The typical individual investor should provide for his liquidity needs through savings accounts, insurance, etc., and look to his stock market holdings as a source of potential benefits, not as a source of liquidity. If liquidity is not a prime portfolio objective, then stocks with *low* liquidity should be preferred. As noted earlier, theory suggests they should provide higher returns. Experience shows that, in fact, they do just that.

"Thin stocks," those with a very small floating supply of shares, are usually among the marketplace's most volatile issues. As we have seen in the previous chapter, high volatility is a desired attribute in a rising market. Hence thin stocks represent a superior investment for many investors.

If a stock with a small floating supply becomes very active, its *Volume Turnover Ratio* (annualized trading volume as a percent of floating supply) will be high. A less actively traded stock with a large capitalization will have a relatively low Volume Turnover Ratio. The Volume Turnover Ratio is therefore useful in isolating highly volatile stocks that might perform exceptionally well in a bullish environment and thus provides us with yet another useful stock selection indicator.

# PART FOUR
## STOCK SELECTION: FROM THEORY TO PRACTICE

## 63 The Synthesis

Synthesizing a single stock selection strategy from the innumerable available techniques involves far more subjective judgment than consolidating the several dozen best market timing indicators into an econometric model. Fortunately, knowledge of the market's future direction, such as we can gain from the econometric forecasting models, is also the primary ingredient of a stock strategy. Even though some stocks are always rising, it is nearly impossible to construct a properly diversified portfolio of long positions that will outperform interest bearing securities such as treasury bills during a bear market. The excellent interest returns available during the last several bear markets indicate that by far the wisest stock strategy in the next major downtrend will be a no-stock portfolio. Proceeding on that assumption, any stock selection strategy should be bull market oriented.

The three stock selection indicators which have been proven to be most profitable during bull markets are based on: (1) volatility, (2) relative price strength, and (3) insider trading.

Volatility studies, in this application, seek to identify

those stocks which will fluctuate the most in the future. As a rising market will cause most fluctuations to be positive, it is desirable to own stocks that will experience the largest percentage fluctuation. A very basic characteristic of stock price behavior works to an investor's advantage at this point. Stock price changes are unevenly distributed — a statistician would say that the distribution is "skewed to the right." In laymen's terms, this means that positive changes are generally greater in magnitude than negative changes. It is obvious that gains can exceed 100%, while losses never can.

Consider this hypothetical example:   Even though the overwhelming majority of stocks rose in the early months of 1976, an investor lucky (or smart) enough to have selected the ten best performing stocks on the New York Stock Exchange *and* unlucky enough to have also picked the ten worst performers would *still* have experienced a gain far above average.   The list of his losers would have shown an average 20% decline, but all his winners would have more than doubled, one nearly tripling.  The overall return on his twenty stock portfolio would have been 65%. Very, very few comparably diversified portfolios would have matched that record during the first four months of 1976.

In other words, *in anything but a sharply falling market*, it is enough to know which stocks will be the biggest movers in *either* direction because the large gainers will almost always more than offset the large losers.

Although Beta statistics are a very scientific way of measuring a stock's potential volatility, the simple Square Root Rule is superior at forecasting future volatility. A useful compromise between these indicators, one of which has a sound theoretical basis (Beta) and one which has an excellent record in actual application (the Square Root Rule) is to mathematically convert both indicators to the same base and combine them.   This can be accomplished by calculating every stock's potential price appreciation during a 10% market rise on the basis of both Beta and the Square Root Rule and averaging the two statistics.  The result, by itself, provides an excellent guide to future price volatility. But even this can be further improved by consideration of other indicators (e.g. Volume Turnover Ratios and size of common stock floating supply) which are also proxies for future volatility.

The result is that low priced stocks with high volatility, small floating supply, and high volume relative to capitalization are potentially the most volatile. Such stocks may constitute a quite risky portfolio, regardless of how you define risk. As we shall see in Part Five, adequate diversification can probably reduce this risk to an acceptable level for most investors. Those investors requiring even more stable portfolios can simply move in from the extreme ranges of each criteria, selecting medium priced stocks with somewhat lower volatility, greater liquidity, and less extreme Volume Turnover Ratios.

Having determined that a market rise is likely and identified stocks expected to be highly volatile, the next step is to fine tune the selection process. Relative strength and weakness analysis provides a superb time tested technique for accomplishing this task. During continuing bull markets, relative strength identifies those issues currently advancing most rapidly. It is axiomatic that as long as a stock's relative strength rank remains high, its advance is continuing. A weakening relative strength rank provides a warning that the otherwise desirable volatility may be about to occur in the wrong direction, and such stocks can then be replaced.

At the very beginning of bull markets and during the tax loss selling season in the last few weeks of each year, the strongest stocks should be temporarily disdained in preference to the relatively weakest stocks. It is at the birth of new bull markets that some of the most dynamic portfolio gains will accrue. The purchase of highly volatile, weak stocks at market lows will often provide doublers in the short span of just a few weeks.

An additional refinement in an overall stock selection strategy is to restrict actual investments to issues exhibiting unusual levels of insider buying. Besides enhancing upside potential, insider buying provides a measure of insurance against extreme losses in the event the bull market prognosis proves erroneous.

Volatility provides few clues as to when to sell. Both fading relative strength and a swing from insider buying to insider selling provide a timing mechanism for moving out of one issue and into new positions for further participation in an ongoing market rise.

Investors can further improve their overall stock selection by restricting purchases to issues with below average Price/Earnings Ratios and above average yields, eschewing all high P/E, low yielding issues. Even though the latter may provide excellent returns over shorter periods, rarely are they attractive holdings through multiple market cycles. Many studies have revealed that P/E Ratios can improve portfolio performance in holding periods as short as one year.

After a decision is made to buy a common stock, the company's capital structure should be examined to see if an alternative to the common stock is available that can yield superior rewards or require the assumption of less risk. Convertible bonds and preferreds, for example, may be converted into common stock at the option of the holder. The bonds can be purchased at lower commission rates and with less margin than common stocks, and both bonds and preferreds frequently provide higher interest or dividend yields than the common. Because of the conversion feature, which causes their prices to be tightly linked to the price of the common stock, these securities also occasionally offer equivalent upside price potential, but less downside risk, than the common stock. Another security worth checking on is a common stock purchase warrant. Issued by corporations, warrants entitle their owners to buy a specific number of shares of common stock from the issuing company at a specified price per share during a specified period of time. Warrants are not unlike market created call options, which give to their holders the option to buy common stock from other investors. Both warrants and options are capable of offering highly leveraged plays on common stock price changes. Furthermore, warrants and options, as well as convertible bonds and preferreds, can be useful in structuring less risky hedging strategies.

The complete stock selection strategy outlined in this chapter may lack the excitement of high volume breakouts, upside down head and shoulders patterns, ascending channels, triple top failures, speed resistance lines, five year earnings extrapolations, esoteric new products, and the hottest news from an analyst "who talked to the company this morning." It has one great advantage, however; it works. Thus, when it comes to performance, the excitement will return.

It is impossible to prove that *some* variant of such seemingly appealing approaches as tick volume, money flows, etc. will not work. All that can be said is that they are not yet of proven value. Each generation likes to believe it has found the key that unlocks the door of ultimate knowledge, but behind every unlocked door there is always another locked door waiting for the key to be found that will open it.

Almost thirty years ago no less a market authority than Garfield A. Drew stated, "The trail of forecasting price trends has been well blazed since the early crude attempts, and it is safe to say that no possible avenue of approach has been neglected." In fact, the years since that was written have witnessed literally hundreds of new stock selection systems — only a few of legitimate value, but all deserving of thoughtful attention and study.

The years ahead will witness more developments and discoveries. Most will be valueless, despite claims to the contrary. The key to investment success is to discard those lacking proven theoretical and practical bases and to adopt those which have such bases. As noted above, the current state of knowledge is transitory. But the stock selection system we have outlined should provide performance at this time that is far superior to that commonly achieved by most investors.

# PART FIVE
## A TOTAL FINANCIAL MANAGEMENT SYSTEM

## 64 Diversification: The First Step

Now that we have seen how to identify the market's direction and select stocks to optimally capitalize on bull moves, we must address the aspect of investment management which the average investor hears so much about and practices so little — scientific portfolio management.

The most fundamental error the average individual investor makes is to fail to properly diversify his portfolio. Indeed, the single most important step most investors can take to immediately improve the long range performance of their portfolios relative to the market is to properly diversify their common stock investments.

During the mutual fund boom of the 1950s and 1960s, many individual investors were led to believe that optimal diversification required a portfolio of 100, 200, or even more issues — the "don't put all your eggs in one basket" theory. The funds boasted that they could provide "instant diversification" at less commission cost than smaller investors would have to pay if they acquired odd lots of over 100 issues.

In the latter part of the 1960s a different breed of fund, managed by the "gunslingers" of that day, argued that superior performance could be achieved by concentrating

holdings in a minimum number of carefully selected issues —
the "put all your eggs in one basket and watch that basket"
concept. As the go-go market evolved to its ultimate denoue-
ment, many individual traders adopted the same practice of
riding with one or two high flyers.

Although neither extreme is optimal, the very widely
diversified funds treated their holders better in the long bear
markets than the under-diversified performance funds.

Given an ability to correctly forecast the direction of the
market, volatility becomes desirable. The object of market
timing is to accurately forecast the direction and magnitude
of general price moves. The object of diversification is to
*assure* that the overall portfolio will move in the same direction as the market, be it with greater or lesser volatility.

Most of the volatility of a one stock portfolio consists of
the volatility associated with only that one company. There
is a substantial risk that the stock will not even move in the
same direction as the market, let alone move as much relative
to the market as we would expect on the basis of the stock's
historical volatility. As additional stocks are added, the portfolio will tend to act more and more like the general market.
The extreme is reached when every stock in the market is
purchased in equal dollar amounts. At that point the portfolio will perform exactly like the market for the simple
reason that it is the market.

Over time investors who leverage or hold volatile stocks
should earn above average returns. However, investors who
lack diversification run the risk that their portfolios will not
provide them with the returns they expect *relative* to the
market.

A wide array of studies has shown that almost all such risk
can be eliminated from a portfolio through a relatively
modest program of diversification. These studies have been
soundly based and conducted with the use of elaborate statistical techniques. There can be no argument as to the validity
of their results. Calculated with mathematical precision, and
using several decades of comprehensive historical data,

TABLE 60

DIVERSIFICATION AND REDUCTION OF RISK

| Number of Stocks in Portfolio | Percentage of Risk Eliminated |
|:---:|:---:|
| 2 | 46% |
| 4 | 72% |
| 8 | 81% |
| 16 | 93% |
| 32 | 96% |
| 64 | 98% |
| 500 | 99% |
| All Stocks | 100% |

Table 60 shows the reduction in this type of risk which results from diversification.

A very important assumption implicit in this analysis is that individual issues in the portfolio are not perfectly, or even closely, related. Unfortunately, most market participants, either consciously or unconsciously, select industries and stocks that are closely related. At any given time the typical investor is attracted to broad stock groupings such as Services, Capital Goods, Raw Materials, or even more specific industry groups. Even technical analysts are likely to discover that stocks of companies with similar characteristics are likely to yield buy signals at about the same time. Consequently the percentage of risk eliminated from a typical investor's portfolio will ordinarily be much less than that indicated in the table. Most investors should therefore diversify among a greater number of stocks than shown in the table in order to achieve a given risk reduction.

For most investors, basic portfolio diversification should consist of holding between 20 and 40 stocks unrelated to one another. Several closely related stocks should be viewed as a single issue for the purpose of establishing breadth of diversification. Furthermore, to the extent that several unusually large positions in certain stocks exist, the balance of the portfolio should be spread over a somewhat greater number of issues to partially offset that factor. It is preferable, however, to reduce the over-concentrated positions.

It is also important to bear in mind that the indicated degree of diversification applies to the common stock portion of an investor's portfolio regardless of how small a portion of his total assets are invested in common stocks. For example, an investor with half of his assets in bonds, one-quarter invested in real estate and the balance in common stock should still hold a minimum of 20 stocks in his portfolio. That is, an investor holding any common stocks at all should hold a diversified portfolio of 20 or more issues since to do otherwise is to expose himself to risk for which he cannot expect to receive commensurate reward.

Investors unable to sufficiently diversify their portfolios would be better off if they were to invest in properly diversified mutual funds.

# 65 Leverage: Multiplying Rewards and Risks

"More bang for the buck" aptly describes the concept of leverage, the employment of financial assets in such a way as to provide a potential reward that is more than proportional to the amount of money invested. In return for the possibility of superior rewards, leverage also requires the assumption of equivalently greater risk.

A total investment may draw upon two primary sources for capital: *equity capital* and *debt capital* (borrowing).

Leverage may then be defined mathematically as the ratio of *total* capital to *equity* capital. The smaller the equity portion of the total, the higher the leverage ratio.

*Company Leverage.* There are several ways to employ leverage in the stock market. One of the easiest is to buy and sell common stocks of companies which are themselves highly leveraged. A company which has a relatively low proportion of equity in its total capital structure is, by definition, more highly leveraged than a company with substantially all equity. The primary objective of profit making organizations is to maximize the percent return earned on "total capital" invested. Since "total capital" includes funds raised from both the sale of common stock (equity) and borrowing (debt), a given percent return on total capital translates into a higher return on the common stock portion of that capitalization.

Assume, as in Table 61, three companies with identical $1,000 total capitalizations but with different proportions of common stock and debt within their capital structures.

## TABLE 61

### EXAMPLES OF COMPANY LEVERAGE

| Source of Funds | Company A | Company B | Company C |
|---|---|---|---|
| Equity (Common Stock) | $ 1,000 | $ 500 | $ 100 |
| Debt (Borrowing) | $ 0 | $ 500 | $ 900 |
| Total Capital | $ 1,000 | $ 1,000 | $ 1,000 |
| Leverage Ratio (Total Capital/Equity) | 1:1 | 2:1 | 10:1 |
| Net Profit | $ 100 | $ 100 | $ 100 |
| Return on Total Capital (Profit/Total Capital) | 10% | 10% | 10% |
| Return on Equity (Profit/Equity) | 10% | 20% | 100% |

Assume further that in a given year each company earns $100, or 10%, on its total capital. (For simplification, interest costs on debt will be ignored.) Now, as Company A's capital structure consists entirely of equity, it will also have a 10% return on the equity portion of its capitalization. Company B, for which equity accounts for only half of total capital and which thereupon has a leverage ratio of 2:1, derives a return of 20% on equity. Company B has thereby earned twice as great a return for its common stockholders as Company A. Company C is most highly leveraged of all, and has a return on equity of 100%, a leverage ratio of 10:1. (Company C is an admittedly extreme, even unlikely, case, but it beautifully illustrates the effect of leverage on equity returns.)

Of course, if each company lost $100, Company A would have lost only 10% on equity, whereas Company B's loss would be 20% and Company C's loss would be 100%, leaving it effectively bankrupt with no equity, or net worth. An equal profit for each company therefore translates into the highest return on equity for Company C, but an equal loss incurred by each company also causes Company C to incur the greatest percentage loss per unit of equity employed.

Hence leverage is a two-way street. Rates of return can be magnified, but so can rates of loss. It is not surprising that the market prices of leveraged companies are more volatile and less stable than those of companies employing little or no leverage within their capital structure.

It will be observed that *leverage* is synonymous with *volatility*. Just as Company C's capital structure is ten times as leveraged as Company A's, so is its rate of return on equity ten times as volatile as Company A's. Similarly, a portfolio of common stocks consisting of 10:1 leveraged companies is theoretically ten times as volatile as a portfolio of common stocks consisting of unleveraged companies, although in practice, many other factors contribute to volatility as well.

*Margin Leverage.* Perhaps the best known use of leverage in portfolio management is the purchase of common stocks on margin. The essence of margin is that an investor borrows some of the funds used for purchasing stock, (debt), and pays only a fraction of the total required capital from his own funds (equity). In concept, the margin technique is identical to the employment of leverage in a company's capital structure.

TABLE 62

EXAMPLES OF MARGIN LEVERAGE

| Source of Funds | Portfolio A | Portfolio B | Portfolio C |
|---|---|---|---|
| Equity (Margin) | $ 1,000 | $ 500 | $ 100 |
| Debt (Borrowing) | $ 0 | $ 500 | $ 900 |
| Total Capital | $ 1,000 | $ 1,000 | $ 1,000 |
| Leverage Ratio (Total Capital/Equity) | 1:1 | 2:1 | 10:1 |
| Net Profit | $ 100 | $ 100 | $ 100 |
| Return on Total Capital (Profit/Total Capital) | 10% | 10% | 10% |
| Return on Equity (Profit/Equity) | 10% | 20% | 100% |

In Table 62, for example, Portfolio A employs no leverage whatsoever. The total investment is financed entirely from the investor's own equity funds. Portfolio B has a 2:1 leverage ratio, and any profits or losses incurred will result in twice the rates of return on the investor's personal equity capital as Portfolio A (ignoring interest and commission costs for the moment for the sake of simplification).

In the 1920s borrowing was essentially unrestricted and speculators put up as little as 10% of the total investment out of their own pockets, borrowing the balance (such as in Portfolio C). In effect they were leveraged by a factor of ten to one. With this kind of leverage, the purchase of stock valued at $1,000 would require only $100 of equity capital to be paid by the investor, with the other $900 borrowed from a bank or broker. All that was required of the stock for a doubling of the individual's personal equity investment was a ten percent rise. The $900 loan could then be repaid, and the investor could retire with $200, twice his $100 original personal investment. Hence, an investment margined at 10% resulted in a 100% return on equity, or a leverage ratio of 10:1.

Of course, the purchase of stock on thin margin requires the assumption of a great element of risk as well. Had the investor been forced to sell the stock for a total of just $900, all of the selling proceeds would have been required to repay the original loan, leaving the investor nothing for himself, and, in effect, a 100% loss on his original equity investment. Even worse, if the investor had not been able to sell the stock until its value had declined to $800, he would have lost not only his original $100 equity investment, but he would have had to raise an additional $100 to fully repay his $900 debt.

During the market crash of 1929-1932, this situation came into play with resounding, even devastating, impact. Banks and brokers lent considerable sums of money to speculators on 10% margin. Lacking funds to meet margin calls, the first time prices declined by 10%, these speculators were forced to sell their stock in order to repay their loans in full. The sale of the stock had the obvious effect of pushing prices lower, which triggered "margin calls" for other speculators, which forced additional sales of stock, which pushed prices still lower, resulting in still further margin calls – a never ending cycle. To prevent recurrence of such a phenomenon, in the early 1930s Congress empowered the Federal Reserve System to establish minimum margin requirements for stock speculation. With but a couple of early exceptions, the Fed has always held the margin requirement at 50% or above.

At this writing it is impossible, or at least illegal, to directly purchase common stocks on anything less than 50% margin. However, there are several highly leveraged investment opportunities still available in the marketplace for the speculatively inclined. It is possible, for example, to purchase mutual funds on relatively thin margin with commercial bank loans. Convertible securities may also frequently be purchased on less than 50% margin. Common stock purchase warrants and put and call options can provide leverage possibilities as great as ten to one, or even higher.

*Volatility Leverage versus Margin Leverage.* Stock volatility, the advantages of which have been explored in Chapters

61 and 64, is, in essence, yet another form of leverage - *stock* leverage.    Most investors seeking leverage choose *margin* leverage in preference to *company* leverage or *stock* leverage, perhaps because it seems so direct and the mathematics appear so simple.    However, stock leverage should always be preferred over margin leverage because of various factors which will be apparent when the alternatives are carefully analyzed.

At first thought a portfolio of average volatility stocks purchased on 50% margin might seem almost identical in leverage to a fully paid portfolio of stocks which have double the normal level of volatility — both strategies being twice as profitable in a rising market as holding an unmargined port-folio of average volatility stocks.    But that is not the case. Regardless of whether the market advances or declines, lever-age obtained through stock volatility is preferable to leverage obtained through a margin account.    Table 63 analyzes the impact of a series of falling prices on a normal volatility cash account, a margin account, and a high volatility cash account, each based on an initial $1,000 equity.

TABLE 63

EQUITY IN THREE TYPES OF ACCOUNTS
DURING A FALLING MARKET

| Net Equity After | Cash Acct. Average Volatility Stocks | Margin Acct. Average Volatility Stocks | Cash Acct. 2:1 Volatility Stocks |
|---|---|---|---|
| Initial 2% Commission | $ 980 | $ 960 | $ 980 |
| Period 1 - Market falls 20% | $ 784 | $ 498 | $ 588 |
| Period 2 - Another 20% fall | $ 627 | $ 109 | $ 352 |
| Period 3 - Another 20% fall | $ 502 | $   0 | $ 212 |

The disadvantages of a margin account (in this case, a 50% margin account), are threefold — first, since twice as much stock must be bought, commission expenses are doubled; second, the margin account must bear substantial interest expense on the margin debt balance (here assumed to be 6% per annum); and third, a falling market increases the leverage ratio in the margin account, finally leading to a total loss of equity in a severe market decline.

Now, perhaps you would expect that the margin account would prove superior in a rising market, but, again, such is not the case. The extra interest and commission expenses, coupled with the *decreasing* leverage as the margin account equity grows relative to debt, once again makes the high volatility portfolio a preferable strategy, as shown in Table 64.

TABLE 64

EQUITY IN THREE TYPES OF ACCOUNTS
DURING A RISING MARKET

| Net Equity After | Cash Acct. Average Volatility Stocks | Margin Acct. Average Volatility Stocks | Cash Acct. 2:1 Volatility Stocks |
|---|---|---|---|
| Initial 2% Commission | $ 980 | $ 960 | $ 980 |
| Period 1 - Market rises 20% | $ 1176 | $ 1282 | $ 1372 |
| Period 2 - Another 20% rise | $ 1411 | $ 1677 | $ 1921 |
| Period 3 - Another 20% rise | $ 1693 | $ 2161 | $ 2689 |

Given the risks involved in margin trading: margin calls, constant changes in regulations, and, most important, the "risk of ruin" (total loss of capital), a high volatility strategy is superior in all regards. It should be pointed out that when margin requirements are as low as 50%, it may be somewhat difficult to identify enough sufficiently volatile stocks to match the margin account in leverage and still obtain proper diversification. On the other hand, when margin requirements are set at very high levels, *only* a high volatility strategy can achieve a reasonably high degree of leverage.

Margin traders may hasten to point out that they cure one aspect of the margin account's deficiency by constantly re-leveraging on the way up (pyramiding) to maintain a constantly high degree of leverage. True as this may be, they then also keep themselves in a constant position of maximum risk whereby a retracement of part of the preceding gains is all that is necessary to wipe out all equity. The high volatility account will still be worth its starting value if the market scores first a sharp advance and then an offsetting decline without the investor having taken any profits. The constantly releveraged margin account can be wiped out in a retracement which merely leaves prices back at their initial level. In the last great bear market, more than one margin investor saw this double edged aspect of releveraging completely extinguish his equity even before prices fell below his original purchase price.

# 66 The Miracle of Compound Interest

Compound growth and loss just might be the ultimate financial miracles. The magic of earning interest on interest to increase the value of a financial portfolio has always enthralled financial analysts.

*The Original "Manhattan Project."* The classic example of the virtues of compound growth is the Dutch purchase of Manhattan Island. When Peter Minuit, First Director General of the Dutch Province of New Netherland, bought the island from the Man-a-hat-a Indians in 1626 for 60 guilders, or about $22.20 at today's exchange rates, he probably had no idea what he was contributing to the investment world. That was 350 years ago. The question, as debated by statisticians (and New York City residents) is: Who got the better deal — the white men or the Indians? The settlers, of course, received land which is today part of a large metropolis.

But the Indians received 60 guilders! Had the Indians invested their 60 guilder fortune in corporate bonds yielding, say, 7% per year, by 1976 they would have over $427 billion, which is well in excess of what Manhattan Island (land, buildings and all) is worth today. Alternatively, had they been wise enough to invest in common stocks on the New Manhattan Stock Exchange and earned a 9% yield year-in and year-

## TABLE 65

## TEN YEARS OF COMPOUND GAIN AND LOSS

| Annual Percent Gain | $10,000 Grows to . . . . | Extra $ Gain Per Extra 1% | Annual Percent Loss | $10,000 Shrinks to . . . . | Extra $ Loss Per Extra 1% |
|---|---|---|---|---|---|
| 0% | $10,000 | . . . . | 0% | $10,000 | . . . . |
| + 1% | 11,046 | $ 1,046 | − 1% | 9,044 | $ 956 |
| + 2% | 12,190 | 1,144 | − 2% | 8,171 | 873 |
| + 3% | 13,439 | 1,249 | − 3% | 7,374 | 797 |
| + 4% | 14,802 | 1,363 | − 4% | 6,648 | 728 |
| + 5% | 16,289 | 1,487 | − 5% | 5,987 | 661 |
| + 6% | 17,908 | 1,619 | − 6% | 5,386 | 601 |
| + 7% | 19,672 | 1,764 | − 7% | 4,848 | 546 |
| + 8% | 21,589 | 1,917 | − 8% | 4,344 | 496 |
| + 9% | 23,674 | 2,085 | − 9% | 3,894 | 450 |
| +10% | 25,937 | 2,263 | −10% | 3,487 | 407 |

| Annual Percent Gain | $10,000 Grows to . . . . | Extra $ Gain Per Extra 10% | Annual Percent Loss | $10,000 Shrinks to . . . . | Extra $ Loss Per Extra 10% |
|---|---|---|---|---|---|
| 0% | $10,000 | . . . . | 0% | $10,000 | . . . . |
| +10% | 25,937 | $15,937 | − 10% | 3,487 | $ 6,513 |
| +20% | 61,917 | 35,980 | − 20% | 1,074 | 2,413 |
| +30% | 137,858 | 75,941 | − 30% | 282 | 792 |
| +40% | 289,255 | 151,397 | − 40% | 60 | 222 |
| +50% | 576,650 | 287,395 | − 50% | 10 | 50 |
| +60% | 1,099,512 | 522,862 | − 60% | 1 | 9 |
| +70% | 2,015,994 | 916,482 | − 70% | 0 | 1 |
| +80% | 3,570,047 | 1,554,053 | − 80% | 0 | 0 |
| +90% | 6,131,066 | 2,561,019 | − 90% | 0 | 0 |
| +100% | 10,240,000 | 4,108,934 | −100% | 0 | 0 |

out (as has been the American investing experience during the last 75 years), their original $22.20 investment would have grown to over $300 trillion (!), a sum many times greater than the value of all the world's assets. The fact that the Indians didn't make such investments in no way impugns the wisdom of their original sale of the land; it merely casts doubt upon the ability of their portfolio manager.

*The Enrichment of Compound Growth.* The Manhattan analysis demonstrates two principles. First, in the long run, it is impossible to earn extremely high rates of yearly return. Second, the ability to earn interest on interest through compound growth can nevertheless greatly increase the value of one's investment portfolio.

Table 65 (page 263) indicates the value to which $10,000 would grow, or shrink, if it were invested for a period of ten years at various rates of gain or loss. For example, $10,000 obviously remains $10,000 if it earns a zero percent annual return for ten years. If a positive annual return of 10% can be achieved, an initial $10,000 investment would grow to $25,937 after a decade.

Of course, 10% interest on $10,000 is $1,000. Without the benefit of compound growth — earning interest on interest — the investor would earn $1,000 in each of ten years, a total profit of $10,000 and an ultimate portfolio value of $20,000. However, because at the end of each year the interest earned that year is reinvested in the portfolio so that it may also earn 10% interest in ensuing years, compound growth enables the portfolio to grow by an additional $5,937.

Very high rates of compound growth are even more dramatic. An annual return of 100% would provide a $10,000 portfolio with a growth of over $10 million in ten years, rather than merely $10,000 profit per year, and a total growth of just $100,000. (Remember this the next time you hear about a stock system that will allegedly double your money every year.)

*The Devastation of Compound Loss.* On the other hand,

compound loss can be disastrous.  A 20% loss each year for ten years causes an initial $10,000 investment to decrease to $1,074, while a decade of 60% annual losses depreciates the initial investment of $10,000 to $1.

Just the same, the table illustrates one of the great advantages of stock market investment:  the limitation of 100% loss, but the potential for unlimited gain.  Obviously, no matter what annualized rate of loss is incurred, the initial $10,000 portfolio cannot decrease to less than zero dollars, or a loss of $10,000.  However, an annual return of a mere 8% is all that is required to realize a $10,000 *profit* in ten years.  As evidenced by the geometrically increasing portfolio values in the table, ultimate returns in the hundreds of thousands, or even millions, of dollars, are also theoretically possible, all with a risk of loss of only $10,000.

*The Importance of 1%.*  A very interesting statistical quirk is illuminated in the table;  namely, that each additional percentage of return is more valuable than the last.  Increasing the annual ten year return from 0% to 1% results in an improvement in portfolio value of $1,046 ($11,046 minus $10,000). The next step' up in return, from 1% to 2%, increases the final portfolio value by $1,144.  An incremental gain from 9% to 10% increases the portfolio by $2,263!

Similarly, the first 10% step shown in the table, from 0% to 10%, shows a $15,937 profit.  But the next step up, from 10% to 20%, provides over twice as much incremental profit, $35,980.  A 10% improvement in annual return from 90% to 100% results in an astounding additional ten year profit of over $4 million.  Therefore, the higher the current rate of return, the more important it is to increase it by some percent.  (Viewing from another perspective, the benefit derived from increasing the annual rate of return a single percentage point from 99% to 100% is almost as great as the total gain which results by increasing the return from 0% to 50%!)

This phenomenon is also evidenced in situations of compound loss.  In this case a 1% decrease in the annual rate of loss is more valuable as the loss approaches zero. For example reducing the annual rate of loss from 10% to 9% improves the portfolio value by $407 ($3,894 minus $3,487), whereas decreasing the annual loss from 2% to 1% results in an $873 advantage ($9,044 minus $8,171), more than twice as great.

*Compound Return and Risk.* The compound interest concept also serves to clarify a misunderstanding which has resulted from studies of historical rates of return on risk bearing securities (We shall use here the classic academic definition of risk — volatility, since that is the one most previous studies have used.)

There is a positive correlation between risk and return among financial assets; that is, the greater the return expected from an investment, the greater should be the risk incurred in achieving it. This is simply common sense. If it were not so, investors would flock to the higher yielding, lower risk security, purchase it en masse, and push its price up to such an extent that it would subsequently provide a lower return and entail greater risk. For example, numerous studies have noted that corporate bonds, which are more risky than government bonds, furnish a higher rate of return as well, and that corporate bonds of a more speculative and riskier grade provide larger returns than high quality, low risk corporate bonds. Similarly, common stocks, which are inherently more risky than bonds, have historically provided a greater return. From 1897 through 1975 the Dow Jones Industrial Average provided a compounded annual rate of return of 9.3%, including dividends and capital gains. In contrast, high grade corporate bonds returned only 4.3% per annum.

However, studies which have focused on common stock returns have noted a peculiarity in the reward-risk relationship. While speculative, higher risk common stocks tend to offer greater returns than low risk stocks, the additional increment in return realized by increasing risk an arbitrary unit tends to decrease as one moves up on the risk scale. For example, an unpublished doctoral dissertation by Shannon Pratt covering all NYSE common stocks between 1926 and 1960 revealed the interesting results of Table 66. (Return includes both percentage price change and dividend yield and is presented here as the mean of the arithmetic and geometric three year returns, converted to an annual basis.)

### TABLE 66

### RISK AND ONE YEAR RETURN SPECTRUM

| Volatility Risk Grade | | Annual Rate of Return | Extra % Return |
|---|---|---|---|
| Lowest | A | 13.2% | — |
| | B | 15.9% | + 2.7% |
| | C | 17.7% | + 1.8% |
| | D | 19.0% | + 1.3% |
| Highest | E | 20.3% | + 1.3% |

Note that a 2.7% additional return was earned by increasing risk from Grade A to Grade B, but that only 1.8% extra return was earned by stepping up to higher risk Grade C. Still lower 1.3% return increments were earned by moving from Grade C to Grade D and from Grade D to the highest risk Grade E.

Table 67 of compound returns illustrates the truth which lies behind this seeming incongruity. In the long run, each additional percent return is more valuable because it earns a higher incremental dollar return due to compounding. Therefore, Pratt's table can be altered to relate risk units with *dollar* returns after, say, 20 years of compound growth.

### TABLE 67

### RISK AND 20 YEAR COMPOUNDED RETURN SPECTRUM

| Volatility Risk Grade | | Annual Rate of Return | Extra % Return | In 20 Years $1,000 Grows to... | Extra $ Return by Increasing Risk One Grade |
|---|---|---|---|---|---|
| Lowest | A | 13.2% | — | $11,938 | — |
| | B | 15.9% | + 2.7% | $19,128 | + $7,190 |
| | C | 17.7% | + 1.8% | $26,033 | + $6,905 |
| | D | 19.0% | + 1.3% | $32,429 | + $6,396 |
| Highest | E | 20.3% | + 1.3% | $40,301 | + $7,872 |

Note that although the *extra percent* rates of return decline as one increases risk, after 20 years the *extra dollar* returns between adjoining risk classes is about the same: $7,000. It can be proven very easily that if returns were compounded for periods longer than 20 years, the incremental dollar returns achieved by moving to higher risk grades would become even greater. As in the final analysis a return must approximately compensate the risk which is incurred to achieve that return, the trade off really boils down to the length of investor time horizons. The number of years of compound growth which equalizes the relationship between risk and dollar return is the long run time horizon of the average investor.

# 67 New Issues: Initial Public Offerings

*New Issues* comprise a category of stocks which falls outside the usual evaluation techniques. A "new issue" is the first sale of stock to the public by a company or its original shareholders.

During the late 1960s newly issued stocks often doubled and tripled overnight as the public clamored to get aboard "new IBM's" and "Xerox's." The price behavior of these new issues reflected the get-rich-quick atmosphere of the times. Of course, subsequent years witnessed the complete demise of many of these companies and crumbling stock valuations for most of the others. Only rarely did the companies go on to become important or dynamic factors in their own industries. When the stock market declined during 1969 and the early 1970s, the performance of new issues also deteriorated, and public interest in these types of issues almost vanished. As future markets will doubtless once again develop a speculative nature and witness a resurgence of new issues, it is worth knowing how to deal with them.

Initial common stock offerings may be made by the company itself, by existing shareholders, or by some combination of the two. As a rule, the greater the proportion of the total offering being newly issued by the company and the lesser the proportion being resold by existing shareholders, the better is the stock's subsequent performance. One study of this phenomenon was made by James D. Blum in a 1971 doctoral dissertation. Blum analyzed 400 new common stock issues from January 1965 through June 1969. The 400 issues were divided into four categories, dependent upon who received the proceeds of the offering. Table 68 summarizes the essential results.

TABLE 68

1965-1969 NEW ISSUE PERFORMANCE
BY DISTRIBUTION OF SALE PROCEEDS

| Weeks After Offering | All Proceeds to Company (181 Stocks) | 50% - 99% to Company (101 Stocks) | 1% - 49% to Company (65 Stocks) | All Proceeds to Shareholders (53 Stocks) |
|---|---|---|---|---|
| 1 | + 46.1% | + 25.7% | + 18.6% | + 15.5% |
| 13 | + 78.6% | + 46.3% | + 24.0% | + 26.2% |
| 26 | + 83.0% | + 62.2% | + 24.2% | + 38.5% |
| 39 | + 83.0% | + 75.9% | + 19.3% | + 33.6% |
| 52 | + 77.2% | + 68.6% | + 15.1% | + 36.2% |

The table brightly illuminates the incredible performance of new stock issues in general during the late 1960s. That once in a generation performance may not be duplicated for many years, or even decades. More to the point is that the greater the proportion of an initial offering that was sold by the company and the less that was being resold by existing shareholders, the better was subsequent stock performance. The principal reason for this phenomenon is probably that money flowing directly to the corporation at least has the chance of earning a return for new investors. Offerings made entirely by large shareholders simply fill their own pockets and do not provide any tangible benefit to the company.

Also apparent from data in the table is that most of the

gains occurred within the first week of the initial issuance of stock. Investors who managed to get a piece of the action at the initial offering and sell out a few days later realized dramatic gains. This performance seems too good to be true . . . and it is. Not everyone could buy these issues. In fact, it was almost impossible during these years to obtain large allotments of "hot" new issues.

The table also shows that substantial gains beyond the first week of the offering were realized, and hence purchase in the open market was also usually rewarded during that period. This is especially evident in the offerings where most of the proceeds went to the company.

*Primary Offerings* are stock sales made by corporations which are already publicly traded. The sale is made either to the public at large or to existing shareholders who receive "rights" to buy shares of the new issue in proportion to their existing equity interest in the company.

Studies of companies making primary offerings reveal that a very slight stock price decline relative to the market usually follows the offering. The question arises, Why should this performance be so markedly different from the performance of new issues? One reason may be that a trading market already exists, and that the marketplace has already had an opportunity to ascribe a value to the stock. Another reason is that the additional supplies of stock thrown into the marketplace has a downward impact on price, as would any new injection of supply into the supply-demand equation. Finally, companies are naturally most inclined to raise equity capital when their physical resources are stretched to the maximum and they need new funds for expansion. They also wish to receive the largest capital infusion possible from an offering of a given number of shares. Both conditions are most likely to prevail when prices are very high. Thus, such offerings proliferate near bull market peaks when generally declining prices are the best prospect.

*Secondary Offerings* are the sale of stock to the public exclusively by existing shareholders. The need for a secondary usually arises when one or several shareholders have a large block of stock which cannot be sold by the regular auction process without unduly affecting the price of the stock and creating havoc in the market. They therefore arrange for a sale of their stock off the exchange floor, usually through a group of underwriters pursuant to a prospectus. As an enticement to potential buyers, the sellers of a secondary usually bear both buying and selling commission costs. Studies of market performance following secondary issues reveal a situation quite similar to that following primary offerings. The price of the stock usually declines modestly. The most logical reason for this would seem to be that the type of shareholders possessing large blocks of stock might well be those who have superior sources of information into the company. Their sale of the stock may reflect their negative feelings about the future earning and dividend trends of the company.

Generally speaking, *primary* and *secondary* stock offerings should be avoided, but *new issues* can, in the proper bull market environment, be unusually rewarding.

(Note: The author is editor of *New Issues,* an investment advisory service designed as the investor's guide to initial public common stock offerings. A complimentary copy of *New Issues* can be obtained by writing to the author at The Institute for Econometric Research, 3471 North Federal Highway, Fort Lauderdale, Florida 33306.)

# 68 Contra-Cyclical Investing With the Gold Price Model

Traditionally, gold mining stocks have tended to rise when the market has fallen and have shown a propensity to decline during periods of broadly rising stock prices. Homestake and ASA, for example, have demonstrated an average historical tendency to advance about 5% for every 10% the market has declined, and to fall 5% when the market rises 10%.

As gold stocks exhibit this contra-cyclical characteristic, they can make sound investments during bear markets; better investments than the two traditional bearish strategies of holding interest bearing cash equivalents or selling stocks short. Short selling, while potentially profitable during bear markets, unfortunately offers an extremely unfavorable reward/risk ratio. Gains are limited to 100%, and potential losses are theoretically infinite. On the other hand, the purchase of gold mining stocks limits downside risk to 100%, while offering a theoretically infinite reward, just the opposite of a short selling strategy.

Given, then, that gold stocks can be good contra-cyclical investments, all that remains is to forecast their price movements. The most obvious way is to forecast the stock market first and hope gold stocks go the opposite way. But gold stocks aren't contra-cyclical all of the time — just most of the time. An alternative gold stock forecasting system is to predict the price of gold — obviously the factor most intrinsic to the profitability of gold mining companies and their common stocks.

The price of gold is sensitive to several factors. The most important is the rate of inflation, or, more precisely, both *changes in the rate of inflation* and *the extent to which actual inflation rates exceed expected inflation rates.* This takes cognizance of the fact that gold is less dependent upon classical commodity supply-demand factors and more dependent upon the emotions of potential public buyers of the metal. Thus, during periods of sharply rising inflation rates, investors and individual citizens have frequently turned to gold as an economic monetary hedge.

Gold has long been a monetary hedge in European and Asian countries. Gold is ideal for this function because it is durable, easily stored, and relatively scarce. When currencies fail, gold has always been a widely acceptable medium of exchange for the basic necessities of life. Hence, it has an underlying true currency value.

It is important to observe that the rate of inflation (or

deflation) per se, is unrelated to changes in the price of gold. For example, constant rates of price change of −5%, 0%, +5%, or +20% will not cause any changes in the gold price. So long as citizens can foresee future inflation rates with a moderate degree of certainty, as is the case if the rate of inflation is *constant*, there is little reason for them to purchase gold as a hedge against future uncertainty. Nor is a *declining* rate of inflation of great concern to the public. So long as prices are declining faster than wages so that purchasing power is increasing, consumers will be content with their economic prosperity. However, if the rate of inflation *rises* rapidly, so that all the public can foresee is a further rising rate of inflation, they may well fear for the safety of their own conventional monetary savings and turn to gold as a hedge against future uncertainty. Thus, a rising rate of inflation can be expected to accompany an increase in the price of gold and both constant and falling rates of inflation can be expected to accompany a decrease in the gold price.

The second important inflationary element that is useful in forecasting the price of gold is the extent to which actual inflation rates exceed expected inflation rates. Regardless of the increases or decreases in inflation rates in the past, if the public has perceived that a given inflation rate will prevail at a given time and if that time arrives with the rate of inflation far above their previous perceptions, their fears of inflation and monetary troubles could well come to the surface. They could then be expected to turn to gold stocks as a hedge against the possibility that future monetary uncertainty could wreak havoc with their hard earned savings.

Let us combine both of these inflation elements into a simple example. If inflation is currently advancing at a 10% rate, and if the rate of inflation one year ago was only 5%, it is clear that the rate of inflation has sharply increased. The public will, in all likelihood, turn to gold as a future inflation hedge, thus increasing its price. In addition, if a year ago investors had *perceived* that the rate of inflation would increase from 5% to only 7%, their expectations would have fallen far short of the actual 10% rate and the current higher rate would compound their uncertainty and fears, and lead to accelerated gold purchases.

We noted earlier that gold cannot be analyzed by classical commodity supply and demand measures. For one thing, the supply of gold is relatively fixed. Increases in the price bring out little new supply. Nor is there very much gold available in this world to begin with. Indeed, if all the gold that has been dug out of the ground in the entire history of human civilization were put together in one spot, it would do little more than fill a very large barn.

On the demand side of the ledger, industrial uses for gold are relatively few and not of great consequence. Gold demand in recent years has been controlled by speculative, not industrial, forces; hence the importance of concentrating on economic price indicators and public emotion when forecasting gold prices.

An extremely useful gold price model can be constructed from (1) the three month change in the twelve month rate of change in the Consumer Price Index; (2) the current rate of inflation minus the expected rate of inflation − the latter estimated by an exponential extrapolation in the rate of change of the consumer price index during the last twelve months; (3) the current market interest rate − for instance, the commercial paper rate; and (4) a price trend following variable calculated by dividing the current price of gold by the average price during the last twelve months.

This model has shown a high degree of proficiency in estimating the current trend in the price of gold. Although the reliability of the model is extremely tentative, given the very short period of time available for testing (the period in which the price of gold has been established by free market forces), it is certainly worth following until an adequate history permits the development of a more sophisticated model.

An elementary gold price model, which can be calculated each month by hand in just a few minutes, consists of the first variable only: the three month change in the twelve month rate of change of the U. S. Consumer Price Index (a proxy for the direction of world inflation) . The twelve month rate of change figure is provided in most newspaper articles describing the monthly release of the CPI. Note: the statistic used is the percent change in the CPI between the latest month released and the CPI one year earlier, *not* an annualized version of the latest monthly change.

The comparable twelve month rate of change that was calculated three months ago is then subtracted from the current calculation. If the answer is positive, gold prices should rise — if it is negative, they should fall. The indicator called the early 1975 bearish cyclical turn in gold prices in January of that year after having been bullish for gold prices ever since 1972.

# 69 The Dividend Difference

It is understandable that investors occasionally get carried away by the glamour and excitement of capital gains and losses at the expense of the mundane world of dividends. Compared to stock prices, which are in a continual state of intriguing, and at times even breathtaking fluctuation, dividends are just plain dull. However, the lesson of history is that in the long run dividend return deserves more attention. As an outgrowth of the depressing market performance from 1968 to 1974, the "total return" concept of investment performance has gained a growing constituency, and deservedly so. The evidence in support of this thesis is considerable and beyond refutation.

*The Chicago Study.* In perhaps the most exhaustive analysis of stock returns ever made, a team of researchers at the University of Chicago, with funding from Merrill Lynch, calculated the monthly investment performance of every New York Stock Exchange common stock for the 35 year period 1926 to 1960. One key part of that study revealed that the average stock returned about 9% per year compounded — but that 47% of this return, almost half, was from dividends. Since 1960 the dividend portion of total return has increased as common stocks have turned in a markedly slower rate of price growth. It is safe to say that the same study, updated for the entire half century 1926 to 1975, would show that over half of the 50 year total return was accrued from dividends alone.

*The Total Return Dow.* A 1975 study conducted at The Institute for Econometric Research analyzed the Dow Jones Industrial Average on price, dividend, and total return bases. The illuminating results of that study are presented in Table 69.

### TABLE 69

### THE DOW JONES INDUSTRIAL AVERAGES

|  | Price Return Dow | Dividend Return Dow | Total Return Dow |
|---|---|---|---|
| On Jan. 2, 1897, the Dow Jones Industrial Averages were . . . | 29.85* | 29.85* | 29.85* |
| but by mid-September 1975 they had grown to . . . | 816.10 | 1196.59 | 32684.99 |
| a portfolio growth of over . . . | 27 fold | 40 fold | 1095 fold |
| which is a compounded annual rate of return of . . . | 4.29% | 4.80% | 9.30% |

(*adjusted for 12/12/14 change in D.J.I. components)

An investor who collected and reinvested only dividends while ignoring all price return (the Dividend Return Dow) actually gained more than an investor concerned with price fluctuation alone (the Price Return Dow). Consideration of both price and dividend return (the Total Return Dow) naturally provided the greatest growth. The Price Return Dow, which furnished the smallest return, is the one you read about in all the newspapers!

*Total Return Indexes.* The unweighted Total Return (TR) Indexes of the New York and American Stock Exchanges are the only publicly available, daily calculated, stock price indexes which explicitly include both price and dividend return. They therefore provide a more accurate historical perspective of investor performance than any other market index. Their perspective of market behavior can often provide striking contrast with less complete market indexes. For example, from the beginning of 1965 through the end of 1975 the capitalization weighted NYSE Composite Index was relatively unchanged, while the Value Line geometric average and a few of the well publicized unweighted indexes actually *fell* about 30%. The more accurate NYSE TR Index indicates that, in reality, the average Big Board issue provided a *positive* total return from price growth and dividends of 40%. Although the error in the other market indexes rests partly in downward mathematical biases their creators have built into them, much of the divergence lies in the exclusion of dividends from measured return.

*IBM or GM?* An enlightening example of the total return concept is provided by an investment performance comparison between perennial growth favorite IBM and the plodding old cyclical, General Motors. If someone asked you whether you would have preferred to own General Motors or IBM in recent years, you most probably would have replied: "IBM." And from mid-1967 to year-end 1975 IBM increased 8% in price, while General Motors declined 26%, proving you right. But only partly right, for if the returns from dividends are included and reinvested, the picture changes dramatically. The total return on IBM was 27% during the eight year period, while General Motors actually performed better, providing a total return of 29%. Of course, these are just two stocks and one time period, but it clearly demonstrates that dividends really can make a difference.

*The Total Return Approach.* The importance of total return in long run investment performance has been proven conclusively. To cement the point it should be noted that dividend return is inherently less risky than price return. Leaving aside the question of inflation adjustment, while speculation in stocks for price changes can often be highly rewarding, it can also lead to the realization of large losses. But dividend cuts are the exception, not the rule, and dividend omissions are comparatively rare.

Given a choice between the two, in the long run dividend return is really superior to price return; it is at least as great and it is less risky.

Fortunately, we do not have to choose between the two — most stocks provide both. However, Part Six, which will examine market indexes, will point out that most (although not all) indexes ignore this total return approach.

# PART SIX
## MEASURING THE MARKET: KEEPING SCORE

## 70 Evaluation of Market Indexes

Market indexes provide the yardstick against which all investment performance is measured. Even such a basic decision as whether or not to invest in common stocks at all is dependent in part upon the long run rate of return provided by common stocks. It is therefore necessary to accurately measure historical market returns. We have constantly stressed the importance of market forecasting to the success of an overall investment strategy. A natural precondition to forecasting where the market is going is to know what and where the "the market" is. This, in turn, requires knowledge of what segment of the market is being forecast, what elements of return are being forecast, and how those forecasts should be interpreted in the light of historical returns of the selected market index.

Market indexes also provide essential standards of investment performance with which to compare actual portfolio returns. Every portfolio must be compared to a market index which is comparable in construction and includes similar types of securities. For all of these reasons, an understanding of market indexes is of the utmost importance to the success of a total financial program.

Everyone wants to know where the market has been and where it is going. But it is first important to know exactly what the market is. In fact, the market comes in all shapes and sizes. A great deal of public confusion has arisen simply from the fact that most observers are not aware of how various market indexes are constructed nor what segments of the market they purport to measure.

The evaluation of a market index should be based on the answers to several questions. First, what stocks are included in the index? Some market averages contain merely a sampling of the thousands of listed stocks; the widely followed Dow, for example, with just 30, or the various Standard & Poor's Indexes, containing a few hundred. Various indexes concentrate on different sections of the U. S. securities market. For example, the New York Stock Exchange Composite Index measures only stocks listed on the NYSE. Other indexes provide a sampling of independent markets such as American Stock Exchange issues and over-the-counter securities, while still others measure returns of stocks in broad industry groups.

Second, given the sample of stocks in an index, how is each individual security weighted? By price (e.g., the Dow Jones Averages); by equity capitalization (e.g., the New York Stock Exchange and Standard & Poor's Indexes); by equal weighting of the daily percent change of each stock (e.g., the Value Line Averages and the Total Return Indexes), or by equal weighting of the simple price change direction of each stock (the Advance/Decline Line)?

Third, how are the prices or price changes of all the stocks in an index combined? Arithmetically averaged, as in the Dow, or geometrically averaged, as in the Value Line Composite?

Fourth, how does the index treat stock splits, mergers, new listings, delistings, etc.?

Fifth, precisely what return does the index attempt to measure? That from price change alone, or dividend return as well?

The following chapters will examine the most widely known market indexes in the light of these questions. The answers are important, for they will explain the short and long term behavior of the indexes themselves. In turn, they will furnish critical information relative to the indexes' value in providing accurate market forecasts, portfolio comparisons, and historical market performance measurements.

Some of the answers may be surprising. For example, we will note that the Dow Jones Averages use a very poor weighting system and adjust for stock splits in a manner so irrational as to make comparisons of the average's level over long periods of time virtually meaningless.

We will also discover that such widely used unweighted indexes as the Value Line and Indicator Digest Averages are so downwardly biased as to render them effectively useless for purposes of long term comparison.

And we shall discover that, on average, every market index save one subtly, but effectively, excludes over half of the total dollar return of its component stocks.

# 71 Dow Jones Averages

"How did the Dow do today?" is probably the most frequently heard question on Wall Street. The answer usually comes back, "Down five points," "Up ten points," or something similar. Exactly what does this mean? It certainly does not imply that the average stock lost $5 per share or gained $10 per share during the day; most component stocks rarely fluctuate more than one or two points daily. Furthermore, during the last ten or fifteen years the Dow Jones Industrial Average has been quoted within a range of 500 to 1000. Obviously, the average price of a Dow stock is not $500 or $1,000, even though the original index measured exactly that — the average price of its component stocks.

The first Dow Jones Average was calculated before the turn of the century. It consisted of just fourteen stocks, representing twelve railroad and two industrial companies. Since then the composition of the average has been changed on numerous occasions. Today, rather than one single Dow Jones Average, there are four, broken down into 30 industrial stocks (the most popularly quoted average), 20 transportation issues, 15 utilities, and a 65 stock composite average.

Critics argue that a sample of as few as 30 stocks is hardly representative of the market; that the average's fluctuations are highly dependent upon the specific sample of stocks. For instance, if IBM had not been pulled from the Dow Jones Industrial Average in 1939 in favor of AT&T, the DJIA would today be more than twice its currently quoted level. The limited sample also occasionally causes interesting statistical fluctuations. On August 9, 1976, by amazing coincidence nine of the thirty stocks went "ex-dividend," automatically causing a 2.31 drop in the Dow on the opening of that day.

In fairness, it should be noted that the 30 stocks in the DJIA are among the largest companies in America, that these companies reflect economic trends unusually well, and that they therefore provide a good sampling of the trends among all other stocks. Hence, even if very short and very long term measurements are misleading, at least cyclical fluctuations are more or less representative. Furthermore, even though the 30 DJIA stocks comprise just 1½% of the total number of issues on the New York Stock Exchange, they contribute about one-third of its total market value. Dow Jones & Company, which maintains the averages, also occasionally makes changes in the component stocks to keep them in tune with current reality. Dow Jones also is not above changing the essence of an average itself to reflect changing circumstances as they did in 1970 when the current "Transportation" average supplanted the traditional, and more homogeneous, "Rail" average.

The Dow Jones Averages have the added virtue of

possessing a continuous record dating back to 1885. This enables current readings and changes to be placed in the perspective of an extensive history.

*Construction of the Average.* In its simplest form, the Dow Jones Industrial Average is computed by summing the prices of its 30 component stocks and dividing by 30. However, when stock dividends and splits are declared, or when changes in the list of component stocks occur, the average must be adjusted to avoid statistical aberrations. For example, if one of the 30 Dow companies declared a four for one stock split with a consequent 75% decline in quoted price from, say, $120 to $30, the sum of the prices of the 30 stocks would also have fallen by $90, or 3 Dow points. Obviously, the average itself should not decline because of a stock split.

Prior to September 10, 1928, the Dow Jones Averages were adjusted as follows: If a stock was split, its price was multiplied by the number of shares into which each share was split. Thus, if General Electric split four for one, its price was multiplied by four to return it to its original basis prior to calculation of the average itself. Using this adjustment technique, the average effectively reflected a simple buy and hold policy for each individual component stock. While this rendered stock splits irrelevant, issues that performed exceptionally well — which rose to very high split-adjusted prices — tended to increasingly dominate the average by virtue of their consequent greater adjusted price fluctuations.

To correct for this "distortion," the method of split adjustment was changed. Since September 10, 1928, adjustments have been made as follows: Assume that the prices of the thirty stocks summed to $3,000. Then the 30 stock average price would be $3,000 divided by 30, or 100.00. If one of the thirty stocks was quoted at $200, but then split two for one so that its price fell to $100, the sum of prices would be only $2,900. To maintain the average at its actual level of 100.00, the divisor of the average is systematically altered. Since $2,900 divided by 100.00 equals 29, the new divisor is set at 29, down from 30, in effect preserving the average price at $100 ($2,900 divided by 29 still equals 100.00). After decades of such adjustments, the divisor has fallen lower and lower. At the end of 1975 it was only 1.6.

Unfortunately, this method of adjusting for stock splits unavoidably causes another arbitrary distortion in the average. In the preceding example, the stock which split originally provided 1/15th of the total weight in the average ($200 divided by $3,000). After it has split, its weight is only 1/29th ($100 divided by $2,900). Consequently, its daily price fluctuations (smaller in magnitude, given its lower price) have less effect on the daily point fluctuations in the average, a change that is devoid of rationale.

However, after all is said and done, the Dow Jones Averages are still the most frequently referred to of all market indexes. The fact that they are the product of the two most widely read financial periodicals in the country – *The Wall Street Journal* and *Barron's* – both Dow Jones & Company publications, doesn't hurt their reputation at all. But if better alternatives are readily available, why not use them? Superior market indexes do exist, and are described in the following chapters.

# 72 Capitalization Weighted Indexes

Capitalization or market value weighted indexes reflect the total common stock investing experience. They do so by measuring the total market value of the common stocks included in the index.

The market value of a stock is calculated by multiplying the number of common shares outstanding by the current price per share. The values for individual stocks are then added to determine the total market value of all stocks in the index.

Each component stock in the index is therefore weighted so that it will influence the index in proportion to its own relative importance in the marketplace.    For example, General Motors, which has 288 million shares outstanding and a total market value of $16.6 billion (based on a year-end 1975 price of $57-5/8), has 16 times the weight of Polaroid, which has only 33 million shares outstanding and a market value of just $1.0 billion (based on a price of $31).

The theory underlying capitalization weighted indexes is that *someone* owns every share of stock that is outstanding. While your own portfolio may not be 16 times as heavily weighted with General Motors as Polaroid, and while no single investor may hold a portfolio of General Motors and Polaroid in a 16 to 1 ratio, it is certainly true that more portfolios hold GM than PRD.   Capitalization weighted indexes reflect this fact.   More importantly, it is a truism that all investors in the aggregate do hold those stocks in the 16 to 1 ratio.   Therefore, a capitalization weighted index is the only index which reflects the total market experience of all investors.

Capitalization weighted indexes provide an excellent performance comparison for large portfolios.   Large investors and institutions are unable to purchase substantial quantities of thinly capitalized issues.   Even if they could manage to buy, say, a million shares of a small Amex stock, they would force the price up enormously in the process.   Any "book profit" would be illusory since the price would have to be pushed back down in order to liquidate the position.   Consequently, capitalization weighted indexes should form the basis of portfolio comparisons for any investment entity with large and diversified common stock holdings.

A capitalization weighted index uses an index number such as 10, 50, or 100 to represent the initial market value of the stocks in the index as of a base date.   The index is then updated, usually at least daily, and the current market value is expressed relative to the base period market value.   For example, the New York Stock Exchange Composite Price

Index was arbitrarily set to equal 50.00 on the base date of December 31, 1965. Ten years later, on December 31, 1975, the index was 47.64, indicating that its current market value was about 5% less than its base date market value a decade earlier.

Stock dividends and stock splits have no effect upon the continuity of a capitalization weighted index because as the number of shares of a stock increases due to a split-up, the price of the stock is reduced by a proportionate amount, holding the total market value constant.

Acquisitions, mergers, new listings, delistings, stock rights, changes in capitalization, etc., are handled by adjusting the base period market value. Changes are made in that value as follows:

$$\text{New Base Value} = \text{Old Base Value} \times \frac{\text{New Market Value}}{\text{Old Market Value}}$$

Capitalization weighted indexes do not count dividend return. They measure the value of stock prices, and hence stock price changes, only, even though dividends are very significant in the long run. Dividends can also have minor short term impacts. When a company declares a regular quarterly dividend, the specialist in that stock automatically marks down the price of the stock. In the case of AT&T, this can result in a one day decrease of about a half-billion dollars in market value — enough to have a perceptible impact on the index change for that day.

*Standard & Poor's Stock Price Indexes.* The most popular capitalization weighted indexes at the present time are the Standard & Poor's group. Standard & Poor's Corporation maintains a comprehensive price record of 500 common stocks divided into four primary statistical groups:

400  Industrial Stocks
20  Transportation
40  Utility Stocks
40  Financial Stocks
500  Stock Composite

The 500 stocks are sub-divided into 95 industry groups and four supplementary groups are maintained as well: Capital Goods, Consumer Goods, High Grade, and Low Priced common stocks. Standard & Poor's also maintains separate industry group indexes which include stocks not among the basic 500. When first inserted into the indexes, each of the 500 stocks must represent a viable enterprise and must further be representative of the industry group to which it is assigned. Preference in stock selection is given to the larger, more highly capitalized companies.

Actually the S&P indexes have included the present total of 500 stocks only since March 1, 1957. On that date Standard & Poor's rebased their indexes to a 1941-1943 value of 10.00. They also standardized the historical daily record from January 1, 1928 to February 28, 1957, to 50 industrials, 20 rails, 20 utilities, and a 90 stock composite. At the same time a monthly extension was made back to January 1918. Finally the monthly Cowles Commission Index was linked to the S&P indexes for the period 1873 to 1917. The end product is effectively a continuous market index record over one century in length. The extensive historical continuity of the indexes and the availability of current quotations has made the S&P indexes of great value to numerous market students.

Complete historical data is contained in Standard & Poor's publication, *Statistics: Security Price Index Record.* The book also contains information on yields, price/earnings ratios, and book values for the primary indexes during the last half century.

*New York Stock Exchange Indexes.* In 1966 the New York Stock Exchange began publishing stock price indexes encompassing every common stock listed on the exchange. The indexes consist of a Composite Index of all common stocks and four sub-indexes:

> (1) Finance Index – (closed-end investment companies, savings and loans, real estate holding and investment companies, and others in commercial

and installment finance, banking, insurance, and related fields).

(2) Transportation Index — (railroads, airlines, shipping, motor transportation, and other operating, leasing, and holding companies in the transportation field).

(3) Utility Index — (operating, holding, and transmission companies in gas, electric power, and communications).

(4) Industrial Index — (includes all NYSE listed common stocks not included in the first three indexes).

All of the indexes were initially set to a December 31, 1965 base of 50.00. (At that time the price of an average NYSE common stock was about $50.) The indexes have been computed on a daily close basis back to May 28, 1964. In addition, from January 7, 1939 to May 28, 1964, the Securities and Exchange Commission calculated a similarly constructed weekly index of 300 common stocks which accounted for about three-fourths of the market value of all NYSE listed common stocks. The New York Stock Exchange has linked their Composite Index to the old S.E.C. Index, making a weekly record of the composite available since 1939. (The entire historical record may be obtained free of charge from: Research Department, New York Stock Exchange, 11 Wall Street, New York, New York.)

For investors desiring to relate their portfolio experience to a market value weighted index of New York Stock Exchange listed common stocks, the NYSE Composite Index is *the* index to use. The NYSE indexes measure common stock behavior in precisely the same manner as do the Standard & Poor's indexes and cover more stocks to boot. They will certainly develop greater usage in the future and may eventually become the most widely followed indexes in the country, next to the Dow Jones Averages.

*American Stock Exchange Market Value Index.* After a period of experimentation with various stock market measuring systems, the American Stock Exchange finally settled on the same type of index as that used by the New York Stock Exchange. The latest Amex indexes were established on August 31, 1973 at base values of 100.00 (which, needless to say, had nothing to do with the average price of an Amex stock.) They represent the aggregate market value of all common stocks and warrants listed on the exchange. Also included are American Depository Receipts (ADR's) which are negotiable securities issued by American banks representing the shares in their custody of foreign corporations. Rights, preferreds, and "when issued" stocks are excluded. In addition to its total market value index, the exchange has divided its stocks into eight sub-indexes:

(1)  Capital Goods – Manufacturing
(2)  Consumer Goods – Manufacturing
(3)  Finance
(4)  High Technology
(5)  Housing, Construction, and Land Development
(6)  Natural Resources
(7)  Retailing
(8)  Services

The sub-indexes, as well as the primary composite stock index, are calculated daily and are reported by most major wire services.

Although the Amex Composite Index does provide a direct comparison with its Big Board counterpart, it suffers from one flaw. A very few companies dominate the total market value of all Amex issues to an even greater extent than a few blue chips dominate the NYSE. For example, at year-end 1975, one stock, Imperial Chemical, accounted for over 8% of the Amex's total market value. Four other issues, British American Tobacco ADR's, Carnation, Gulf Oil of Canada, and Imperial Group ADR's accounted for an additional 14%. Hence, a mere five stocks furnished almost one quarter of the weight in the index. Since most American Stock Exchange issues represent fairly young or small companies, in all likelihood the typical American Stock Exchange investor will find that his portfolio will diverge markedly from the American

Stock Exchange Index.

*M/G Composite Market Value Index.* The *Financial Weekly* published by Media General Corporation in Richmond, Virginia, calculates a daily composite market value index encompassing all NYSE and Amex listed common stocks as well as more than 700 issues traded over-the-counter. The index was initially established on January 2, 1970, with a base value of 100.00 and has been calculated daily since that date.

The only source of current index readings is the Financial Weekly itself, a $100 per year service. The index suffers from a lack of historical data, although interested followers of the index could link it to the NYSE Composite, Standard & Poor's 500, or some other index if they so desired. Furthermore, although the index is calculated daily, the readings are only presented in the service at the end of each week. Against these drawbacks, the index does include an exceptionally broad range of common stocks, and is therefore probably the best multi-market capitalization weighted index available.

# 73 Advance/Decline Line

The Advance/Decline (A/D) Line has traditionally been one of the most widely used measures of market performance. The A/D Line is easily calculated by counting the number of stocks which advanced in price within a given period of time (say, a day or a week) and subtracting the number of issues which showed price declines during the same period. The periodic net differences are then accumulated to establish perspective through time.

The index's popularity is chiefly a product of two factors: First, it measures, however crudely, the price performance of every listed stock. Second, it is extremely easy to calculate.

As the index is based upon a periodic count of the number of stocks rising and falling in price, no weight is given to the extent (dollar or percent) of a price change, nor is any attention paid to the price level or capitalization of a stock. Therefore, every stock is treated equally. Until the recent advent of large scale data processing systems, it was an extremely difficult and time consuming task to continually calculate average prices, percent changes, total capitalizations, and related statistics necessary for the construction of sophisticated and theoretically sound market indexes. However, it has always been a relatively simple matter to count the number of advancing and declining stocks.

To calculate an Advance/Decline Line, start with an arbitrary base number, say 10,000. If, on a given day (or week) 700 stocks advance in price while 300 decline, a net of 400 stocks have advanced, and the Advance/Decline Line moves from 10,000 to 10,400 (10,000 + 400). If, on the succeeding day, the situation is reversed with 700 stocks declining and only 300 advancing, a net of 400 declines, the Advance/Decline Line retreats to an even 10,000 (10,400 − 400).

Of course, the number of issues listed on the major exchanges has steadily expanded through the years. While a net of 400 advances on the New York Stock Exchange was very sizable even 25 years ago when there were relatively few issues traded, a net of 400 advancing stocks in 1976 is only moderately favorable because of the greater number of issues listed. It is a relatively simple matter to adjust for this trend. Again, start with an arbitrary Advance/Decline Line base number of, say, 100. As in the preceding example, if 700 stocks advance while 300 decline, the net Advance/Decline Line change for that day is not +400, but +0.40, calculated by dividing the net of advances minus declines, +400, by the sum of the total number of stocks which advanced or declined, 1,000.

$$\frac{700 - 300}{700 + 300} = \frac{400}{1000} = +0.40$$

As before, the A/D Line is updated merely by adding the change for that day to the preceding index value, in this case, adding 0.40 to 100, which equals 100.40.

A 0.40 change in the revised Advance/Decline Line would also result if twice as many stocks were traded on a given day and twice as many advanced. The preceding example of 1,000 total issues changing price might well have occurred in the 1950s. Today, a precisely equivalent situation would exist if 1,500 stocks changed price, with 1,050 advancing and 450 declining. The net number of advances, +600, divided by the total number of stocks changing in price, 1,500, again equals +0.40. This refinement of the revised A/D Line provides index consistency through time.

In return for simplicity of calculation and broadness of base, the A/D Line is a theoretical nightmare. The index is especially subject to criticism for failing to measure the extent of price changes. A stock might decline by an eighth of a point on each of five consecutive days and advance by one full point on the sixth day, resulting in a net *positive* price change for the full six day period. However, the A/D Line would reflect one up and five down ticks, a net of *minus* four.

Now, one may argue that the opposite situation might occur just as frequently, thus eliminating any bias. However, the Advance/Decline Line has, in fact, exhibited a long term downward trend. (The NYSE A/D Line peaked out some two decades ago and has been trending down ever since.) The downtrend can be attributed principally to the bias introduced from this factor. Academic studies have *proven* that over any given time interval, trade to trade, hour to hour, day to day, week to week, or even year to year, average price advances are larger than average price declines. This follows, in part, from the elementary observation that, although the degree of any price decline is limited to 100%, there is no limit to the amount that a stock price can increase in any fixed period of time. A fair market index should reflect this natural phenomenon. The Advance/Decline Line does not. The net result is a long term downward bias.

An additional element of bias in advance and decline counts may ensue from the inclusion of preferred stocks which fluctuate independently of common stocks.

At the minimum, any use of the Advance/Decline Line as a comparative market index should factor into it some reverse adjustment to eliminate its downward bias. The Advance/Decline Line is an extremely crude measure of broadly based market fluctuations. Its method of calculation and resultant bias suggest that it should be used with particular care.

# 74 Geometric Averages

The Value Line Averages are often referred to as unweighted geometric averages; and, in fact, they are the only continuously calculated market indexes which give equal geometric weight to the daily percentage changes of a large group of common stocks. Calculated since January 1962, the Value Line Composite Average consists of all common stocks under continuous review by the *Value Line Investment Survey*. Although Value Line divides all monitored stocks (currently numbering about 1,600) into three major groups — industrials, rails, and utilities — the Composite Average has gained the broadest following. Most stocks included in the Composite Average are listed on the New York Stock Exchange, although a few Amex issues and a handful of over-the-counter stocks are also included.

The indexes are updated daily by geometrically averaging the percent changes of the monitored stocks. For example, if the geometric average percent change of the 1,600 stocks on a given day is +2% and the previous day's reading of the Value Line Average is 100, then the average increases by two points (2% x 100), resulting in a new reading of 102. The Value Line Averages thus assign each of the stocks contained therein equivalent percentage weights. IBM, which carries a price in the hundreds of dollars and a market value in the tens of billions, is treated no differently from, say, Benguet Consolidated, which in 1975 was priced at about $2.00, with a total market value of just $20 million. The daily percent change of each stock is treated equally. If IBM increases 6% from $200 to $212, the effect on the Value Line Average is the same as if Benguet should increase 6% from $2.00 to $2.12.

Unfortunately, the Value Line Averages suffer from one flaw, a flaw so serious that it is, in fact, fatal. The flaw is that the percent price changes are averaged *geometrically*. A geometric average, calculated by averaging the "logarithms" of each term and finding the "anti-logarithm" of the average, is widely conceived on Wall Street to constitute the perfect averaging system. However, as recognized for some time by mathematicians and learned financial scholars, this conception is false. When different price changes of two or more stocks are averaged, the geometric method will always produce a result that is below the true answer. This can be demonstrated easily with but a single example. Say you own two stocks, A and B, in equal dollar amounts. If, on a given day, stock A increases 25%, but stock B declines 25%, the simple average of the changes is zero, and therefore your total portfolio change is zero. Right?

A geometric average such as Value Line's says, "Wrong: you have a net loss of 3%."

There are two points worth noting here. First, you are right and the geometric average is wrong. Second, the error in the geometric average is that its net return is *less* than the correct one. A geometric stock market average will *always* be below a simple average. Value Line calculates its geometric average of percent changes every day. Every day it is wrong. Every day its measured average return is too low. Every day it either shows a greater loss than it should, a smaller gain than it should, or a loss when it should show a gain. And it has made this downward error every day for the last 14 years. The cumulative consequence is that the Value Line Average is so biased downward that its current level, placed in the perspective of its own history, is utterly without meaning.

And yet the Wall Street myth persists that geometric averages provide the ultimate index of market behavior. Nothing could be further from the truth. Consider this: If you established an initial portfolio of stocks equivalent to the Value Line Composite Average, held them in equal proportions, as does the Value Line Average, added and removed issues in accordance with the Average's system — in short, if you attempted to exactly duplicate the Average's performance through time — you would face an impossible task. Your portfolio would *always* provide returns superior to the Value Line Average itself. (Index fund managers take note!)

The Value Line averaging system does handle stock splits and related phenomena in an efficient manner. If a stock splits, its previous closing price is adjusted downward in the same ratio as the split so that it is put on an equivalent basis with the post-split price for computing the percent change.

New stock listings are ignored on their first day of trading so that they can establish an initial closing price on which to base a percent change calculation.

Stocks which disappear because of merger, delisting, bankruptcy, etc. are ignored on the day they disappear — that is, they are not counted in the average because they do not have a current price. The only drawback to this sytem is in the case of a stock which disappears from trading because its price falls to zero (for example, delisting due to a bankruptcy filing). In effect, its return on that final day is minus 100% (a total loss), and a market index should treat it as such. Unfortunately, the index that does so is almost non-existent. The Value Line Average's excuse for this omission is simply that the geometric averaging procedure is mathematically incapable of handling a minus 100% return.

In conclusion, the Value Line Averages fail to perform the essential task of which every good market index should be capable: At least approximately replicate the behavior of the stocks contained in the average. Due to the downward bias, historical comparisons of their own trends are meaningless and comparisons of individual portfolio performances with the averages are also meaningless.

# 75 Unweighted Market Indexes

Within the past decade a new breed of market index has blossomed forth upon the investment scene — the so-called "unweighted market index." Unweighted indexes are based upon the premise that price weighted barometers such as the Dow Jones Averages, or capitalization weighted measures such as the NYSE, Amex, and Standard & Poor's Indexes, do not properly, or adequately, reflect the price fluctuations of the great mass of stocks traded on the New York and American Stock Exchanges.

To correct for this deficiency, unweighted indexes usually measure the price fluctuations of all stocks on an exchange, giving equal weight to every issue.

The underlying mathematical basis of an unweighted index is the calculation of the percent change of each stock in the population under study. For example, if a stock appreciates from $10 to $20, it has gained 100%. But a stock which appreciates from $100 to $110 (also 10 points) has advanced only 10%. An index consisting of only these two stocks would advance 55% because the average of the two percent changes is 55% (100% + 10%, divided by 2). Note that the change in the index is based upon the percent price changes of the component stocks. It is related neither to the dollar price change of each stock, nor to the price of those stocks, nor to the size of their common stock capitalizations. (In this example, a price weighted index like the Dow Jones Industrial Average would show an *18%* increase.)

After calculating the average percent change of each stock on a given day, the index itself is derived as follows:  Start with an arbitrarily established index value; say, 50.00. If the average stock appreciates 1%, the new index value is 1.01 times 50.00, or 50.50. By similar logic, if the average stock declines 1%, the new index value is equal to 0.99 times 50.00, or 49.50. This is an eminently fair and reasonable method of calculating stock market indexes. Every stock receives equal treatment, regardless of price or capitalization. The index's fluctuations furnish particularly good comparisons with portfolios which are as likely to contain low priced, thinly capitalized issues such as Atlas Corporation or Benguet Consolidated as high priced, highly capitalized stocks such as IBM or AT&T.

Stock splits have no adverse impact on unweighted indexes. Prior to calculating the daily percent price change of a stock which has just split, its preceding day's pre-split price is simply adjusted downward to place it on a comparable basis with the price of the stock after the split.

Unweighted indexes received their initial foothold in the financial community from a computer study of common stock price performance conducted at the University of Chicago. The study yielded, in part, several "unweighted indexes" based upon monthly price and investment returns of all NYSE listed stocks from 1926 to 1960. A few of the indexes have since been updated through 1972.

Virtually all unweighted indexes currently in popular use are based upon data calculated by Quotron Systems, Inc. The average percent changes of all New York and American Stock Exchange stocks appear on Quotron's electronic stock quotation devices throughout each trading day. The daily closing statistics are published in several weekly financial periodicals, notably *Barron's* and *Media General's Financial Weekly*.

The most widely known of the Quotron based indexes is the Indicator Digest Average ("IDA"), computed by the *Indicator Digest* advisory service. Identical indexes have been constructed by *The Zweig Forecast* (the "ZUPI"), *The Professional Tape Reader* (the "NYUA"), and several other investment advisory services (all of which assign their own names to the same index).

Unfortunately, the Quotron data suffers from a critical error which downwardly biases every index using it. The error, which resides in the method  of calculating percent changes, is incredible on its face. As described above, a stock which moves from $10 to $20 has properly increased 100% in price. However, Quotron calculates the percent change not by dividing the $10 change by the $10 starting price, but rather by dividing the $10 change by the $20 ending price. In this case, the method results in a percent change not of 100%, but 50%. Note that Quotron's percent change is biased *downward* — the calculated gain is less than the actual gain.

The downward bias also exists when stocks decline in price. In the extreme case of a stock which declines from $10 to $1, Quotron divides the $9 decrease by the $1 ending price, deriving a change of −900% (!), not −90% as would be obtained by properly dividing the $9 decline by $10. Again, the bias in the calculation is *downward*. Just as the extent of a gain is always understated, so the extent of a loss is always overstated. This fundamental error persists for every stock on the New York and American Stock Exchanges every day of every year.

Although the extent of the downward bias may be relatively insignificant from day to day, over the span of several months or years, it is very considerable indeed. For example, the Quotron based indexes of NYSE stocks should have been approximately twice their December 31, 1975 level to properly reflect the returns of their component stocks during the previous ten year period! Unfortunately, these indexes are incapable of correcting themselves because even more downward bias will be injected into them in the future, removing them ever further from reality.

The extent of the bias is a function of the volatility of price changes of the component stocks. Hence, the downward bias is greater in more volatile periods, when the error of calculated price changes is greater.  It is not surprising, then, that the bias has been more pronounced in the volatile markets of the last few years than it was previously.

For the same reason, the Quotron based indexes of the generally more volatile Amex stocks have been biased more severely downward than indexes of NYSE issues.  Virtually every index of Amex price behavior, properly calculated or not, shows that an all time peak was established in early January 1969.  The peak (at this writing) has not yet been reached.  How much appreciation is required to once again attain that peak is a function of the measuring index used.  Thus, in July 1976, the Amex Total Return Index (see next chapter), calculated by The Institute for Econometric Research, required a gain of about 63% to reattain the 1969 top.  To reach the same objective, the incorrectly calculated Quotron based unweighted indexes required a near quadrupling (a 300% gain)!

Users of the Quotron based indexes point out the similarity of cyclical fluctuations between their indexes and those of the Value Line Average and the Advance/Decline Line, as if by the three way confirmation they are all accurate.  To the contrary, it proves that all three are wrong, albeit for three different reasons — Quotron based unweighted indexes from an erroneous method of calculating percent changes, the Value Line Average from an unfortunate misuse of the geometric averaging concept, and the A/D Line from a failure to consider the *extent* of price changes and the non-symmetrical distribution of those changes over any time interval.

It is worth noting that Quotron's data does take into account the return from dividends and hence "IDA" "ZUPI," "NYUA," and similar indexes do, in a sense, measure "total return."   The problem, of course, is that while dividend return is correctly added, the other element of return, price change, is incorrectly calculated.

Unweighted indexes, properly constructed and correctly calculated, constitute an excellent measure of market fluctuations, as we shall see in the next chapter.

# 76 The Total Return Indexes

The Total Return (TR) Indexes for the New York and American Stock Exchanges, regularly published in The Institute for Econometric Research's *Market Logic,* are unique and valuable tools for gauging market performance. They provide an unsurpassed view of the true breadth and performance of the market.

While the perfect stock market index does not exist, we have seen that most popular indexes suffer from one particularly objectionable bias or another and therefore do not truly reflect market fluctuations.

The Total Return Indexes are unweighted, that is, they give equal weight to every common stock listed on each Exchange. The superiority of the TR Indexes lies in two characteristics not found in any other continually calculated and published index.

First, the TR Indexes give equal arithmetic weight to the correctly calculated, daily percent price change of every common stock, regardless of whether its price is $1 or $100, or whether the company is large or small. This characteristic is unique, irrespective of claims made for similar unweighted market measures. The common feature among all of the other averages is that they are downwardly biased.

The second key advantage of the TR Indexes is that they include dividend return as well as price changes — both integral components of total return. As we have seen in Chapter 69, over half of the total return of all common stocks through history has been from dividends. While price fluctuations may be the primary feature of stock returns in the short run, over long periods of time dividends assume an increasing importance in the total return.

Changes in the TR Indexes are equivalent to the returns

from a well diversified, randomly selected portfolio. Since such returns can be duplicated with minimal effort, only returns in excess of those shown by the TR Indexes can generally be considered indicative of superior investment management.

Figure 1 (page 6) shows the weekly movements of the *New York Stock Exchange Total Return Index* since 1964. It is interesting to note that the NYSE TR Index presents a picture of recent market cycles that more closely conforms to the average investor's experience than the performance of the Dow Jones Industrial Average. The TR Index reached a top in April of 1972, falling 10% short of the 1968 peak, and then turned downward. The Dow Jones Industrial Average continued erratically upward during the balance of 1972 to a new all time high in December. More recently, the TR Index shows that the bear move ended in September, 1974 for the broad market, even though the Dow did not bottom out until three months later, in early December. The major cyclical movements of the NYSE TR Index during the past decade are shown in Table 70.

TABLE 70

NYSE TOTAL RETURN INDEX TURNING POINTS

| Event | Date | NYSE TR Index | % Change |
|-------|------|--------------|----------|
| High | Apr. 21, 1966 | 147.16 | |
| Low | Oct.  7, 1966 | 112.17 | − 23.8% |
| High | Dec. 13, 1968 | 230.51 | + 105.5% |
| Low | July  7, 1970 | 117.04 | − 49.2% |
| High | Apr. 12, 1972 | 209.15 | +  78.7% |
| Low | Sep. 13, 1974 | 96.55 | − 53.8% |
| Recent | July  14, 1976 | 211.91 | + 119.5% |

Both the chart and the table show that the 1966 decline was small relative to the crashes of 1968-1970 and 1972-1974. They also indicate that a similar degree of loss was suffered in the two latter bear markets, whereas the DJIA showed a much sharper loss in the last bear market than in 1968-1970.

Finally, in moves completely contrary to those experienced by the other so-called unweighted indexes, the NYSE TR Index has, at this writing, very nearly regained all of the ground it lost between 1968 and 1974.

The *American Stock Exchange Total Return* has experienced a somewhat more pronounced downward movement during the past seven years than its NYSE counterpart. As shown in Table 71, the junior exchange has been devastated by the one-two onslaught of the recent bear markets, and would still have to travel a long upward path from recent levels to recapture its 1969 peak.

### TABLE 71

#### AMEX TOTAL RETURN INDEX TURNING POINTS

| Event | Date | Amex TR Index | % Change |
|-------|------|---------------|----------|
| High | Jan. 3, 1969 | 335.97 | |
| Low | July 7, 1970 | 122.00 | − 63.7% |
| High | Mar. 9, 1972 | 228.66 | + 87.4% |
| Low | Sep. 16, 1974 | 98.31 | − 57.0% |
| Recent | July 14, 1976 | 205.60 | + 109.1% |

The *Combined Total Return Index* consolidates the NYSE and Amex Indexes into a single measure of total return for all listed stocks. Its major cyclical swings during the last seven years are shown in Table 72.

### TABLE 72

#### COMBINED TOTAL RETURN INDEX TURNING POINTS

| Event | Date | Combined TR Index | % Change |
|-------|------|-------------------|----------|
| High | Dec. 13, 1968 | 267.76 | |
| Low | July 7, 1970 | 119.50 | − 55.4% |
| High | Mar. 9, 1972 | 218.41 | + 82.8% |
| Low | Sept. 13, 1974 | 97.42 | − 55.4% |
| Recent | July 14, 1976 | 209.78 | + 115.3% |

In conclusion, the Total Return Indexes are the only publicly available market indexes which give equal weight to the daily percent price change and dividend return of every listed common stock. The TR Indexes are therefore the broadest and most accurate gauges of daily market behavior in existence. The total gain or loss from every common stock must, by definition, be reflected in the TR Indexes, and analyses of their trends and cyclical patterns provide an unparalleled technical view of the U. S. stock market.

# PART SEVEN
## USING MARKET LOGIC

## 77 How to Use Market Logic

We have explored a sophisticated and logical approach to making profits on Wall Street: first, forecasting the market; second, selecting stocks to fit the market environment; third, constructing an efficient portfolio; and finally, evaluating alternative measures for comparisons of portfolio performance. The informational input necessary to continuously update and adhere to such an approach is beyond the facilities of most individual investors.

The Institute for Econometric Research (of which the author is President and Research Director) is dedicated to scientific investigation of the stock market and providing investment advice to its clients through sophisticated computer technology.

Several newsletters are provided to guide investors through the frequently tricky financial markets. *New Issues* is the investor's guide to initial public offerings. Its 254 stock recommendations have appreciated an average of +112%. *The Insiders* provides continuous investment ratings on over 3,000 common stocks. These Insider Ratings are based on the buying and selling activity of corporate insiders, America's most knowledgeable investors. *Income & Safety* is the consumer's guide to high yields. It includes safety ratings and yield forecasts for money funds, insured money market accounts, and CDs, plus best buy and avoid recommendations for long-term bond funds. *Mutual Fund Forecaster* features Profit Projections and Risk Ratings on several hundred equity mutual funds for traders and investors. *Fund Watch* is a chart service for mutual fund traders and investors. *Mutual Fund Buyer's Guide* is an in-depth compilation of ratings, evaluations, performance, and key investment data on over 1,500 equity and bond funds. *Investor's Digest* offers a compendium of market timing and stock recommendations from dozens of other investment services.

The heart of The Institute's service is *Market Logic*, which provides a complete market-timing and stock-selection system, utilizing the principles expounded in this book.

Any reader of this book who desires a sample copy of one of these newsletters may obtain it *gratis* by calling the author toll-free at The Institute for Econometric Research, 1-800-442-9000.

# 78 Scanning Market Logic

A typical eight-page issue of *Market Logic* contains many valuable features to help every investor achieve his or her goals. The Institute's *Current Forecasts* from its econometric models of the U.S. stock market is featured at the top of Page 1. This information is followed by a succinct, unhedged statement of currently recommended market policy under the heading *Summary & Recommendation*. This short paragraph, which constitutes the heart of the issue, either confirms The Institute's basic investment policy as unchanged or clearly sets forth any change in recommended strategy. It is followed by *Current Position*, which elaborates upon The Institute's market outlook. This article discusses the causes of recent market behavior and the logic underlying The Institute's forecasts of future price trends. The front page is completed by a chart of either The Institute's *Major Trend Model* or the comprehensive and unique *NYSE Total Return Index*.

The remainder of *Market Logic* elaborates upon the front-page features and provides more detailed market, industry, and stock information. *Indicator Review*, which usually leads on Page 2, presents analyses of the factors contributing to the current market forecasts, including readings and comments on literally dozens of fundamental, monetary, technical, and trend indicators. The Institute's own proprietary computer research on these indicators, including many original discoveries, are presented as well.

Page 3 of *Market Logic* is devoted to individual stock selection, including comprehensive technical data, charts, and narrative follow-ups on all previously recommended securities in the *Master Portfolio*. (Every stock recommended in *Market Logic* is continuously followed up until its liquidation from investment portfolios is formally advised.) The average performance of all previously and currently recommended stocks is presented at the bottom of Page 3 of every issue.

While the rest of the issue is generally more flexible in format, Page 4 frequently begins with a *Featured Indicator*, which offers an in-depth analysis of some aspect of market action, or a particularly interesting market-timing indicator that has special current significance.

Page 5 presents the *Actual Option Portfolio*. Option recommendations are made when warranted by bullish short-term, intermediate-term, and long-term market forecasts, and position follow-ups are contained in every *Market Logic* issue. The *Mutual Fund Selector*, including buy recommendations on the top-performing no-load funds is presented on Page 6. Buy and sell trading recommendations of these funds are also keyed to The Institute's current forecast of future market trends. All recommended funds are continuously followed up until liquidation is formally advised.

The balance of the issue presents such features as *Research Reports*, which bring to our readers new discoveries and insights to stock selection and portfolio strategy; *Market Opinion*, based on a regular perusal of thousands of dollars worth of investment, economic, and financial letters; The Institute's exclusive *Seasonality Indicator* (see Chapter 44); economic and monetary analysis; insider buying and selling favorites; the market's strongest stocks; and the *Gold Price Model*.

Occasional *Market Logic* features include specialized computer scans, reviews of important investment books, recommended trading tactics, news on tax developments and commission rates, and special-situation recommendations.

*Forecast Results.* The Institute believes that the reader of every investment advisory service is entitled to know its historical market-forecasting record. Many services hedge so completely as to make it impossible to ascertain their market position at any given time. Not only is the reader unable to understand current market forecasts, but he is also unable to precisely recall past predictions.

The Institute has designed *Market Logic* to avoid these problems. The econometric forecasts and *Summary & Recommendation* on Page 1 are explicitly presented and leave no doubt as to The Institute's position on the present and future trend of stock prices.

To dramatize its commitment to an unhedged position, each issue of *Market Logic* contains a brief table entitled *Forecast Results*, which reviews the outcome of each econometric forecast published three, six, and twelve months, and three and five years earlier. The author knows of no other market letter that constantly reminds its readers of its exact prior forecasts in every issue.

# 79 Market Logic: The Complete Service

*Summary & Recommendation.* The lead article in every issue of *Market Logic* is Summary & Recommendation, designed to present The Institute's current policy recommendations in a clear and succinct manner.

Accordingly, Summary & Recommendation should be the first article read in every issue. It consists of three short statements which impart the essence of the market's current standing and the policy recommended by The Institute to profit therefrom: first, what the market has done in the immediate past; second, what primary forces have directed that behavior; and third, what action should specifically be taken now vis a vis the stock, option and mutual fund recommendations provided in *Market Logic.*

A client can read Summary & Recommendation to the exclusion of all other articles in *Market Logic* and come away with a knowledge of what to do in his current market operations. In fact, after reading Summary & Recommendation, it is necessary only to turn to the Master Portfolio and Actual Option Portfolio pages to note specific security recommendations. Of course, The Institute believes that a well rounded, soundly based understanding of the market environment — past, present and future — is desirable. The remaining pages of *Market Logic* are devoted to providing that background and understanding. However, if you are short of time and wish to know only The Institute's basic market policy, Summary & Recommendation is the one article in *Market Logic* you should read. It is the unhedged condensation of market policy from our entire computer and human research complex.

*Current Forecasts.* The nucleus of The Institute's stock market forecasting approach is the set of econometric models which are used to ascertain the primary trend of the market, as well as to predict intermediate and long range price changes. Each issue of *Market Logic* begins with the Current Forecasts box placed prominently at the top of Page 1.

The first forecasts provided in the box are based on our finely tuned array of econometric models. These forecasts are calculated for two stock market indexes, the Standard & Poor's 500 Index and the broadly based NYSE Total Return Index. They encompass six time frames — three and six months, and one, two, three and five years.

The final forecast provided in the box is the Major Trend Model, which is The Institute's econometric estimate of the current long term trend of the stock market. Model readings over 0.50 are graded bullish, while values below 0.50 are bearish. As a general rule, however, readings in the 0.40 to 0.60 range may be considered approximately neutral. Values around 1.00 are extremely bullish, while readings close to zero are overwhelmingly bearish.

It is often possible to determine The Institute's basic long term position with a mere glance at the model forecasts. For example, if the Major Trend Model is well above 0.50 and all forecasts of future price change are positive, The Institute will be bullish long term and, as a practical matter, you need not read further to ascertain the current long term recommended investment position — it will be bullish. Conversely, if the Major Trend Model is well below 0.50 and all forecasts are negative (that is, a unanimous prediction of lower prices), The Institute will be bearish long term.

The Institute's assessment of the short term market position (less than three months) is not presently included under Current Forecasts, but is stated elsewhere on Page 1 — see Summary & Recommendation and Current Position. (The Institute is presently in the process of developing several short term forecasting models. As these models attain perfection, they will be included in Current Forecasts with those models which have already achieved a high degree of forecasting accuracy.)

If there is an apparent statistical disagreement among the various econometric forecasts, readers should consult the Summary & Recommendation and Current Position articles for clarification and recommended long term policy. Nevertheless, the econometric forecasts always form the basis of recommended investment policy.

Market index forecasts are presented with a slight lag, a condition necessitated by the publishing schedule required for *Market Logic*. *Market Logic* is sent to press and mailed during the day on Friday so that clients may receive it the following day or by Monday or Tuesday morning at the latest. As data on many important indicators is not available until the weekend, or in some cases Monday, the forecasts must reflect the models' condition as of a few days earlier.

For example, a typical model forecast is calculated on the Tuesday prior to the Friday publication, with the predicted market changes based upon the preceding week's price levels. The forecasts on both the Standard & Poor's 500 Index and the NYSE Total Return Index are based upon an average of the daily closing values for the week.

The models use a wide variety of information, including various interest rate indicators, margin and reserve requirements, free reserves, volume trends, recent price changes, short interest ratio, several market breadth measures, money supply, inflation, new stock offerings, a number of short sale statistics, mutual fund cash positions, and several indexes of speculative conditions.

*Current Position.* This article appears directly below Summary & Recommendation on Page 1 of each issue of *Market Logic.* Its primary purpose is to elaborate upon the comments and policy suggestions already stated in the previous article.

To that end attention is given to important news and economic events which have recently affected stock prices or which might have an effect on them in the future. Recent moves of significance by the major indexes contained under Current Price Levels are also provided.

The Major Trend Model is placed in historical perspective for easy understanding, and any required interpretation is furnished. The present positions of the econometric forecasting models are elaborated upon as well, with predictions of special significance discussed in some detail. To facilitate interpretation of the current standing and recent changes in the model forecasts, the indicators which are contributing most importantly to them are also mentioned.

Current Position always concludes its narration with a clear and concise statement of current recommended market policy for the short and long term. Finally, a chart of one of the Total Return Indexes alternates with a chart of the Major

Trend Model directly below the narrative at the bottom of the page.

*Indicator Review.* The purpose of Indicator Review is to provide elaboration upon Current Position. As The Institute's fundamental market policy is based upon its econometric stock market forecasts, it is worthwhile to periodically review the numerous forecasting indicators which contribute to those models. Indicator Review is designed to furnish readers with the most significant developments in a broad array of indicators, ranging from monetary to sentiment, from fundamental to technical.

Although most of the indicators discussed in the review are included in the econometric models, this is not universally the case. Many valuable clues to market behavior come from indicators which are extremely difficult to quantify and incorporate into objective forecasting models. Such indicators are studied continuously nonetheless, and when they appear to be signalling important messages, they are discussed in this column in some detail.

One of the most valuable features of the review is the presentation of historical perspective through probability studies and detailed analyses of important indicators. Charts of significant indicators are also often presented in issues of *Market Logic* to provide visual perspective.

Most of the indicators covered in the review section of *Market Logic* are discussed in detail in earlier chapters of this book. Should you at any time have difficulty understanding either the indicators themselves or The Institute's comments on them, or should you desire additional background information, you should consult those chapters.

*Featured Indicator.* Most issues of *Market Logic* single out one market indicator for in-depth analysis. The indicator is usually one of current importance that is contributing significantly to the econometric model forecasts. Featured Indicator is designed to provide readers with the results of The

Institute's own research during recent years. These articles are intended to be an educational course in themselves. The studies which are related are usually based upon several decades of market data and are the product of intensive computer and scientific analysis.

While the indicators covered are generally above average in their market prediction qualities, The Institute does not feel obligated to solely present those indicators which are providing a particularly valuable or meaningful message. It is just as important not to act on misinformation as to act on correct information. Consequently, indicators which are not working well or which have been ballyhooed out of all legitimate proportion by the investment community are also featured from time to time.

Up to a full page is often devoted to a Featured Indicator. It is The Institute's hope that by the time an investor has read *Market Logic* for one year, Featured Indicator alone will have substantially broadened his investment perspective and increased his stock market acumen to the point where this single series will have repaid the investment in *Market Logic* many times over.

*Total Return Indexes.* A regular feature of every issue of *Market Logic* is a table containing daily readings of The Institute's three Total Return (TR) Indexes as well as several important timing indicators. The TR Indexes (see Chapter 76) are market indices of all listed common stocks which not only give equal weight to all stocks but measure their total return from price change *and* dividends. All daily closing readings for the NYSE, Amex and Combined Total Return Indexes since the previous edition of *Market Logic* are shown in each issue.

Of course, day-to-day market fluctuations *can* weigh too heavily in the investor's mind. It is important not to lose sight of the big picture. Hence, appearing directly below the daily TR Indexes themselves are the percentage changes recorded by each of the three Indexes since their last major cyclical low or peak. These long term changes provide a perspective in which to assess the market's recent short term patterns.

Appearing in conjunction with the Total Return Indexes are current readings on several important technical market indicators. The content of this list is subject to change, but at present includes the percent of stocks in long, intermediate, and short term price uptrends, as well as the percent of issues currently priced above their support levels. "Support" is defined as the average weekly closing price of a stock during its last thirty weeks of trading (see pp. 333-334 for additional details).

To provide a continuing reminder of the market's underlying fundamental condition, we also present current readings for both the New York and American stock exchanges on three classical fundamental tools: (1) the percent of stocks currently priced below their net book value per share; (2) the average dividend yield of all stocks; and (3) the median price/earnings ratio of all issues. (See Chapter 3 for guidance on interpreting and applying these indicators to market timing.)

Finally, we let you be a market predictor, too. Twice every month, *Market Logic* conducts a random-selection survey of several hundred of its readers. Based on this continuing survey, we show the percent of *Market Logic* readers who believe the stock market will be higher in six months. This fascinating and unusual indicator is called the "Market Logic Reader Index." Developed in 1982, the ML Reader Index still has too short a history to draw reliable conclusions as to its forecasting accuracy. In fact, it is still unclear whether it measures sophisticated investor sentiment or should be treated as a contrary indicator. Early readings revealed, however, that *Market Logic* subscribers were themselves much more firmly committed to the record 1982-1983 bull move than were the nation's most popular investment advisory services.

*Insider Insights.* We learned in Chapter 60 that insider

trading activity has been proven to be the most consistently useful criterion on which to base stock selections. It is so valuable, in fact, that The Institute publishes a separate advisory service, *The Insiders,* to provide in-depth coverage of this one topic. Its very importance, however, compels coverage of insider trading highlights in *Market Logic* as well. Insider Insights, which appears regularly in every issue of *Market Logic,* does just that, pointing out to investors the stocks that are being most heavily accumulated and liquidated by corporate insiders, America's most knowledgeable investors.

*Stock Recommendations.* The Institute places first priority upon prediction of the current market trend and prospects for future market change. When the investing climate is favorable, the next task is to select stocks for purchase.

To this end The Institute has programmed its computer system to monitor every common stock listed on the New York and American Stock Exchanges, as well as hundreds of OTC issues. Each week the computer sorts through the entire list of stocks, calculating and analyzing dozens of technical and fundamental indicators on each security. In a typical week, the computer scans over 3,000 stocks and flags ten to twenty issues on the basis of pre-programmed criteria relating to insider buying, relative strength or weakness, volatility, and other factors.

The staff of The Institute examines these stocks, applies other objective and subjective standards to them, and narrows the group down, usually to around a half dozen issues. Following more comprehensive analysis of the remaining issues, one or two may finally be recommended for purchase in *Market Logic.*

The thrust of The Institute's stock research is to synthesize space age computer technology with plain old-fashioned hard work. The computer first identifies stocks with desirable characteristics, and the staff of The Institute then subjects these stocks to further analysis.

Finally, after the entire process has resulted in the selection of one or more stocks, The Institute checks to see whether a convertible security, warrant, or option is available for those stocks which might provide opportunities to obtain higher yielding investments, leverage, or lower risk hedges. After final selection of the appropriate security (or securities), the stock is assigned to one of The Institute's continuously monitored portfolios. (See Master Portfolio and Actual Option Portfolio.) In that portfolio it is subjected to continuous attention and analysis until final sale is advised.

Upon initial recommendation of any security, a special *Stock Recommendations* column in *Market Logic* discusses the reasons and logic behind its recommendation. During the course of its holding in one of the portfolios, technical and fundamental developments in the stock are discussed in each issue of *Market Logic*, both through statistical updates in the Master and Option Portfolios and through periodic narrative comments in this column on recent developments and future prospects for the company. Finally, when formal sale of the security is advised, the reasons for the sale recommendation are stated.

The entire process is designed to provide you with the best security recommendations possible, and then to follow up those securities continuously so that clients holding positions are never left in doubt about what to do with them.

Affiliates and employees of The Institute usually establish concurrent positions in each recommended security. Thus, your profits and losses are our profits and losses, and you may be sure that we are doing our very best to bring to you the finest investment and speculative opportunities of which we are capable.

*Master Portfolio.* The Master Portfolio on Page 3 of every issue of Market Logic provides a continuing technical and fundamental update on all previously recommended common stocks. As new stock recommendations are made, they are added to the Master Portfolio in the *Market Logic* issue following their initial recommendation. The stocks are continually monitored until such time as liquidation of holdings is specifically advised.

The Master Portfolio is divided into three components, the first consisting of stocks most suitable for aggressive portfolios, the second for conservative portfolios, and the third, special situations. Although a distinction between aggressive and conservative companies is not possible on purely objective grounds, the latter are basically distinguished by their ability to withstand severe national economic stress. These companies are generally leaders in their industry and will, in all probability, maintain a sound earnings base even during periods of economic crisis. Such stocks are usually sound long term holdings.

Aggressive stocks, on the other hand, represent companies which are generally smaller and less firmly situated than their competitors. Their earnings are likely to be more volatile, leading therefore to greater potential gains for investors willing to accept greater risks. These stocks are more likely to represent trading positions.

The conservative list may contain some issues also suitable for aggressive portfolios when dynamic developments seem likely to produce better than average growth. On the other hand, conservative investors should generally eschew positions in aggressive stocks except to the extent that excess funds may be set aside especially for speculative purposes.

The basic table of the Master Portfolio provides many pieces of technical and fundamental information, including recent prices, apparent major price support levels, Strength Ratings, price trends, volume measures, Volatility Ratings, current price/earnings ratios, dividend yields, and evidence of significant insider activity. In addition, the originally recommended price for each stock is provided and current trading advice (buy, hold, sell) is explicitly stated.

The average annualized percent price changes since original date of recommendation are provided at the bottom of the table for all issues currently in the Master Portfolio and for all closed out recommendations.

Master Portfolio issues held by The Institute, affiliates, or employees are also specifically identified.

In addition to the Master Portfolio table itself, several stock charts provide a visual presentation of significant price moves by Master Portfolio stocks in recent days and months.

*Actual Option Portfolio.* The expanding role of stock options on the investment scene requires a continuing and comprehensive update of current opportunities. The Institute devotes nearly a page of every issue of *Market Logic* to the world of options, including a trend analysis of every stock with a listed option, as well as specific option purchase recommendations.

Option trading is a highly complicated and speculative field of investment endeavor. A comprehensive treatment of the advantages, disadvantages, risks, and potential rewards which are inherent in the multitude of potential option positions would require a volume in itself.

The Institute makes specific option recommendations based upon the information contained in the Actual Option Portfolio table and other technical and fundamental criteria. A portfolio of stock options is maintained by an affiliate of The Institute, identically matching *Market Logic* recommendations. The current value of this Option Portfolio is updated in every issue and a detailed record of its history is available from The Institute upon request and a stamped, self-addressed envelope, as is a complete history of all *Market Logic* stock recommendations.

All specific option recommendations are reviewed in every issue until final liquidation of positions is advised.

By their very nature, stock options are highly volatile investment mediums. Continuous attention should be devoted to current portfolio holdings, and clients trading individual recommendations should monitor the twice-weekly *Hot Line* recording (see Chapter 81) which includes The Institute's latest option buy and sell advise.

A key ingredient of the option presentation is a relative

strength analysis of every stock with a listed option. The ranking serves two purposes.

First, it provides technical information on the stocks underlying all listed options. A fair value for any option is based upon the current market price and future prospects of the common stock. The Option Portfolio allows investors to make judgments on the technical merits of the underlying stocks, to winnow out those with poor qualities, and to concentrate on those exhibiting superior potential.

Second, because stocks must generally meet fairly rigorous requirements before exchange option trading can commence, the Option Portfolio serves as a relative strength and technical analysis of the nation's largest, most widely owned, and most important companies.

The Option Portfolio printout is constantly expanded to include new stocks as they are listed for trading on the various option exchanges.

*Mutual Fund Selector.* The Institute's comprehensive coverage of investment opportunities includes a computerized performance ranking of over 150 mutual funds. Leading no-load funds are periodically recommended for purchase in *Market Logic* in conjunction with important market upswings. "Money market" funds, which invest only in very short term, low risk government securities, bank certificates of deposit, and commercial paper, are also monitored by The Institute and are recommended during periods of expected market declines. The ranking is based only on *no-load* funds, which do not charge a commission for purchase of their shares. The ranking excludes load funds, which levy initial sales commissions as high as 9% of the amount invested.

Several mutual fund performance studies have proven conclusively that there is no appreciable difference in investment performance between load and no-load funds. A sales charge, after all, does not buy superior fund management (all funds, load and no-load, charge a "management fee," usually less than 1% per annum, for that). All a sales charge buys is a salesman. It obviously makes little sense to pay more for the same performance. Therefore, all other things equal, a no-load fund is a preferable investment to a load fund.

Still, no-load funds are not totally commission-free. They do incur commission costs in stock transactions and these costs are passed on to the fund shareholders in the form of reductions in net asset values. However, most funds turn over their portfolios relatively infrequently, and so do not pay many commissions. Most funds, especially the larger ones, also buy and sell stocks in very large quantities and can take advantage of the lower percentage commission rates applicable to such transactions.

Diversification is the most important benefit provided by mutual funds. In relatively small portfolios, extensive diversification is difficult to achieve unless one is willing to purchase small numbers of shares in each of a large number of stocks. Mutual funds provide investors access to portfolios consisting of dozens, or even hundreds, of stocks — all for a very small minimum investment.

Mutual funds also enable investors to conduct convenient switching programs. One of our most popular techniques used in *Market Logic* is periodic switching between a common stock mutual fund and a money fund managed by the same group. During bullish market periods, an investment may reside in a common stock fund, and during bearish periods (or in a time of high interest rates) the investment can be switched to the money fund without any commission. Such switches are frequently as easy to make as picking up your telephone and calling the fund toll-free.

Each issue of *Market Logic* presents a statistical analysis, along with the address and telephone number, of each of the currently recommended no-load funds. Toll-free WATS line numbers are provided where available and are indicated by an 800 area code. To contact other funds, you should first call collect, as some will accept the charges; others will not.

An investor's relative preference for mutual funds or common stocks should ultimately rest on his own relative skills in market timing versus stock selection. An investor more proficient in stock selection should obviously avoid funds, and buy and sell his own stocks. However, an investor expert in timing market swings will find mutual funds ideal investments. Since most mutual funds (specialized funds excepted) have well diversified common stock portfolios, their net asset values usually fluctuate directly in concert with the market itself. Thus, all the investor has to do is select the best performing funds – and, of course, know when to buy and sell them. Such a strategy lends itself well to trading both long and intermediate term market swings. During broadly based price uptrends, the trader should be invested in the best performing no-load funds. During market downswings, he should withdraw his money and purchase low risk securities such as treasury bills or commercial paper, or no-load money market funds which invest directly in those types of securities themselves.

Three primary factors should be considered in no-load fund investing. First, while most funds move in the same direction as the market – up when prices are advancing, down when the averages are declining – some, by virtue of their individual investment philosophies, are inherently more volatile than others. The relative degree of volatility peculiar to each fund tends to persist through time. Our long term measure of fund volatility, *Beta,* is based upon a computerized examination of a fund's performance relative to the market during the last two years. Beta expresses the rate of a fund's percent price change that has accompanied a 10% rise in the market. A Beta of 13, for example, indicates that a fund has historically advanced, and will likely continue to advance, at a 13% rate when the market goes up 10%, and should decline 13% when the market falls 10%. A Beta of 10 denotes a fund which is expected to advance and decline at the same rate as the market, while a zero Beta denotes one whose price fluctuations are totally unrelated to those of the market.

Investors wishing to maximize rewards in rising markets (albeit with a concomitant maximization of risk in declining markets) should purchase high Beta funds, while more conservative investors should concentrate on funds with lower Betas.

The second important factor in selecting mutual funds is more recent price growth.   Our measure of growth is the "Strength Rating."   (The Strength Rating is the percent by which the average price of the fund over the last thirty weeks is above or below the average thirty week price of a date thirteen weeks earlier.)   Given comparable volatilities, the fund with the highest Strength Rating should be preferred.

While fund volatility does tend to persist through time, deviations from the historical volatility norm can occur as funds move in or out of tune with the current market environment.   For instance, individual funds might concentrate on broad categories or groups of stock which are leading or lagging the market, or fund managers might simply be wrong on the market itself, holding too much or too little cash at key turns.   Consequently, recent strength is just as important in forecasting future strength as is historical volatility.   All other things equal, the higher the Strength Rating, the better the fund has performed in the past few months, the more in tune with the market it is, and the better it should perform in the future relative to all other funds.   The recommendations in *Market Logic* are therefore based upon Strength Ratings, and investors should normally concentrate on funds with superior Strength Rating ranks.

To complement the current Strength Rating, the five week change in the Strength Rating of each fund also appears in the table.   The five week change is simply the difference between the current week's Strength Rating and the Strength Rating of five weeks earlier, providing a measure of short term strength or weakness.

Finally, as an adjunct to the Beta volatility and long and short term strength measures, long and short term Performance Ratings are calculated, which measure the extent to which each fund is exceeding or falling short of expected performance based upon its historical volatility (Beta).   The long term Performance Rating is based upon an interaction of the Strength Rating and Beta, while the short term Performance Rating is determined by an equivalent calculation using the five week change in the Strength Rating and Beta.

To determine a fund's long term Performance Rating, the Strength Rating the fund *should* have achieved, given its historical volatility, is subtracted from the current Strength Rating which the fund *actually* achieved. Assume that a fund has a historical volatility (Beta) of 16% — indicating that it advances or declines 16% for every 10% the market advances or declines. Assume further that the average volatility among all funds is just 8%. It follows that the fund should increase twice as fast as the average fund in a rising market because it is twice as volatile. If the average no-load stock fund has a Strength Rating of, say, 10%, then this fund should have a Strength Rating twice as great, or 20%. By subtracting this expected Strength Rating from the fund's actual Strength Rating, the long term Performance Rating is derived. If the actual Strength Rating is +25%, the long term Performance Rating is an excellent +5% (25% − 20% = +5%). But an actual Strength Rating of only 15% yields a poor long term Performance Rating of −5% (15% − 20% = −5%).

The short term Performance Rating is determined in precisely the same manner, using the five week Strength Rating change in lieu of the Strength Rating.

By definition, the average long and short term Performance Ratings for all funds are always zero. The computer carries all of the calculations out to several more digits than appear on the table so occasionally a Performance Rating may be one point above or below a figure computed by hand —but the computer calculation will be the more accurate of the two.

The most attractive funds in *bull markets* are usually those with high Betas, high Strength Ratings, *and* high Performance Ratings. If a fund has been able to achieve superior performance in both the short and long terms, so much the better. All of these measures taken together constitute a comprehensive analysis of the funds' recent performance and provide valuable information for determining which funds should lead the market in the next period of rising prices.

*Industry Groups.*   Market observers have long recognized the tendency of stocks in homogeneous industry groups to move together. One study which analyzed 63 stocks between 1928 and 1960 discovered that in certain instances, up to one-third of a stock's price fluctuation may be ascribed to industry influences to the exclusion of all other factors.

There are sound theoretical reasons for this phenomenon. Companies within an industry group are often similarly affected by economic developments. As a consequence, most Wall Street research houses are geared to analyzing industry groups first and companies within those groups second. It comes as no great surprise, then, that large institutions often commit investment funds in diversified sub-portfolios aimed at particular industry groups. The price correlation also leads to similar price, volume, and other technical patterns which gain the attention of technical analysts. So, when technicians make market commitments, they too are frequently attracted to issues in similar industries, a fact which only serves to accentuate industry co-movement in the market.

The Institute continually monitors the performance of sixty primary industry groups.   Every New York and American Stock Exchange listed company is classified into one of the sixty sectors, which are then examined by computer for price strength and weakness.

To determine a group's long term price strength, The Institute utilizes Strength Ratings of all stocks in the group, together with five week changes in the Strength Ratings. The ratings for every stock in an industry group are averaged to yield an Industry Group Strength Rating (long term price strength) and an Industry Group Strength Rating Change (short to intermediate term price strength). The sixty groups are then rank ordered from one (strongest) to sixty (weakest) by each of the two measures.

Each issue of *Market Logic* identifies the groups which are leading the market in long term price strength. The strongest stocks in the leading groups are usually flagged as well. In addition, industry groups which are lagging far behind the market are noted, as are groups which are strongest or weakest on a short to intermediate term basis.

*Research Report.* This occasional feature condenses major studies of stock price behavior that have been conducted at The Institute, in academia, and on Wall Street.

*Investor's Digest.* Each week the staff of The Institute examines literally scores of advisory services, economic letters, professional journals, and other financial periodicals. Aside from the obvious value of expanding our own investment knowledge and horizons, several ancillary benefits flow from this study, including a regular *Market Logic* article entitled Investor's Digest.

The Digest distills and presents for your perusal the best (and occasionally the worst) investment insights from these publications.

While the thoughts from a widely diversified range of publications are presented, emphasis is given to the stock market advisory services. This enables you to see what the largest investment letters are currently recommending, as well as what your favorite and our favorite letters have to say.

As the staff of The Institute surveys the dozens of stock market advisory publications each week, it ascribes to each a rating of its bullishness or bearishness on the market. The individual service ratings are tabulated and summarized in an Advisory Sentiment Index, which presents the percentage of services that are bullish at the present time. This index has value as a market forecasting tool in itself since the aggregate of advisors are usually (and unfortunately) wrong in their opinions at critical market turning points. However, as discussed in Chapter 22 of this book, the Advisory Sentiment Index does require a degree of interpretation because, while advisors are usually wrong at turning points, they are often

correct during extended market trends. An ancillary indicator, the *Market Timers Index*, reveals the recommended
percent commitment to equities by leading market timing
investment newsletters. Current readings and the requisite
interpretation of both the Advisory Sentiment Index and the
Market Timers Index are provided in the *Indicator Review*
section of every issue.

*Million Dollar Glamour Stock Index.* The Glamour Stock
Index represents a hypothetical investment of one million
dollars on December 31, 1972, divided equally among seventeen market high flyers. In the late sixties and early seven-
ties, institutional investors created a two tier market as they
became enamored of "one decision stocks," so-called because
investors had only to decide when to buy the issues. (Presumably, it would never be desirable to sell them.)

As 1972, and the bull market, drew to a close, *Institutional Investor,* a monthly magazine catering to mutual and
pension fund managers, announced the agenda for a major
investment conference to be held in New York during March,

FIGURE 22.   Million Dollar Glamour Stock Index (month end).

1973. The editors singled out seventeen stocks with then impeccable growth credentials for special presentations at the conference: American Home Products, Avon Products, Coca Cola, Walt Disney, Eastman Kodak, IBM, IT&T, Johnson & Johnson, S. S. Kresge, Eli Lilly, McDonalds, Merck, MGIC, Minnesota Mining, Polaroid, Sears Roebuck, and Xerox.

At the time, these issues were high flyers in the truest sense of the word, with some selling at price/earnings ratios that appear astronomical in retrospect. The median P/E was 48, but multiples ranged as high as Polaroid's 91.

These same seventeen issues became The Institute's Million Dollar Glamour Stock Index. As illustrated in Figure 22 (page 325), the Glamour Stock Index declined in value in 19 of the 21 months of the long 1973-1974 bear market, in the process losing over 60% of its beginning capital. From the September 1974 low, the portfolio moved upward during the first half of 1975, although at nowhere near the rate of the preceding decline. It may well take many years for the old highs to once again be attained.

A close monitoring of the Million Dollar Glamour Stock Index can provide important clues to the action of the institutions which are drawn to these highly capitalized issues. The relatively lethargic recovery of the Index coming off the September 1974 low, for example, provided compelling evidence that investors would do better to avoid the "high flyers" and concentrate on either cyclical issues or smaller and less widely known companies. As institutions often dominate market fluctuations, the Glamour Stock Index can also often furnish valuable indications of major trends and cycles in the broad market as well. For example, the 15 month consecutive downtrend in the Index from July 1973 through September 1974 clearly defined one of the great bear market crashes in recent history.

*How to Read Market Logic in 60 Seconds.* We don't think for a minute that that's all there is to *Market Logic*. But if you're in a hurry, or if detailed explanations of market behavior, indicators, industry groups, strongest stocks, or advisory opinion is just not your bag . . . in short, if all you want to know is what to do now in the market and what securities to buy or sell, here's how to do it:

(1)  Read Summary & Recommendation on Page 1.  In three quick sentences, it tells you what the market has done, why it has performed that way, and what you should do now. Time:  15 seconds.

(2)  Quickly scan the Master Portfolio (Page 3) for stocks rated Buy or Sell. Time:  25 seconds.

(3)  Flip over to Page 6 for the currently recommended option and mutual fund trades. Time:  15 seconds.

Add 5 seconds for turning pages.

Total time:  60 seconds.  A minute for the essence of . . . dare we say it . . . just possibly the greatest investment advisory letter in the world.

# 80 Key Market Logic Statistics

*Market Logic Volatility Ratings.*  One of the most valuable statistics included in the Strongest Stocks, Master Portfolio, and Option Corner tables of *Market Logic* is the Volatility Rating.  The Institute for Econometric Research also regularly publishes a supplementary report providing Volatility Ratings for all listed stocks. A copy of the latest report is available free of charge to readers of this book, and to Market Logic subscribers, from The Institute for Econometric Research at 3471 North Federal Highway, Fort Lauderdale, Florida 33306.

*Calculation of Volatility Ratings.*  As we saw in Chapter 61, high volatility is a very desirable individual stock or portfolio attribute in a rising market. The Volatility Ratings are an average of the classic Beta measure of volatility and a statistic derived from the Square Root Rule. (Both concepts are also explained in Chapter 61.)

The Beta used here is a fifteen quarter exponential moving average of quarterly Betas. (The more recent quarters receive more weight in the average.) In turn, each stock's quarterly Beta is derived from a comparison of its daily price fluctuations with the daily price fluctuations of the New York Stock Exchange Composite Index. The final Beta is multiplied by ten, so it is expressed in terms of the percentage stock price fluctuation that has historically accompanied a 10% move in the market. This relationship is expected to hold in the future, regardless of the direction in which the market moves. If the Beta is 15, it means the stock should rise 15% if the market rises 10%, and fall 15% if the market falls 10%.

Square Root Volatility is based on the premise that lower priced stocks show greater price movements in both directions than higher priced stocks. To calculate Square Root Volatility we first determine the dollar increase that will occur in the *square root of the price* of the average priced stock in the market if that average stock were to rise 10%. The Square Root Volatility for any stock can then be calculated by first adding that same increment to the *square root* of the stock's present price. The result is then squared (multiplied times itself). The squared number represents the projected price of the stock. It can be readily compared to the actual current price of the stock to determine its expected percent price gain if the market goes up 10%. (If the market goes *down* 10% instead, the stock is expected to *fall* by the calculated percentage.) The percentage itself is the Square Root Volatility for the stock.

The final Volatility Rating is simply the average of the Beta statistic and the Square Root Rule statistic. (If the Beta is negative, such as is the case for contra-cyclical issues like gold mining stocks, the Square Root Rule statistic is made negative as well, before averaging.) A final Volatility Rating less than 10% means that the stock is less volatile than the market, a value of exactly 10% means the stock has average volatility, and a value greater than 10% indicates a stock has above average volatility. For example, a stock with a Volatility Rating of 20% is twice as volatile as the average stock. During rising prices it should increase twice  as fast as the market, and during a period of falling prices, it should decline twice as fast.    Remember, one of the major purposes of Volatility Ratings is to single out fast moving stocks to buy and hold during rising markets.

*How To Find The Volatility of Your Portfolio.* Just as the Volatility Rating of an individual stock indicates how fast that stock should move relative to the market, a Volatility Rating for a portfolio of stocks provides an estimate of how much that portfolio will rise or fall, given a certain swing in the market.

If your portfolio consists of approximately equal dollar amounts of a number of stocks, calculating a Volatility Rating for the portfolio is very easy — just find the average of the Volatility Ratings of the stocks. (Simply add up all the individual Volatility Ratings and divide by the number of stocks.)

In the more likely case that your portfolio consists of unequal amounts of various stocks, a bit more work is required to find the portfolio's Volatility Rating. But it is a simple, straightforward technique. First, multiply the Volatility Rating of each stock by the *market value* of that stock. (If you own 200 shares of Boeing priced at $40, its "market value" is $8,000.)   Second, add together all the numbers calculated in the first step (which we shall call "Dollar Volatilities").   Third, divide that sum by the total market value of your entire portfolio. The result is the Volatility Rating of your portfolio.

Here is an example of how to calculate a Volatility Rating for a portfolio of more than one stock (*any* number of stocks can be used).   After multiplying each stock's Volatility Rating by its market value to determine "Dollar Volatility," the individual market values and "Dollar Volatilities" are totaled.   Finally, total "Dollar Volatility" is divided by market value.    As $120,000 divided by $10,000 equals

| Security | Volatility Rating (%) | | Market Value | | "Dollar Volatility" |
|---|---|---|---|---|---|
| Boeing | 10 | x | $ 8,000 | = | $ 80,000 |
| Woolworth | 20 | x | $ 2,000 | = | $ 40,000 |
| Total | | | $10,000 | | $120,000 |

12, the Volatility Rating for this portfolio is 12%.    The portfolio should rise or fall slightly faster than average.    If the market rises 10%, the portfolio should rise 12%.    If the market falls 10%, the portfolio should decline 12%.

If the same portfolio contains cash, treasury bills, or similar completely non-volatile investments, the total portfolio volatility is lower.    To find out just how much lower, the calculation is repeated, adding in the amount of non-volatile liquid assets (we shall assume $10,000 worth here).    These liquid assets *always* have a Volatility Rating of zero.

| Security | Volatility Rating (%) | | Market Value | | "Dollar Volatility" |
|---|---|---|---|---|---|
| Boeing | 10 | x | $ 8,000 | = | $ 80,000 |
| Woolworth | 20 | x | $ 2,000 | = | $ 40,000 |
| T-Bills | 0 | x | $10,000 | = | $    0 |
| Total | | | $20,000 | | $120,000 |

Dividing the portfolio's total "Dollar Volatility" (still $120,000) by its total market value (now up to $20,000), equals 6%, the Volatility Rating of this partly cash portfolio. The substantial liquid position has dropped the Volatility Rating to well below average.

Just as a cash reserve decreases volatility, buying stocks on margin increases volatility.    Taking the first example, but assuming half the investment was borrowed, we will now *deduct* a $5,000 margin debt from the market value before making the final calculation.

| Security | Volatility Rating (%) | | Market Value | | "Dollar Volatility" |
|---|---|---|---|---|---|
| Boeing | 10 | x | $ 8,000 | = | $ 80,000 |
| Woolworth | 20 | x | $ 2,000 | = | $ 40,000 |
| Funds Borrowed | 0 | x | $ (5,000) | = | $ 0 |
| Total | | | $ 5,000 | | $120,000 |

Dividing $120,000 by the $5,000 net equity equals 24%, the Volatility Rating of this margin leveraged portfolio — indicating the portfolio *equity* will rise or fall nearly 2½ times as fast as the market. Of course, interest expenses on the debt will actually cause any gain to be slightly less than expected and cause any loss to be slightly sharper. (See Chapter 65 for an analysis of how interest and commission expenses impact upon margin account trading.)

*Technical Note.* For readers interested in the mathematics of computing Volatility Ratings, here is the formula The Institute uses each week to calculate the Volatility Rating of every common stock:

$$K_1 \cdot R_{MS} \cdot \frac{\sigma_S}{\sigma_M} + \left\{ \frac{\left( \sqrt{P_S} + \lambda \right)^2}{P_S} - K_2 \right\} \cdot K_3$$

The terms to the left of the braces represent the widely used Beta statistic, while the remainder of the equation is a quantification of the Square Root Rule. The formula is constructed so as to give equal weight to each of these two measures, which is the same as calculating them separately and averaging the two.

The three left hand terms are: K1, a constant always equal to 5.0; Rms, the correlation coefficient showing how closely the fluctuations of the stock have been related to the fluctuations of the market to find the stock's relative volatility. The two symbols which look like a small "o" with a squiggle are lower case forms of the Greek letter Sigma. Mathematicians sometimes use Greek letters to stand for an entire  commonly used formula – in this case the formula is for standard deviation. (Mathematicians also sometimes use Greek letters just so nobody else will know what they are doing.)

The other half of the equation is somewhat more complex. Ps stands for the price of the stock, and the symbol which looks like an upside down "Y" is another Greek letter; in this case, Lambda, standing for the amount the square root of the average priced stock will rise if the actual price of that stock rises 10%. What this particular part of the formula tells us to do is: first, find the square root of the price of the stock we are analyzing, add the amount represented by Lambda to that square root, square the sum, and then divide it all by the price of the stock. This gives us the ratio of the future price to the present price. We then subtract K2, a constant always equal to one, and multiply the result by K3, a constant always equal to 50. Adding this result to the Beta result obtained from the left half of the equation, we have our Volatility Rating.

Now, aren't you glad *Market Logic* does this for you?

*Market Logic Strength Rating.* Second in importance only to The Institute's Volatility Ratings are The Institute's weekly Strength Rating calculations for every common stock listed on the New York and American Stock Exchanges. These ratings appear regularly in the *Trend Scan Highlights, Master Portfolio,* and *Actual Option Portfolio* tables. All relative strength rankings used in *Market Logic* are based on the Strength Rating unless otherwise specified.

*Calculation of the Strength Ratings.* The stock price as of the close of trading in New York on the last day of the week is used to construct and update a 30 week simple moving average of price. (No claim is made that a 30 week average has any mystical powers, despite its popularity among market technicians. The same calculation based on a 20 or 40 week moving average would yield very similar results. If this were *not* the case, the whole strength concept would be suspect.) *The Strength Rating is simply the percent change between the current value of the 30 week moving average and the moving average 13 weeks earlier,* after adjustment for any stock dividends or splits. The higher the percent change, the stronger the stock has been. The Strength Ratings for all listed common stocks (over 2,500) are arranged in order of rank, strongest to weakest. The 25 stocks on both the New York and the American Stock Exchanges with the highest Strength Ratings are sorted out for listing in *Strongest Stocks.*

As a second step, each stock's Strength Rating is compared with its Strength Rating of five weeks earlier to measure whether the stock's strength is improving or worsening on a shorter term basis.

Long, intermediate, and short term price trends for each stock are determined from various aspects of this relative strength analysis. If the 30 week moving average, upon which the Strength Rating is based, is rising (higher this week than last week), the *long* term trend is said to be "up" (+); otherwise the trend is "down" (−). This is the equivalent of defining the long term trend as "up" (or "down") if this week's stock price is greater (or lesser) than the stock price 31 weeks ago. Again, these are not magical numbers; they are intended only as an approximation of trend.

Next, the *intermediate* term price trend is determined by examining the one week change in the Strength Rating. If the current Strength Rating is above its level of a week earlier (i.e., is rising), the intermediate term trend is defined as "up" (+). If the current Strength Rating is below its level of a week ago (i.e., is falling), the intermediate term trend is classified "down" (−).

To calculate the third and last price trend direction, the *short* term, the ratio of current price to 30 week moving average is calculated and reduced to a percent difference. This percentage is compared with the Strength Rating (which is the percentage by which the current moving average is above or below its moving average of 13 weeks earlier). If the price to 30 week moving average percentage is greater than the Strength Rating percentage, the short term trend is defined as "up" (+).   When the price to 30 week moving average percentage is less than the Strength Rating percentage, the Strength Rating will soon decline (in the absence of a quick price rally) and the short term price trend is graded "down" (−).

To reiterate, the choice of moving average length in these calculations (30 weeks) is *not* absolutely critical.   If it were, the system itself would be suspect.   We are only dealing with approximations of trend.

Using this basic long, intermediate, and short term price trend information, the following table traces an idealized stock through a six phase cyclical price movement:

| Price Trends | Phase | Cyclical Position |
|---|---|---|
| − − − | (1) | Stock in established and continued downtrend |
| − − + | (2) | Conditions for coming reversal forming |
| − + + | (3) | Increasing intermediate term strength |
| + + + | (4) | Main trend up; all technical conditions agree |
| + + − | (5) | Conditions for coming reversal forming |
| + − − | (6) | Increasing intermediate term weakness |
| − − − | (1) | Downtrend firmly established |

Finally, the basic 30 week moving average is also used as a hypothetical support level.   Again, this is an approximation of where short term declines may find support, and should be viewed as the mid-point of a range, not as an absolutely critical value.   In cases where the price is already below the moving average, the support level in the table reads "NONE."

*Volume Turnover Ratio.*   This ratio is calculated by dividing the total trading volume in a stock over the last six months by the total number of shares outstanding.   The result is multiplied by two to convert it from a six month to a twelve month *annual* basis.   For example, a 20% Volume Turnover Ratio results if 10% of the total outstanding shares of a stock have traded in the past six months.   A high Volume Turnover Ratio is typical of volatile, thinly capitalized stocks of small companies, whereas a low Volume Turnover Ratio is associated with less volatile, broadly capitalized stocks of larger companies. The Volume Turnover Ratio's principal value is as an additional measure of prospective volatility. A notation "M" next to the Volume Turnover Ratio signals that there are less than one million shares of the common stock outstanding. Such issues tend to be particularly volatile.

*Volume Trend* is a measure of whether relative volume in the issue is currently increasing or decreasing. It is calculated as the percent difference between average daily volume during the last one month and average daily volume during the last six months. A positive Volume Trend reading shows that the most recent month's volume is above the six month average level, while a negative Volume Trend reflects a fall off in volume. The Volume Trend shows whether a high Volume Turnover Ratio (see above) is a product of a recent upsurge in trading activity.

*Price/Earnings Ratio and Yield.* These fundamental measures of value are calculated each week on the basis of latest reported twelve month earnings and indicated annual dividend rates, respectively. "NE" stands for negative earnings. Stock dividends and extras are, of course, ignored in the yield calculations.

*Insider Activity.* The symbols "B" and "S" in this column indicate insider buying or selling in the stock over the latest reported three month period. The precise parameters for insider buy and sell signals are flexible and take into account the various problems which arise in analyzing this extremely valuable, yet sometimes highly erratic, data. (See Chapter 60, "The Insiders," for discussion.)

*Market Logic Trend Scan.* The same computer analysis which each week produces all of the statistics and tables for the Market Logic Master Portfolio, Actual Option Portfolio, and Mutual Fund Selector, as outlined above, also provides *Market Logic's* editors with a number of additional rankings and scans, many of which, although they do not appear in Market Logic, are useful in the stock selection process. For example:

(1)   A listing of stocks with preliminary buy signals. These are issues which currently meet special buy signal criteria based on the expected market environment, which, in turn, is based on the output of the econometric model market forecasts.

(2)   A list of stocks with preliminary sell signals, an identification similar to (1) above, which is immediately compared with all Master Portfolio holdings.

(3)   The 50 stocks with the highest Strength Ratings.

(4)   The 50 stocks with the lowest Strength Ratings.

(5)   The 50 stocks with the largest positive five week Strength Rating changes.

(6)   The 50 stocks with the largest negative five week Strength Rating changes.

(7)   The 50 stocks most above their 30 week average.

(8)   The 50 stocks most below their 30 week average.

(9)   The 50 stocks with the highest positive change in Volume Trend.

(10)   The 50 stocks with the highest Volume Turnover Ratios.

(11)   The 50 stocks with the fewest shares outstanding.

(12)   The 50 stocks with the highest Beta volatility statistics.

(13)   The 50 stocks with the highest Square Root Rule volatilities.

(14)   The 50 stocks with the highest combined Volatility Ratings.

(15)   The 50 stocks whose price fluctuations are most highly correlated with those of the market.

(16)   The 50 stocks with the lowest P/E ratios.

(17)   The 50 stocks selling at the greatest discount from their companies' net book value.

(18)   The 50 stocks with the greatest insider buying.

(19)   The 50 stocks with the greatest insider selling.

(20)   A special comprehensive tabulation and analysis of all stocks with listed put and call options.

Finally, a Master Printout consolidates all of the above data for every NYSE and Amex stock, and provides additional data such as the time duration of each stock's current short, intermediate, and long term trends, a five year compounded annual earnings growth rate, the percent by which current price is above or below book value per share, and the industry group data used to compile the Industry Group Rankings and the Industry Group Diffusion Index (see Chapter 39). This vast array of constantly updated data in computer accessible format permits the generation of any specified listing desired. For example, it can be used to identify stocks with particular technical and fundamental qualities, such as the highest yields, the greatest discounts from book value, the most vigorous and persistent price uptrends, unusual volume patterns, etc.

# 81 Hot
## Line

*Twenty Four Hour a Day Service.*  The *Hot Line* telephone service provides instant access to The Institute's latest market forecasts and specific stock and option recommendations.  The *Hot Line* telephone number is provided immediately to all new *Market Logic* subscribers.

Updated at regular intervals, usually every Tuesday and Friday at 7:00 p.m. (Eastern Time), except when otherwise specified in *Market Logic,* the *Hot Line* also provides the present status of the Major Trend Model, The Institute's stock market forecasting model readings, and developments affecting key market indicators.  In those weeks when *Market Logic* is published, the *Hot Line* also presents the complete *Summary & Recommendation* feature from the current issue.

*Market Logic Preview.*  One of the primary purposes of the *Hot Line* is to improve timeliness of receipt of information contained in the current issue of *Market Logic.* Although some readers receive their copies on Saturday, most subscribers in large cities around the country get delivery on Monday. In a few sections of the United States, the Post Office is unable to effect delivery before Tuesday. Because many subscribers require more timely receipt of the information contained in *Market Logic* than the U. S. Postal Service is able to furnish, the *Hot Line* message goes on the air far in advance of mail delivery. With the *Hot Line,* subscribers can receive, assimilate, and act upon stock recommendations and timing advice as early as the market's opening on the day *Market Logic* goes to press.

*Interim Updates.* The *Hot Line* also provides updates between *Market Logic* issues. All changes of market policy and new stock and option recommendations are included in these interim *Hot Line* messages, as are The Institute's assessments of recent important developments on the investment scene.

Clients trading *Market Logic's* option portfolio recommendations are particularly advised to keep in touch with the *Hot Line* messages. Common stock options are the most volatile sector of the securities market. Consequently, the earliest possible action on recommendations is required, making the *Hot Line,* with its instant access to The Institute's current recommendations, especially useful in this area.

*Hints on Hot Line Usage.* Remember that phone rates are highest during business hours, lower in the evening, and still lower on weekends and between 11:00 p.m. and 8:00 a.m. (your local time). All interstate telephone tolls on direct dial calls are now calculated with a one minute minimum, so it is possible to call The Institute from anywhere in the contiguous 48 states for a maximum of 29 cents for the first minute and not more than 20 cents for each additional minute. The *Hot Line* recorded message is normally less than three minutes in length. Therefore, a call from anywhere in the 48 states costs 69 cents or less if dialed direct during the reduced rate night and weekend periods. Even during weekday business hours, the maximum cost of a transcontinental direct dialed call is only 74 cents for the first minute and 49 cents for each additional minute.

The Institute also suggests that you consider using a cassette recorder to transcribe *Hot Line* messages. This will allow you to play back the message, while noting names of stock recommendations and other details you may have missed.

# 82 Research Program

The Institute maintains a continuous program of stock market research. Many of the research results, such as the investigation of new security investment opportunities, provide input directly to *Market Logic*. Other research is directed toward improvements of existing prediction systems and toward the development of theoretically sound short term market forecasting models.

Even though the current market forecasting models are among the most comprehensive and most accurate ever developed, opportunities for improvements in the model forms, as well as the development of new indicators and improvements to existing indicator forms, are continually presenting themselves. The staff of The Institute investigates and studies these opportunities on an ongoing basis.

Relative to a short term market model, it is The Institute's belief that no such prediction system currently in existence gives proper attention to the theoretical and practical problems and opportunities involved. Most currently operating systems are based upon one or two indicators and afford only "hit or miss" reliability. Furthermore, without exception, even multi-indicator systems are very crudely constructed. A great opportunity exists, then, for the development and implementation of a theoretically sound and practically satisfying short term market timing model.   A significant portion of The Institute's research efforts are directed toward the construction of such a system.

The entire research program is conducted with *Market Logic* clients in mind.   They will be the direct, and first, beneficiaries of all new discoveries and developments.   But, above all, clients may be assured that when new stocks, indicators, and forecasting models are presented in *Market Logic,* they will have been rigorously researched and analyzed, and based upon a thoroughly sound theoretical and practical foundation.

# PART EIGHT
## THE MUTUAL FUND ALTERNATIVE

## 83 Winning The Easy Way

Most investors should utilize the three-pronged investment approach of market timing, stock selection, and portfolio strategy presented in the first eight parts of this book. Nevertheless, this approach may be impractical for individuals who lack sufficient time to devote to the investment decision-making process, or whose portfolios are simply too small to permit adequate diversification with individual stocks. For such investors, mutual funds are the preferred alternative.

Mutual funds provide investors with professional management and instant diversification, thus solving two of the most difficult parts of the investment puzzle. Funds buy and sell stocks in such large blocks that they pay significantly lower commission rates than individual investors. These savings largely offset the management expenses incurred by funds.

Margin regulations enacted in 1984 even permit mutual funds to be purchased on credit just like common stocks. Because well-diversified mutual funds track the market closely, they are also an ideal vehicle for traders who want to handle their own market timing without the concern of selecting stocks. To top it off, carefully selected funds can significantly beat the market averages, sometimes with less than average risk. Finally, most mutual funds can be bought and sold in small amounts — and frequently with no, or very low, commissions — enabling investors to obtain all these benefits on a shoestring investment.

Investors have a choice of hundreds of funds, including many specialized types of funds offering unique investment opportunities — and pitfalls.

*Telephone Switch Funds.* An innovation of the 1970s, telephone switch funds offer investors the ability to transfer investments between an equity mutual fund and a money market fund with a single phone call.

Many mutual fund groups that have both an equity fund and a money market fund offer this service. Still other equity funds have arranged with money funds in other fund groups to permit switching with nearly equal ease. In some cases, investors are provided a toll-free number to the fund's order department for making switches. And most switch funds do not charge sales or redemption fees, so the whole process can be accomplished without incurring any expense.

Ideally, the account is invested in the equity fund when the market outlook is bullish and in the money fund as a risk-free holding during prospectively poor market periods. It's a veritable trader's delight.

The only drawback is that most telephone switch funds place some limitation on the frequency of switches. Typically, investors are restricted to three or four switching transactions a year. Active traders must move to a new fund group when they exhaust their permissible switches.

*Index Funds.* This is the ultimate way to "buy" the market. An index fund attempts to precisely emulate a selected market index. For example, a fund can mimic the Standard & Poor's 500 Index simply by buying the 500 stocks in that index in exactly the same proportion as the 500 issues are weighted in the index.

An index fund will never beat the market — because it *is* the market. On the other hand, for the price of a smaller-than-average management fee, an index fund enables investors to exactly match the market's performance. For some investors, that can be a big plus. For those who want to *beat* the market, it's nothing to write home about.

*Gold Funds.* Owing to its occasional contracyclicality (see Chapter 69), perhaps no other stock group has such a loyal allegiance as gold. The most popular gold fund is ASA, a closed-end fund (see below) that invests in South African mining stocks and whose American Depositary Shares trade on the New York Stock Exchange. Because it is a closed-end fund, ASA's stock price can fluctuate independently of the value of its portfolio, and it is also subject to the considerable political and international risks inherent in South Africa.

In recent years, several open-end mutual funds specializing in gold and "hard money" investments have appeared on the market scene. Their policies are wide-ranging. Some own gold bullion. Some buy only gold stocks. Others buy stocks of companies whose primary business is in other precious metals. Some invest around the world, including South Africa, while others concentrate on North American securities. All of them, particularly those with no sales or redemption charges, offer a convenient way to profit from gold bull markets.

*Closed-End Funds.* Most investors are familiar with the standard, or so-called "open-end", mutual fund, which always stands ready to redeem its shares at a price equal to the value of the fund's investments. In contrast, a "closed-end" fund is freely traded in the market. Its price varies with supply and demand, and may deviate radically from the value of the fund's investments. A closed-end fund is bought and sold through a securities broker just as with any other stock. Some closed-end funds own a broadly diversified portfolio of stocks. Others concentrate on specific industries, enabling investors to buy a portfolio of stocks in particular areas of the economy.

The difference between the price of a closed-end fund and its underlying asset value presents both investment reward possibilities and risks. Shares of closed-end funds typically sell at discounts from their underlying value. However, when investors become particularly optimistic about the market's overall prospects or about the prospects for a particular fund, they may bid up the price of the shares to a premium above their actual value. By purchasing closed-end funds when they are out of favor and selling them at their peak of popularity, investors can, in effect, get a "double whammy." They can profit not only from the rise in value of the fund's investments, but also from the appreciation of the fund's stock price relative to those investments. Of course, the reverse of this effect can make closed-end funds extra risky in bear markets.

*Penny Stock Funds.* In 1984, a new breed of mutual fund hit the investment scene. As the name implies, these specialized mutual funds invest exclusively in low-priced stocks, usually issues trading below $5 a share at the time of purchase. (The more liberal the definition of "penny," the wider the universe of potential equity investments.)

Very low-priced stocks generally represent companies that are small and earning little or no money, or even recording losses. Perhaps more than with any other type of investments, broad diversification is essential when dealing in penny stocks. Yet most investors who are attracted to this dynamic area of the market fail to adequately diversify their portfolios. The new penny stock funds automatically serve that function. Because information on small companies can be difficult to obtain, expert management is all the more important for a penny stock portfolio. Again, a fund can fill the bill.

The fundamental disadvantage of penny stock funds is their high cost structure. Management fees usually approximate 3% per annum, salaries of officers of the funds' management companies are sometimes paid directly out of the funds' own assets, and the commission costs of trading penny stocks for the funds' portfolios is often extremely high. Merely to offset all these expenses and match the riskless return of treasury bills, some penny stock funds must obtain an approximately 20% annual portfolio appreciation – an exceedingly difficult task.

In any but the most dynamic bull markets, the cost disadvantage of penny stock funds outweighs all their advantages. However, when the market environment is right, penny stocks soar and these funds can give investors more "bang for the penny" than any other fund vehicle.

*International Funds.* The primary appeal of owning common stocks is the potential to profit from the very long-term growth of corporate dividends and earnings that is generated by nationwide and worldwide economic growth. This growth creates new wealth, enabling all market participants ultimately to be winners.

But the long-term reward carries with it a shorter-term risk – occasional, and sometimes severe, bear markets. Some analysts think one way to avoid bear market risk is to diversify across international borders. If stock market fluctuations in various countries are essentially independent of one another, a bear market in one nation will be more or less canceled out by bull markets in others. A portfolio of stocks from many countries should therefore be relatively stable, hardly ever subject to major losses. Meanwhile, worldwide economic growth (which in many countries exceeds that in the U.S.) should provide a good long-term rate of return across all markets.

The performance of international mutual funds suggests that this "have your cake and eat it, too" concept may have some merit. Studies covering the last two decades show: (1) Foreign stock markets have returned a percent or two more per year on average than the U.S. market; (2) while not completely independent of the U.S., the typical foreign market is nevertheless about 50% to 60% independent of it; and (3) this degree of independence is sufficiently great that investors can moderately reduce their total portfolio risk by diversifying worldwide.

Several dozen mutual funds specialize in international securities. Some of these funds include liberal holdings of

U.S. stocks, while others concentrate almost exclusively on foreign companies. Still others focus on a single foreign market; e.g., Japan, Mexico, or Korea. Those that diversify widely across different economies are most likely to achieve a true reduction in risk. But be careful! Regional conflicts, exchange-rate fluctuations, currency controls, foreign capital freezes, and the like can impose extra risks that must be considered before committing your savings to funds that invest abroad.

# 84 Fund Performance Indicators

Is it possible to determine in advance which mutual funds will perform best? Given the caveat that, in the investment world, absolute certainty about anything in the future is impossible, the answer is, Yes. In this and the following chapter, we shall examine some tools that can be used to forecast fund performance, develop a logical approach to fund selection, and finally, show how that approach can be applied in the real world. The starting point is to classify funds by certain basic characteristics.

*Fund Size.* Many academic studies have examined the correlation between the size of a fund and its performance. Although every one of these analyses has been methodologically flawed, it is still possible to draw several conclusions.

First, large mutual funds will rarely be among the top performers in a rising market, and they will hardly ever be among the worst performers in a falling market. Large funds are constrained by their sheer size to invest in highly capitalized stocks which are generally among the least volatile in the marketplace. Smaller funds can be more flexible. With only a few million, or few tens of millions, of dollars to invest, they can take positions in relatively small equities. While such stocks tend to be among the worst performers in bear markets, they are usually the best in bull markets.

But smallness is not beneficial per se. A badly managed small fund will still be a bad investment. Further, management fees and expenses are relatively higher for small funds, penalizing their performance before the game even starts. A billion dollar fund typically incurs annual costs of about half of one percent, while a $10 million fund normally pays out expenses equal to two to three times that.

The major advantage of smallness, then, is that it gives a fund an *opportunity* to manage its portfolio in a superior manner. Aggressive investors and traders can therefore use fund size as a preliminary step to selecting funds with the best chance of beating the market.

*Load v. No-Load.* Funds that levy a sales charge on investments are called "load" funds; those that do not are aptly called "no-load" funds. Loads can range up to 9.3% of the amount invested.

Numerous studies have demonstrated that there is *no* correlation whatsoever between a fund's performance and the amount, if any, of its load. Regardless of whether a fund charges a sales fee or not, it is just as likely to be among the best performers, the worst performers, or in the middle of the pack. There is also no correlation between performance and the size of a fund's annual management fees, redemption charges, or hidden loads. (The latter are pernicious charges levied on the shareholders of some funds to support sales efforts.)

In the absence of rare overriding performance considerations, no-load funds are a better buy than load funds. Short-term traders should use no-load funds exclusively. However, investors who contemplate holding a fund for many years should recognize that an apparently heavy initial sales charge may ultimately be inconsequential. This is especially true if the planned investment is large enough, typically $10,000, to entitle you to a discounted load charge. In these instances, the prospective reward and risk associated with owning a fund's shares is what really counts.

*Fund Price.* We saw in Chapter 61 ("Volatility Analysis") that the price of a stock can provide an excellent indication of its prospective performance. However, a mutual fund's price is completely arbitrary, usually established by the fund's management merely to maximize its sales potential to new investors. Most funds try to keep the price below $20 a share and will split the stock if necessary to do so. There is no reason why a fund whose net asset value is, say, $100 per share, should not be just as good, or bad, a performer as a fund whose share price is $10 or $1.

*Type of Fund.* Mutual funds are commonly classified by their investment objective; e.g., growth, aggressive growth, income, etc. Such classifications can provide a useful guide to what an investor is buying, but only preliminarily. Some funds classified in relatively more conservative categories are actually managed more aggressively than funds in a more speculative category.

What counts is performance. Regardless of claimed objectives, funds are best categorized on the basis of a purely statistical analysis of how they *actually* perform in the marketplace.

*Past Performance.* Were the simple historical performance of a mutual fund a perfect prologue to its future performance, the selection question would be very easily solved. Past can indeed be prologue, but even here a warning is appropriate. Nearly all of the mutual fund investment advice now provided to investors relies exclusively on simplistic historical performance data. Every year, dozens of publications present historical fund ratings and, implicitly, advocate simple past performance as a fund-selection guide. Frequently, though, funds that are on top of the pack one year are at the bottom the next, and vice versa.

A mutual fund's performance must be analyzed not in absolute terms, but in relation to the market. A fund that is twice as volatile as the market is likely to be a performance leader in bull markets and among the worst performers in bear markets. The author has developed a more sophisticated approach to forecasting fund performance, utilizing a separate econometric model for each fund. In effect, a model is created for every fund similar to that used illustratively in Chapter 50 ("An Econometric Model of Your Own"). This method is described in the next chapter.

# 85 Mutual Fund Forecasting

The future performance of most mutual funds can be estimated with considerable accuracy using econometric modeling techniques. These forecasts are based on four premises:

First, it is possible to predict the market's future performance. We have discussed market prediction at length in Parts 1 and 2 of this book. In terms of forecasting future mutual fund performance, it is worth keeping in mind that the market is more easily predicted over long periods of time, such as one to five years, than over shorter periods of, say, less than twelve months. The market indicators and forecasting methods we have perfected can generate market predictions that will be right far more often than they will be wrong, both as to the market's likely future direction, up or down, and the actual magnitude of its change.

Second, price changes of most mutual funds are well correlated with those of the market. We saw in Chapter 64 that diversification significantly reduces a portfolio's fluctuations that are not related to the market. While only index funds are completely diversified, most mutual funds are sufficiently well diversified that they act very much like the market. For example, in the five-year period ending in mid-1992, the average equity fund (omitting international and specialized industry funds) was 66% correlated with the S&P 500 Index. Only a third of their price fluctuations was related to other factors.

Third, the volatility of a fund's price changes relative to the market is usually consistent over time. Funds whose price changes have been, say, 1½ times as volatile as the market in recent months will tend to continue to be about 1½ times as volatile in the future, and funds whose relative volatilities have been, say, half that of the market, or equal to the market, will usually continue to possess those degrees of volatility, too. It is therefore possible not only to identify those funds that will behave very much like the market, but also to calculate just how much the funds will appreciate or depreciate when the market moves some particular amount. This factor is known as a fund's "beta."

Fourth, some funds are managed in a consistently superior manner, and even in a completely flat market can be expected to provide a positive return. Other funds are consistently inferior to the market and tend to decline even in a sideways moving market. This superiority or inferiority of a fund's performance is called its "alpha."

The result of this four-stage statistical analysis is an econometric model that provides a scientific estimate of how any individual fund will perform in the future – a "Profit Projection" if you will. For example, say the market is expected to rise 10% over the next year. If a statistical analysis reveals that a fund's price fluctuations are very highly correlated with the market and that the fund is normally about 1½ times as volatile as the market, we should expect that fund to advance about 15%. Then, if the fund's alpha is, say, +5% per year (indicating that on an annual basis, it tends to consistently beat the market by that amount, regardless of what the market does), the final Profit Projection is +20%. Factors discussed in the previous chapter, such as relative fund size, can then be used to "fine-tune" the projected performance.

*Risk Rating.* Reward and risk generally go hand in hand, so it is desirable to have at least a general idea of the risk that is involved in owning any particular fund.

Risk, of course, is related to prospective losses that a fund shareholder might incur. Two good risk measures are the sensitivity of a fund to the market's fluctuations (the "beta" factor discussed above) and a fund's own historical price variation propensity (statistically called "standard deviation"). The former is useful because if the market declines, funds most sensitive to the market's fluctuations will also decline. The latter is used to flag funds whose behavior is so volatile that they could decline significantly independently of the overall market trend. For example, some gold and international funds don't really track the U.S. stock market very closely and therefore have low "betas," but they may still be vulnerable to occasional large price declines. Because risk is always worth avoiding, the measure that shows a fund to be riskiest – beta or standard deviation – should be utilized as the basis for a Risk Rating.

*Buying Mutual Funds for Your Portfolio.* The funds to buy are those that have the highest Profit Projection for a given Risk Rating. Conservative investors will wish to incur only a moderate amount of risk, while traders may be willing to accept a very high degree of risk. In either case, the risk level appropriate to an investor's objectives should be identified first, and then the fund or funds with the highest Profit Projections in that risk category should be purchased. Finally, keep in mind all of the costs that might be associated with purchasing a particular fund. For example, a short-term trader should not purchase a load fund even if it has the highest Profit Projection of all mutual funds.

*Mutual Fund Forecaster.* The author is Editor of the nation's only investment advisory service that provides Profit Projections and Risk Ratings for mutual funds. This advisory, *Mutual Fund Forecaster*, also maintains a Ratings-Performance-Service Directory on all funds, recommends portfolios for long-term investors and short-term traders, and analyzes individual funds and investment strategies. Every issue highlights the "Best Buy" funds for investors and traders, based on their Profit Projections and Risk Ratings. Special coverage is given to gold funds, international funds, and closed-end funds. Published monthly, the service is supplemented by a weekly Hot Line that features current buy, sell, and avoid recommendations, market trading signals, and the top-rated funds.

*Mutual Fund Buyer's Guide.* This monthly publication, which the author also edits, provides comprehensive information and professional evaluation in a tabular format on every stock and bond mutual fund (except some state tax-free funds), both open-end and closed-end funds, approximately 1,700 funds in all.

Among the information presented is an All-Star Rating, performance scoreboard, current yield, up and down market ranks, Safety Rating, worst-ever loss, market correlation, switching privilege, investment loads, tax load, fund telephone number, portfolio description, 52-week high and low, and much more.

*Fund Watch.* The Chinese say a single picture is worth a thousand words. That is why charts are so popular on Wall Street. Peter Lynch, the guiding hand at Fidelity Magellan Fund for more than a decade, says, "I keep a long-term chartbook close to my side at the office, and another one at home . . . What most people get out of family photo albums, I get out of these wonderful publications." The author's *Fund Watch* advisory is the nation's preeminent mutual fund chart service, with each issue featuring price and moving-average charts of the top-performing and highest-potential funds. Profit Projections, Risk Ratings, and other key performance and investment information accompany each fund chart.

*Income & Safety.* This is the author's publication for income-oriented and low-risk investors. Subtitled "The Consumer's Guide to High Yields," *Income & Safety* is the only comprehensive and objective guide in America to earning the highest returns on income mutual funds, money funds, tax-frees, insured bank accounts, and certificates of deposit. The publication features Yield Forecasts, Safety Ratings, buy-sell-avoid recommendations, and more for all of these investments. Its specific goal is to increase readers' take-home pay on their income and savings investments by 20% to 40%.

A complimentary copy of *Mutual Fund Forecaster, Mutual Fund Buyer's Guide, Fund Watch,* or *Income & Safety* may be obtained by calling the author toll-free at 1-800-442-9000.

# PART NINE
## A RUN DOWN
## RANDOM WALK STREET

## 86 The Non-Random Character of Stock Market Prices

The purest form of the random walk hypothesis (or theory) as it is applied to the securities markets, says that stock prices have no memory; that it is impossible to accurately predict tomorrow's or next week's price changes from yesterday's prices or price changes. Stronger versions of the theory, such as the "efficient market" hypothesis, insist it is impossible to successfully time stock or market swings, even using all available information about all companies, about the market, about the economy, about the world . . . about everything.

A large group of market students, mostly members of the academic community, has risen to support this theory, and countless books, dissertations, journal articles, and manuscripts have been written attempting to demonstrate its truth.

However, to cement their theory with demonstrable facts, the random walk adherents have had to bend it into some rather interesting contortions and grant some very large allowances — allowances so large it almost no longer matters whether the theory exists or not.

The earliest "crude" forms of the theory, for example, suggested that tomorrow's expected price change of a stock or the market was zero. But experienced market observers quickly pointed out that a long term uptrend existed in the nation's economy, and in the stock market as well.

Hence, *even if* all other parts of securities movements were random (a proposition not admitted), price changes must at least be granted a positive average. The random walk theorists consented, and the first exception to the random walk theory was made. (The theorists began to call the market a "random walk with drift.")

Since that time several studies of price movements have demonstrated that extremely crude (crude to the extent that *no one really uses them*) trend following or filter techniques using only historical price information can differentiate between positive and negative future price changes, or at least between average and below average returns. The random walkers were at first startled by this evidence, but then analyzed the data more carefully in an attempt to reconcile it more closely to their theory, or perhaps reconcile their theory to the observed phenomenon. To this end they proposed a test: that to disprove the random walk theory (or to prove non-randomness), a stock or market timing system had to show trading profits superior to those of a simple "buy and hold" strategy over the identical time period, after commission costs. As buy and hold has always been a profitable strategy over the long term in the U. S. securities markets, this test ignores the possibility that in the future a marginally profitable timing system might be substantially superior to buy and hold in a persistently falling market.

But even for rising markets, the random walkers' test is wrong. In point of fact, a profitable in-out, buy-sell strategy is not necessary to disprove randomness or to make data profitably useful in stock or market timing. It is sufficient that a system differentiate between returns of a different magnitude or small returns of opposite direction. For example, every time an investor has new investable funds, he is faced with the simple task of determining whether or not to invest that money in the market on that day. If all of his studies and analyses could but determine whether the day's price change was to be up or down, he would certainly have useful and profitable knowledge – even though his system might be unprofitable to trade on an in-out basis. For example, if you plan to purchase a stock, knowing that it will decline a half-point today permits you to profitably delay buying. According to the test random walkers use, your knowledge of the day's price change is useless because you could not sell the stock short today, cover tomorrow, pay two commissions . . . and still have a profit. (The argument can, of course, be extended from daily to weekly, monthly, or longer time periods, and from individual securities to the entire market.)

Random walk proponents also tend to concentrate their condescending remarks on the cruder and generally less defensible of the technical tools, such as chart reading. However, many technical methods in current use go far beyond such simple concepts. To name just one well known stock market tool completely ignored by the academicians, the Non-Member Short Sales Ratio has proven again and again to be extremely proficient in forecasting important market turning points, passing in the process the most rigorous formal tests of statistical significance. And this is but one of many reliable indicators, almost none of which has received the attention of the random walkers. In truth, every market indicator of even marginal value is a refutation of the random walk or efficient market hypothesis.

About the only market forecasting indicator the academic world has yet examined in any detail at all is money supply, and there their analyses were so inconclusive (i.e., the indicator occasionally did work) that they seemingly gave up on indicator analysis altogether.

As for individual security selection, studies of relative price/earnings ratios, insider trading activity, and relative strength, to name just a few, have proven the random walk theory invalid. In response, the random walkers usually just ignore the evidence. For example, they have never presented a single paper even attempting to refute the usefulness of insider trading data.

Another hole in the random walk theory was revealed by the publication of studies of price behavior which discovered that the *volatility* of price changes among individual securities tends to persist. Stocks which fluctuate, say five to ten percent up or down per week, tend to continue fluctuating with that degree of volatility, while stock volatilities of only one or two percent up or down per week also tend to persist. The studies which have measured this phenomenon have stood the test of time and random walkers ultimately had to acknowledge their validity.

As usual, a hole plugging solution was proposed; a solution that, as one might expect, merely twisted the random walk theory into another strange contortion: the academicians *defined volatility as risk* and went on to say that the higher the risk, *naturally* the higher the expected return. The latter portion of this statement is certainly true . . . investments which contain greater risk must in the long run provide a higher average compensatory rate of return, and investments which offer higher average returns generally entail greater risk.   However, to say that volatility is risk is another large step indeed;   a step backward, in fact.   It certainly does not appeal to common sense (which says that the prospect of *loss* is risk).

Of course, the random walkers have offered a rationale for their volatility risk definition.   For example, two such theorists, Chris Mader and Robert Hagin *(The Dow Jones — Irwin Guide to Common Stocks,* Dow Jones — Irwin, 1976, p. 116 ) representatively ask, "Would you feel 'safer' with a stock that typically had weekly price changes of 1% or 2%, or one that had wide weekly swings of as much as 10%?" They go on to answer their question, "Intuitively, most investors would feel an extra margin of safety with a stock that experienced relatively stable price movements." Ergo, the degree of volatility, or its opposite, the degree of stability, is the only valid risk measure.

What Mader, Hagin and the rest of the random walk community overlook, or at least don't quite get to, is that it is not the *volatility* of the more broadly fluctuating security which makes it riskier (if, in fact, it is riskier), but rather that some of its swings might be on the downside, therein producing at least interim *losses*. (Volatility itself is desirable in a rising market.) Hence it is loss, and not volatility, that is risk. To the extent that volatility is not *perfectly correlated* with loss (and at least half the movements — the gains — are not), predictable volatility is a violation of the random walk hypothesis, not an integral component thereof.

A major problem with the classical academic view of volatility as a risk measure is that it incorrectly ascribes undesirable characteristics to desirable results and favorable characteristics to unfavorable results. For example, a security which has only positive expected returns (no expected losses) would nonetheless be judged risky if those expected positive returns were highly variable, week to week or year to year. Conversely, a security which offers a single, absolutely certain *negative* expected return (i.e., a loss) would be called riskless. (A special case of the latter is a portfolio consisting solely of cash which, with its 0% rate of return, would provide a net "riskless" loss of 6% in an era of constant 6% inflation.) Clearly the classical risk definition fails in these circumstances, as it would in similar but less extreme situations, a factor which casts considerable doubt upon its general validity.

To cite an example, if a highly volatile stock gained 50% one month, doubled the next, tripled the next, rose 50% the next — in short, exhibited month after month of rising prices, but never showed a loss during that time — who in their right mind, based solely on that evidence, would call the stock risky? The answer is, no one would . . . in their right mind. But the academicians would, because of the stock's exceptional volatility. Conversely, the academicians would declare to be riskless a stock that constantly fell in a smooth and uninterrupted pattern until it was worthless. Such inverted logic leads some observers to believe that the risk random walkers fear most is the risk of having their pet theory disproven.

Clive Granger and Oskar Morgenstern, in their book *Predictability of Stock Market Prices,* acknowledge the largest loophole of all in the random walk theory: "The random walk is about *absolute* prices and says little about *relative* price moves." In other words, if you can identify now the one stock which will outperform all others over the next year, it will not, in the eyes of the theorists, constitute proof that the random walk hypothesis is incorrect. But that is what stock selection is all about, identifying and buying the better relative performers. With loopholes like this, one can make millions. (For example, an initial $1,000 invested successively in the best performing NYSE stock each year for the past five years — from 1971 to 1975 — would have grown to over $3 million.)

Thus violations of the original crude form of the random walk hypothesis abound. The random walk theorists either ignore the evidence when it goes against them, or attempt to explain it away, always doing so, however, in a manner so abstract and bearing so little resemblance to the real world that it cannot be called sensible. It is for this reason that the random walk theory has gained such little respect in the practical investment community.

The random walk theory is not valid! It is disproven on page after page of this very book. But should this presentation manage to convince even a few random walkers, the rest will doubtless fall back upon their last line of defense: that any system, however valid it has been in the past, will cease to work in the future when it gains a universal following, since everyone using the system will enter identical buy and sell orders thus bidding prices to a point where any margin of profitability ceases to exist.

This objection does not meet the test of practicality any more than does the random walk hypothesis itself. Common sense dictates that universal agreement on anything is impossible.  Regardless of the validity or usefulness of any market forecasting technique, it is certain to be disregarded by the majority ·of investors.  Like the random walkers, they will refuse to believe that any approach is valid save their own.

The intrinsically non-random character of stock market prices suggests that logical and scientific analyses of the market should be well rewarded.  However, the majority of investors habitually ignore new market timing indicators, stock selection techniques, and analytical methods.  Therefore, superior investment returns will accrue to the intelligent minority of stock market participants who are both able to appreciate and willing to utilize these more sophisticated approaches.

# TECHNICAL NOTE: ECONOMETRICS

(This note is intended for individuals conversant with the terminology of advanced mathematics, especially regression.)

*Introduction.* The development of econometric models requires rigorous application of the appropriate scientific theories and technical methods, along with a thorough knowledge of the prediction system under study. A complete discussion of the techniques involved in the development of The Institute's models would consume several hundred pages. This note will briefly discuss the theoretical and methodological problems which were considered and the mathematical techniques which were used in their resolution.

*Computer Program Selection.* Numerous computer programs were examined, and several programs were actually obtained, tested, and rejected prior to selecting the final program and actual running of the problems. The programs were tested by use of sample problems proposed by Longley and Wampler (see *Selected References*). These problems were designed to test for multicollinearity and related data problems. Selection of a final routine also rested upon other considerations, including estimated computer running time and costs (literally tens of thousands of dollars), and the need for programs which could efficiently analyze a large number of variables and observations. The latter was especially important in view of the practical necessity to study a large array of potentially valuable regressor (independent) variables over a lengthy period of time using weekly data (k exceeding

75, n exceeding 1600).

The forward stepwise routine BMD-02R, developed by the Health Sciences Computing Facility at the University of California, Los Angeles, was selected as the primary program and was used both for regression analysis and two group discriminant analysis. (This program was disc stored and used on IBM 360-65 and 370-168 processing equipment.) The program selection was made with the knowledge that a forward stepwise routine is by no means optimal. However, cost and other considerations also played a role in the selection, and comprehensive *a priori* study of variables and data can improve the efficiency of the stepwise process several fold.

Factor analysis and principal component analysis programs were rejected on grounds of statistical theory. At the present time, experimentation with linear programming routines for the purpose of testing mean absolute error regressions is also being conducted.

*Model Forms:* The Institute's published stock market forecasts for three, six, and twelve months ahead are based on single equation multiple regression models, calculated with 13, 26, and 52 week percent change regressand (dependent) variables respectively. The Major Trend Model is a single equation discriminant analysis model estimated by a regression program using a dichotomous dummy variable regressand.

*Regressand Variable Selection.* Most previous applications of econometrics to the prediction of stock prices have specified the level of a market index as the dependent variable. The Institute preferred to use percent changes in an index. Percent changes afford a superior means of analyzing regressand-regressor relationships and aid as well in the interpretation of results. The distortion which can arise from the time trend alone in "level estimation" regressions is evidenced by the following ex-post result which uses the current level of a stock price index to forecast the level of that index thirteen weeks later for all 1,618 overlapping 13 week periods from 1941 through 1971.

ln S&P 500 (+13 weeks) = .03972 + .99378 ln S&P 500 (current)

The correlation coefficient from this equation is .9964, the coefficient of determination is .9928, and the Error Reduction (see *Measurement of Results*) is .9151. In addition to confusing the relationship of what is close to a random series (ex-cyclical and secular trends), this result also demonstrates the ease with which high correlations may be obtained when regressing levels of time series possessing secular trends. In contrast, the following equation shows the relationship between the relatively independent adjacent 13 week percent changes over the same time period.

S&P 500 % Change (+13) = 1.88289 + .12095 S&P 500 % Change (−13)

The equation's correlation coefficient is now just .1208, the coefficient of determination is only .0146, and the Error Reduction is a minuscule .0073. Since profits are made in the stock market by predicting changes, not levels, and since many of the prospective regressors did not contain a significant secular trend, transformation of the regressand into percent changes was deemed appropriate.

Of the previous econometric modeling studies which have somehow managed to elude the dangerous, yet seemingly alluring, attraction of specifying the dependent variable in terms of market index "levels," most have instead turned to equally perilous specifications; namely, percent changes or log first differences of quarterly indexes which were, in turn, based upon an average of daily price closes within each quarter. The dependent variable averaging process causes predictions made one quarter ahead to result in significant serial correlation, thereby seriously biasing the regression results upward. A coefficient of determination of about .25, for example, would be obtained by chance alone. (Holbrook Working, "Note on the Correlation of First Differences of Averages in a Random Chain," *Econometrica,* October 1960, pp. 916-918.)

An econometric study by a no less eminent authority than Sir Maurice Kendall (Kendall, et al. "Lagged Relationships in Economic Forecasting," *Journal of the Royal Statistical Association,* 1969, pp. 133-163) specified another dangerous dependent variable form.    A linear time trend was first extracted from the raw series by pre-regression.    Of the residual series, the cyclical component was believed to dominate, leaving it as the dependent variable representation in a cyclical prediction model.    The error in this technique lies in the assumption that a single secular growth rate runs through the middle of all (or, at least most) of the observed cycles.    In fact, the only statement of long term stock market secularity which may be made with strict accuracy is that it has been "up."    The growth rate has varied significantly as the decades have rolled by and, as likely as not, price departures from a single trend line erroneously identify their true place on the cyclical plane.

Due to its theoretically fair construction and the availability of extensive historical data, the Standard & Poor's Composite Index was selected as a basic representation of the market.    The index was transformed to a weekly basis by averaging within each week the daily closing index values. The averaging process served to eliminate small random fluctuations.    It did not result in any serious aggregation effects, as the primary intervals used for forecasting (13, 26, and 52 weeks) were of sufficient time spans to effectively eliminate intrinsic variable collinearity.    For example, the correlation between all non-overlapping, equal interval, percent changes in the transformed index from 1941 to 1971 (1,618 weekly observations) are as follows:

| Intervals | Coefficient of Determination |
|---|---|
| 4 weeks | .0012 |
| 8 weeks | .0022 |
| 13 weeks | .0146 |
| 26 weeks | .0007 |
| 52 weeks | .0538 |

All signs are positive except the adjacent 52 week intervals which are negatively correlated. The degree of correlation evidenced between past and future market changes is insignificant relative to the actual regression results which were subsequently obtained. For example, the 52 week percent change model presently being used by The Institute furnished a coefficient of determination in excess of .70. Higher correlations were derived for certain sub-periods, and substantial improvements in the results could easily have been obtained if variables with "wrong" signs or if variables which were statistically significant but theoretically unsound were allowed to enter the equation.

As an alternative regressand measure, a weekly Advance/Decline Line for the New York Stock Exchange was calculated as the running cumulative sum of the quantity advances minus declines divided by the quantity advances plus declines. The resulting series was differenced over various intervals (13 weeks, 26 weeks), and the series of differences were transformed so that the first and second moments of the dependent variable series equaled those moments for the dependent variable series of corresponding differencing lengths based on the Standard & Poor's Composite Index.

As stated above, for each prediction period studied, all overlapping observations were analyzed (e.g., weeks 1-14, 2-15, 3-16, etc. in the 13 week regressions). Obviously, successive observations were highly dependent, overlapping by 12/13ths (92%) in the 13 week regression, 25/26ths (96%) in the 26 week regression, and so on. However, a practical application of econometric models for real time forecasting requires predictions at least weekly and not just once every 13, 26, or 52 weeks. Furthermore, appropriate analyses of residuals was satisfactorily accomplished by simply analyzing observations 13, 26, or 52 weeks apart.

Prior to actual regression, each of the percent change dependent variables was analyzed for normality as gauged by their distribution moments. The mean, variance, skewness, and kurtosis of each of the prospective dependent variables were analyzed over a 31 year time period (1941-1971). The distribution analyses revealed significant negative skewness on 13 week percent changes, non-significant negative skewness on 26 week changes, and non-significant positive skewness on 52 week changes. Non-significant leptokurtosis was observed on 13 week changes, while a non-significant tendency toward platykurtosis was in evidence on 26 and 52 week changes.

The dependent variable for the Major Trend Model was based on an ex-post judgment regarding which prior time periods constituted bull markets and which constituted bear markets. The lowest week of a market cycle was considered part of the ensuing bull market, and the highest week of a cycle was treated as part of the ensuing bear market.

*Regressor Variables.*    Regressor (independent) variable selection rested both on statistical and theoretical grounds. In no case was a variable of high statistical significance allowed in a model without an underlying theoretical justification, and only rarely was a theoretically justifiable variable lacking in statistical significance allowed a place in a final "real time" equation. This policy led to an *a priori* exclusion of several potentially useful variables, but improved the models' ex-ante forecasting reliability.

Prior to actual testing, each prospective independent variable was analyzed for seasonality and secular trend, as well as linearity and potential interaction with past market changes and other variables. Rather than use a non-linear regression program, every attempt was made to transform intrinsically linear variables and nonlinear variables into a linear form. Where seasonal or secular influences were discovered, they were eliminated through prior transgeneration. Seasonal factors were held constant through time. Non-stationary seasonal factors as, for example, those emanating from the standard X-11 Variant of the Census Method II Seasonal Adjustment Program were avoided. (The Census Bureau program was used for data analysis, however.)

In certain cases dummy variables, usually based upon signs,

were used in place of the original variables.

Multicollinearity, as it usually is in multivariate applications, was a severe problem. Every effort was made to include in the final econometric models only those variables which retained the correct theoretical sign. Suppressor effects were examined closely on theoretical grounds and in most cases were found wanting. Inclusion of the many variables which contained suppressor effects would have greatly increased the ex-post significance of the models. However, in certain cases, usually when an independent variable was found useful in forecasting only rising or falling markets, a suppressor variable system was used to effectively retain only one side or the other for forecasting purposes.

In several instances, sub-models were estimated to forecast the behavior of certain groups of market participants (e.g., odd lot short sellers and mutual fund managers), after it was discovered that their behavior patterns were particularly amenable to prediction, and that their behavior had forecasting significance for the general market only when it deviated from predictable expectations. In these cases, the residuals of the sub-models became regressors in the main models.

Independent variables were examined for lead-lag relationships with market changes. Arithmetic, exponential, and polynomial distributed lags were studied. In the final analysis, exponential distributed lags were primarily used. Contrary to the rather strange, and potentially misleading, convention established by Almon, Keran, and others, polynomial distributed lags were approached with extreme caution. In no case was the degree of polynomial under experimentation beyond that which could legitimately be expected from the regressand-regressor system on prior theoretical considerations. In the final analysis, *no* polynomial distributed lags were used. Exponentially weighted distributed lags, which *were* used, served several useful purposes. They helped to eliminate random disturbances in the independent variables, they served to approximate leading relationships of the independent variables with the dependent variable, and they systematically assigned greater weight to the more recent, and usually more important, observations.

Needless to say, all data series were examined intensively for error and outliers through both computer programming techniques and simple eye examination.

Extreme care was also taken to assure that regressor values were available by the time of the "forecast." This required, of course, allowance for variable degrees of reporting lag times. Unfortunately, similar care has not always been exercised by other students of the market, especially as to the availability of earnings reports.

In the actual regression runs, "F" statistic limits for variable entry were established at 1/10th of 1%, approximately 1/50th of the level which is conventional in studies of this nature.

Finally, it was recognized, as has not been recognized in so many other practical applications of regression analysis, that variables tested but not included in the regression implicitly had been assigned a zero coefficient and caused a loss of degrees of freedom.

*Measurement of Results.* The overall ex-post "predictive" success of each model was measured by several statistics based upon the fundamental coefficient of determination. However, this conventional means of measurement was felt to lend an upwardly biased interpretation of equation significance due to the fact that it relates solved squared units to total squared deviations from the mean. Since we are more interested in solving units of deviation per se and less interested in solving squared units, we developed and used a statistic we have termed Error Reduction (ER). ER is directly related to the coefficient of determination by means of the following formula: 1.0 minus the square root of, 1.0 minus the coefficient of determination. Or, alternatively, ER is equal to: 1.0 minus the ratio of squared standard error to regressand variance.

Observe that Error Reduction is always lower than the

coefficient of determination. Moving upward from zero, the distance between them widens until the Coefficient of Determination, Error Reduction point (.75, .50) is reached. Thereafter the gap closes.

As an example of the different perspective ER gives, consider the following relationships:

| R | $R^2$ | ER |
|------|------|------|
| 1.00 | 1.00 | 1.00 |
| .87 | .75 | .50 |
| .71 | .50 | .29 |
| .50 | .25 | .13 |
| .00 | .00 | .00 |

The so-called adjusted coefficient of determination, which simply reduces the coefficient of determination in a manner designed to account for the fact that a k variable, n observation regression will result, on average, in a $k/(n-1)$ coefficient of determination by mere chance, was employed as well. The same adjustment technique was applied to the Error Reduction (ER) statistic to form adjusted ER. The adjusted forms are, of course, always lower than their unadjusted counterparts. Used in a forward stepwise model, however, the former were never allowed to fall from step to step for the simple reason that they fall only when the partial F (or t) statistic of an entered variable is less than 1.00. F's to enter were always held far above 1.00.

*Analysis of Residuals.* Regression residuals were examined for independence, heteroscedasticity, and serial correlation by means of the Durbin-Watson statistic, the Thiel-Nagar statistic, the autocorrelation coefficient, and a runs test. These tests were performed in two ways: first, on adjacent residual observations which, due to the overlapping nature of the time series, naturally evidenced a high degree of serial correlation, and second, on observations w weeks apart, where w was the prediction interval (such as 13, 26, or 52 weeks) being studied. On the latter basis, final results indicated little or no significant serial dependencies among the residuals. In addition, for each regression model the mean absolute error, the standard error, the absolute and relative skewness, and the absolute and relative kurtosis of the residual series were examined.

*Time Period of Testing.* The models were developed and tested ex-post over a primary 33 year period, 1941-1973. Regressions were performed over numerous subperiods as well, such as 1941-1956, 1956-1973, and 1945-1973 (post war) to test for coefficient stability, etc. Two or more years of time were always reserved for ex-ante testing. Of course, forecasting models currently in use are brought as closely up to date as possible.

*Ex-Ante Results.* The various models have been estimated and used ex-ante since different dates in mid-1974. Contrary to the expected result, the standard errors of the models' ex-ante forecasts have been substantially *below* their ex-post standard errors. The present working hypotheses are (a) that during the past two years the stock market has been unusually amenable to forecasting on the basis of the historical relationships fitted by the models, and (b) that the models' standard forecast errors in some future subperiod[s] will exceed their ex-post standard errors, resulting in overall ex-ante standard forecast errors greater than their ex-post standard errors. After all, in the long run, it is difficult to imagine any model which is "better" ex-ante than ex-post.

*Comments.* As this research is ongoing, the author welcomes comments, suggestions, and criticisms.

# TECHNICAL NOTE: RISK

The classical academic definitions of risk are either absolute volatility (standard deviation) or relative volatility (Beta).

An important objection to the volatility risk measure is that it does not appeal to the common sense. Most investors intuitively feel that risk should have something to do with losing money, or at least the possibility of losing money. Volatility simply does not qualify in this regard. As we have seen, volatility (absolute or relative) is highly desirable in rising markets. It seems remote from the subject of loss and hence from investors' common sense perceptions of risk.

Nor do the statisticians' semi-standard deviation or semi-variance volatility risk measures help in this regard. Once one finally acknowledges that the volatility risk measure leaves something to be desired and starts concentrating on the loss portion of the distribution, he might just as well go all the way and acknowledge that it is the loss, not the volatility of it, that counts as risk.

Appeal to the common sense is important. One would hope, after all, that the investing public would utilize, and want to utilize, a correct risk measure. If not, the measure would have no practical application and would merely constitute an academic exercise. Of course, a legitimate theoretical construct should not be discarded merely because the layman does not understand it. But if, after an extended period of concerted lobbying, no appreciable progress is made in furthering its acceptance, it is perhaps the better part of wisdom to redefine terms to correctly reflect the real world.

A new system of risk measurement for stock prices is needed. The following paragraphs will attempt to develop a framework for such a system.

First, to define terms: *Reward* will be a probability estimate of expected investment gains; *Risk* will be a probability estimate of expected losses; and *Return* will be a synthesis of risk and reward expressed in the form of a joint probability estimate of expected net gain or loss (specifically, reward minus risk.)

Assume that the probabilities of future gains and losses for a security are as presented in Table 73. It is important to note that one, and only one, of the probabilities will materialize, so the distribution of probabilities should *not* be viewed as an estimate of future volatility or as a measure of risk in and of itself. The analysis is based on the assumption that expected returns below zero constitute risk and expected returns above zero constitute reward. However, a strong case can be made for considering any expected gain below a required rate of return to constitute risk, in which case the reward-risk relationship would be somewhat altered. In such an event the required rate of return should be subtracted from the original column of expected gains or losses before proceeding with the analysis. Hence, if the required return is

TABLE 73

EXAMPLE OF REWARD – RISK – RETURN ESTIMATION

| | Prob-ability | | Expected Gain/Loss | | Return | |
|---|---|---|---|---|---|---|
| | .05 | x | + 200% | = | + 10% | |
| Probability of Gain = .55 | .20 | x | + 50% | = | + 10% | Expected |
| | .20 | x | + 20% | = | + 4% | Reward = + 25% |
| | .10 | x | + 10% | = | + 1% | |
| | .10 | x | − 10% | = | − 1% | |
| Probability of Loss = .45 | .20 | x | − 20% | = | − 4% | Expected |
| | .10 | x | − 30% | = | − 3% | Risk    = − 13% |
| | .05 | x | − 100% | = | − 5% | |
| | 1.00 | | | | + 12% = | Expected Return = + 12% |

+9%, an expected 200% gain is really only a 191% gain, the 100% loss case becomes a 109% loss, etc., and the net expected return would be +3%, not +12%.

If the stock market is at all efficient, it should provide the opportunity of a reward approximately compensatory for the degree of risk assumed. Therefore, the overall expected return should be a net positive number; i.e., positive to such an extent that the expected reward adequately compensates for expected risk. It follows that exceptionally risky investments must also offer opportunities for exceptional reward so that the final probability weighted expectation of return is reasonable. Or, to put it the other way around, exceptional reward opportunities must also be offset by greater risk.

The effects of diversification can now also be observed. Assume diversification into two stocks possessing identical, though independent, probability distributions of expected returns such as that presented in Table 73. Now there is only a .05 x .05 chance of a 100% portfolio loss; that is, a .0025 probability that each security would produce a catastrophic loss. Of course, there is now also only a .05 x .05, or .0025, probability of the largest possible assumed gain, 200%. Completely working out the joint probabilities of the two stock example leads to an expected gain (reward) of 20.2%, down from 25% in the one stock portfolio, and an 8.2% expected loss (risk), down from 13%. Diversification thus results in reduction of both risk and reward, fitting neatly with existing theory. The expected overall return of the two stock portfolio is unchanged from the one stock portfolio, as it must be since the two stocks have the same expected return distributions.

The foregoing framework leaves unanswered how the individual probabilities within the joint probability distribution are to be estimated. The author can offer no solution, merely the hypothesis that the foregoing describes risk as it is perceived in the marketplace. Anyone seeking to quantify risk bears the burden of rejecting this hypothesis prior to relying on volatility measures of purported risk.

# SELECTED
# REFERENCES

This list of Selected References is divided into three sections:

A - Stock Market Techniques and Security Analysis

B - Investor Behavior and Psychology

C - Mathematics, Econometrics, and Computer Techniques

Due to space and other limitations, each section is of necessity extremely abbreviated. The quantity of works in each of these areas is immense, and complete lists of references would in themselves require several volumes. A number of the articles and books contained in these lists have been selected because they are among the classic works in their field. Many others with a lesser reputation are included nonetheless on the basis of their generally excellent content and ability to inform and educate the reader. Finally, several of the works are very obscure and may therefore provide new and appealing areas of investigation for those who are interested in further enlightenment in these fields.

Note: Most doctoral dissertations may be purchased in microfilm or photocopy format from: University Microfilms, Inc., 300 N. Zeeb Road, Ann Arbor, Michigan 48106.

## A – STOCK MARKET TECHNIQUES AND SECURITY ANALYSIS

Allen, Frederick Lewis. *Only Yesterday*. New York: Harper & Row, 1931.

Bachelier, Louis. "Theorie de la Speculation." Docteur es Sciences Mathematiques thesis, Academy of Paris, 1900.

Translated by A. James Boness. *The Random Character of Stock Market Prices.* Edited by Paul H. Cootner. Cambridge, Massachusetts: The M.I.T. Press, 1964.

Black, Fischer, and Scholes, Myron J. "The Valuation of Option Contracts and a Test of Market Efficiency," *The Journal of Finance* 27 (1972) 399-417.

Blum, James D. "An Analysis of the Price Behavior of Initial Common Stock Offerings." Ph.D. dissertation, Michigan State University, 1971.

Bolton, A. Hamilton. *Money and Investment Profits.* Homewood, Illinois: Dow Jones-Irwin, 1967.

Brealey, Richard A. *An Introduction to Risk and Return from Common Stocks.* Cambridge, Massachusetts and London, England: The M.I.T. Press, 1969.

Brealey, Richard A. *Security Prices in a Competitive Market.* Cambridge, Massachusetts and London, England: The M.I.T. Press, 1971.

Brealey, Richard A., and Pyle, Connie. *A Bibliography of Finance and Investment.* Cambridge, Massachusetts: The M. I. T. Press, 1973.

Comer, Harry D. "Low Priced Versus High Priced Stocks." *Financial Analysts Journal,* April 1945, pp. 15-20.

Conrad, Klaus and Juttner, Johannes. "Recent Behavior of Stock Market Prices in Germany and the Random Walk Hypothesis." *Internationale Zeitschrift fur Sozialwissenschaften.* Switzerland. 26 (1973): 576-599.

Cooper, Richard V. "Money and Stock Returns." Ph.D. dissertation, University of Chicago, 1971.

Cootner, Paul H., ed. *The Random Character of Stock Market Prices.* Cambridge, Massachusetts: The M. I. T. Press, 1964.

Drew, Garfield A. *New Methods for Profit in the Stock Market.* Wells, Vermont: Fraser Publishing Company, 1966, (Revision of 1948 publication).

Edwards, Robert D., and Magee, John. *Technical Analysis of Stock Trends.* Springfield, Massachusetts: John Magee, 1966.

Fisher, Lawrence, and Lorie, James H. "Rates of Return on Investments in Common Stock: The Year-by-Year Record, 1926-65." *The Journal of Business of the University of Chicago.* 40 (1968): 1-26.

Graham, Benjamin; Dodd, David L.; and Cottle, Sidney. *Security Analysis: Principles and Technique.* New York: McGraw-Hill, 1934.

Granville, Joseph E. *A Strategy of Daily Stock Market Timing for Maximum Profit.* Englewood Cliffs, New Jersey: Prentice-Hall, 1960.

Hamilton, William Peter. *The Stock Market Barometer.* New York: Harper & Bros., 1932.

James, Francis E., Jr. "The Implications of Trend Consistency in Portfolio Management." Ph.D. dissertation, Rensselear Polytechnic Institute, 1967.

Jones, Charles P. "The Value of Quarterly Information in Predicting Future Stock Price Changes." Ph.D. dissertation, University of North Carolina, 1969.

King, Benjamin F. "The Latent Statistical Structure of Security Price Changes." Ph.D. dissertation, University of Chicago, 1964.

Livermore, Jesse L. *How to Trade in Stocks.* New York: Duell, Sloan & Pearce, 1940.

Lorie, James H., and Brealey, Richard A., editors. *Modern Developments in Investment Management.* New York: Praeger Publishers, 1972.

Malkiel, Burton G., and Quandt, Richard E. *Strategies and Rational Decisions in the Securities Options Market.* Cambridge, Massachusetts and London, England: The M. I. T. Press, 1969.

Mandelbrot, Benoit. "The Variation of Certain Speculative Prices." *The Journal of Business of the University of Chicago.* 36 (1963): 394-419.

Markowitz, Harry M. "Portfolio Selection." *The Journal of Finance.* 7 (1952): 77-91.

Markowitz, Harry M. *Portfolio Selection.* New Haven: Yale University Press, 1959.

Merkle, Daniel R. *Relative Strength and Stock Market Timing.* Alton, Illinois: 1967.

Merrill, Arthur A. *Behavior of Prices on Wall Street.* Chappaqua, New York: The Analysis Press, 1966.

Officer, Robert B. "An Examination of the Time Series Behavior of the Market Factor of the New York Stock Exchange." Ph.D. dissertation, University of Chicago, 1971.

Parker, Glen King. *The Non-Random Character of Stock Market Prices.* Fort Lauderdale, Florida: The Institute for Econometric Research. Forthcoming.

Pepper, Neal A. "The Money Demand and Supply Determinants of Stock Prices." Ph.D. dissertation, University of California at Los Angeles, 1971.

Pratt, Shannon P. "Relationship Between Risk and Rate of Return for Common Stocks." Ph.D. dissertation, Indiana University, 1967.

Pratt, Shannon P., and DeVere, Charles W. "Insider Trading and Market Returns." Unpublished manuscript. Portland State University, September 1968.

Schreiner, John C. "Historically Successful Portfolio Selection Rules." Ph.D. dissertation, University of California at Los Angeles, 1970.

Smith, Edgar Lawrence. *Common Stocks and Business Cycles.* New York: The William-Frederick Press, 1971.

Watkinson, Wells G. "A Multivariate Relative Performance Security Selection Model." D.B.A. dissertation, University of Oregon, 1971.

Weisman, Benjamin B. "An Empirical Study of 21 Investment Criteria Employed in Common Stock Selection." Ph.D. dissertation, New York University, 1970.

Williams, John Burr. *The Theory of Investment Value.* Cambridge, Massachusetts: Harvard University Press, 1938.

Zimmer, Robert K. "An Empirical Analysis of Stock Market Price Determinants." Ph.D. dissertation, Ohio State University, 1964.

## B – INVESTOR BEHAVIOR AND PSYCHOLOGY

Le Bon, Gustave. *The Crowd.* France: 1895. Reprinted by The Viking Press. New York: 1960

Mackay, Charles, LL.D. *Memoirs of Extraordinary Popular Delusions.* London: Richard Bentley, 1841. Reprinted by The Noonday Press. New York.

Neill, Humphrey B. *The Art of Contrary Thinking.* Caldwell, Idaho: The Claxton Printers, Ltd., 1967.


## C – MATHEMATICS, ECONOMETRICS, AND COMPUTER TECHNIQUES

Anscombe, F. J. "Graphs in Statistical Analysis." *The American Statistician.* February 1973. pp. 17-21.

Beale, E. M. L.; Kendall, Maurice G.; and Mann, D. W. "The Discarding of Variables in Multivariate Analysis." *Biometrika* 54 (1967): 357-365.

Box, George E. P., and Jenkins, Gwilyn M. *Time Series Analysis Forecasting and Control.* San Francisco: Holden-Day, 1970.

Brown, Robert Goodell. *Smoothing, Forecasting and Prediction of Discrete Time Series.* Englewood Cliffs, New Jersey: Prentice-Hall, 1962.

Croxton, Frederick E.; Cowden, Dudley J.; and Bolch, Ben W. *Practical Business Statistics.* Englewood Cliffs, New Jersey: Prentice-Hall, 1969.

Daniel, Cuthbert, and Wood, Fred S. *Fitting Equations to Data.* New York: John Wiley & Sons, 1971.

Darlington, Richard B. "Multiple Regression in Psychological Research and Practice." *Psychological Bulletin.* 69 (1968): 161-182.

Dixon, W. J., editor. *BMD Biomedical Computer Programs; Series* O, P, and X. Berkeley, Los Angeles and London: University of California Press, 1973-1975.

Draper, Norman, and Smith, Harry. *Applied Regression Analysis*. New York, London, Sydney: John Wiley & Sons, 1966.

Eisenbeis, Richard A., and Avery, Robert B. *Discriminant Analysis and Classification Procedures*. Lexington, Massachusetts: Lexington Books, 1972.

Goldberger, Arthur S. *Econometric Theory*. New York, London, and Sydney: John Wiley & Sons, 1964.

Jolliffe, I. T. "Discarding Variables in a Principal Component Analysis. I: Artificial Data." *Applied Statistics* 21 (1972): 160-173.

Kendall, Sir Maurice G. "A Course in Multivariate Analysis." Unpublished manuscript. 1973.

Kendall, Sir Maurice G., and Alan, Stuart. *The Advanced Theory of Statistics*. New York: Hafner Publishing Company, 1968.

Longley, James W. "An Appraisal of Least Squares Programs for the Electronic Computer from the Point of View of the User." *Journal of the American Statistical Association.* 62 (1967): 819-841.

Merton, Robert C., and Samuelson, Paul A. "Fallacy of the Log-Normal Approximation to Optimal Portfolio Decision-Making Over Many Periods." *Journal of Financial Economics.* May 1974.

Miller, Merton H. "Discussion." *Journal of Finance.* May, 1972. pp. 294-298.

Pindyck, Robert S. and Rubinfeld, Daniel L. *Econometric Models and Economic Forecasts*. New York: McGraw-Hill, 1976.

Taylor, Lester D. "Estimation by Minimizing the Sum of Absolute Errors." *Frontiers in Econometrics.* New York and London: Academic Press, 1974.

Wampler, Roy H. "An Evaluation of Linear Least Squares Computer Programs." *Journal of Research of the National Bureau of Standards.* April-June 1969, pp. 59-90.

## THE BEST INVESTMENT BOOKS
## EVER WRITTEN

Bolton, Hamilton A. − *Money and Investment Profits* (1967)

Braeley, Richard − *An Introduction To Risk and Return from Common Stocks* (1967), and *Security Prices in a Competitive Market* (1971)

Cootner, Paul, ed. − *The Random Character of Stock Market Prices* (1964)

Graham, Benjamin; Dodd, David; and Cottle, Sidney − *Security Analysis: Principles and Technique* (1934)

Heiby, Walter A. − *Stock Market Profits through Dynamic Synthesis* (1965), and *The New Dynamic Synthesis* (1967)

Levine, Sumner N., ed. − *Financial Analysts Handbook I: Methods, Theory, and Portfolio Management* (1975)

Lorie, James, and Brealey, James, ed. − *Modern Developments in Investment Management* (1972)

Mackay, Charles − *Memoirs of Extraordinary Popular Delusions* (1841)

Markowitz, Harry M. − *Portfolio Selection* (1959)

Merrill, Arthur A. − *Behavior of Prices on Wall Street* (1966)

Rolo, Charles J. − *Gaining on the Market* (1982)

Smith, Adam − *The Money Game* (1967) and *Supermoney* (1972)

Smith, Edgar Lawrence − *Common Stocks as Long Term Investments* (1924)

Williams, John Burr − *The Theory of Investment Value* (1938)

# INDEX